FOR NO REASON AT ALL

FOR NO REASON AT ALL

The Changing Narrative of
the First World War in American Film

Jeffrey A. Hinkelman

University Press of Mississippi / Jackson

The University Press of Mississippi is the scholarly publishing agency of the Mississippi Institutions of Higher Learning: Alcorn State University, Delta State University, Jackson State University, Mississippi State University, Mississippi University for Women, Mississippi Valley State University, University of Mississippi, and University of Southern Mississippi.

www.upress.state.ms.us

The University Press of Mississippi is a member of the Association of University Presses.

Copyright © 2022 by University Press of Mississippi
All rights reserved

First printing 2022

∞

All quotations of intertitles or dialogue from films are the author's direct transcriptions from film prints or video copies.

Library of Congress Cataloging-in-Publication Data

Names: Hinkelman, Jeffrey A., author.
Title: For no reason at all : the changing narrative of the First World War in American film / Jeffrey A. Hinkelman.
Description: Jackson : University Press of Mississippi, [2022] | Includes bibliographical references and index.
Identifiers: LCCN 2021046866 (print) | LCCN 2021046867 (ebook) | ISBN 9781496836946 (hardback) | ISBN 9781496836939 (trade paperback) | ISBN 9781496836960 (epub) | ISBN 9781496836953 (epub) | ISBN 9781496836984 (pdf) | ISBN 9781496836977 (pdf)
Subjects: LCSH: World War, 1914–1918—Motion pictures and the war. | Motion pictures—United States—History—20th century. | Historical films—United States—History—20th century. | War films—United States—History—20th century. | World War, 1914–1918—African Americans. | World War, 1914–1918—Women. | Comedy films—United States—History and criticism.
Classification: LCC D522.23 .H56 2022 (print) | LCC D522.23 (ebook) | DDC 791.43/658—dc23/eng/20211201
LC record available at https://lccn.loc.gov/2021046866

LC ebook record available at https://lccn.loc.gov/2021046867British Library Cataloging-in-Publication Data available

Dedicated to the memory of my grandfathers, Oswald Hinkelman and William Roxer, and to my son, David, who was not even a gleam in my eye when this project was begun but who now brightens my every day.

CONTENTS

ACKNOWLEDGMENTS IX

INTRODUCTION 3

CHAPTER ONE—The Cradle of Courage: Warfare in American Film in the 1910s and 1920s 13

CHAPTER TWO—Combat, Literature, and Film: Combat Veterans and the Production of Narratives of Wartime Service, 1925–1930 46

CHAPTER THREE—Comedies, Cartoons, and Carnage: World War I in American Comic Short Films 81

CHAPTER FOUR—Race Film and the Depiction of African American Military Service, 1918–1939 109

CHAPTER FIVE—Girls in Hell: The Changing Depiction of Women in the First World War 136

CHAPTER SIX—For No Reason at All: Homecoming, Disillusionment, and the Failure of Tradition 169

CHAPTER SEVEN—Morals and Muck: From Suicide to Superheroes . . 192

CONCLUSION 211

NOTES 215
BIBLIOGRAPHY 226
FILMOGRAPHY 234
INDEX 246

ACKNOWLEDGMENTS

To paraphrase Vivien Leigh's exemplary Oscar acceptance speech, if I were to thank everyone involved in making this book possible, I should have to entertain you with a list of acknowledgments longer than the book itself. The journey of this manuscript from inception to completion has taken many years, and many of the people I met along the way might not even know that they have affected the eventual result. I first thank David Shumway, Kathy Newman, and Andreea Ritivoi, who helped to guide the project to completion. A cadre of other scholars took the time to review or discuss all or part of the work in progress, including Steven Schlossman, Scott Sandage, Katherine Lynch, and Jim Duesing. Equally (if not more) important are the family and friends who have provided various kinds of support and encouragement. Fully cognizant of the potential inequities of singling anyone out, I nevertheless plunge forward to thank Elizabeth Heffelfinger, who read and commented on various drafts of the manuscript, as well as Evan Beach, who did the same. Evan and Zheng also hosted me on a research trip to New York that enabled me to see William Wellman's *Young Eagles*. Similarly, the hospitality of Steve and Mary Margaret Stone repeatedly facilitated trips to Washington, DC, to do research at the Library of Congress. Dave Petty was a valuable sounding board at every point in the book's development, and our frequent rambles and conversations have always been rewarding. I am regularly grateful that the all-important question of where to sit in the cafeteria for lunch as a high school freshman brought together Dave, Steve, and me and that we have subsequently remained friends.

Less specifically but no less importantly, I thank the many students and faculty I have been privileged to know and work with during my tenure at Carnegie Mellon University. I have tried to always keep my door open to those who wish to discuss anything related to film (or to many other subjects, I suppose), and that policy has amply profited me by bringing many supportive and cherished friends into my circle. In addition to Elizabeth and Evan, this group includes Barry Luokkala, whose weekly lunch appointments provide a sea of calm in a sometimes hectic world, and an entire extended network of friends with whom I still keep in regular touch despite the ever-increasing number of years which relentlessly conspire to separate us, especially including (in rough order of seniority) Richard Schall, Christal Sanchez, Darya Leyzarovich, Bill Savage, Min Kim, Karen Han, Chee-Yuen Hung, Steve Tsou, Krissy Choi, Polly Harrison, Jon Kush, Karen Choi, and Leila Garcia. The final revisions of the manuscript took place under the shadow of COVID-19, so I also thank my Pandemic Pals (Omoye Odiase, Peter Geyer, Sabrina Clarke, and Margaret Mertz) as well as Nina Edwards and all of the members of her Film Club, for weekly, sanity-maintaining conversations that provided a welcome social outlet in a not-very-social year.

Finally, I recognize the importance of my family to this entire endeavor. I celebrated the completion of my dissertation by flying in a vintage B-17 bomber, which I considered an homage to my late grandfathers, Oswald Hinkelman and William Roxer, both of whom were proud of their World War II military service. Unlike so many of the characters discussed in these pages, they never doubted the necessity of that service, but they also understood the high price exacted by war. I hope that their counsel and wisdom is properly reflected in what follows. My only regret is that the extended duration of this project prevented them as well as my late grandmothers, Alice Roxer and Louise Hinkelman, from witnessing its completion.

My siblings, Christy and Tom Hinkelman, have lent their ears as needed over the years of research and writing. Special mention goes to my sister, who has read the manuscript multiple times and has been a valued critic, trusted confidant, and frequent co-conspirator since both of us learned to talk. My wholehearted gratitude also goes to my parents, Alan and Ruth Hinkelman, for their unstinting support. My mother always claims that she had sons so that my father would have someone to take to the movies, an arrangement of which I am happy to be the beneficiary and the results of which are written on every page of this book.

Most important, I thank my wife, Hannah Rosen, for being the perfect companion—whether exploring ancient ruins, being flabbergasted by our initial screening of *The Mad Parade*, or raising our son, David. Her love, patience, and support lighten the load and made possible the completion of this project.

FOR NO REASON AT ALL

INTRODUCTION

IN EARLY DECEMBER 2009, A WEST VIRGINIA FARMER TESTIFIED BEFORE A congressional committee on behalf of a public memorial. In and of itself, that fact would be of no particular note, but this was not an ordinary farmer. Frank Buckles was 109 years old and the last remaining American veteran of the First World War. At sixteen, he had talked his way into the U.S. Army (after being rejected by the marines and the navy) and driven ambulances in France.[1] As the "last doughboy," Buckles had come to Congress to support legislation to commemorate that conflict. The proposal was simple. Though the National Mall was officially closed to further development, a small memorial to veterans from the Washington, DC, area already existed. The rededication of that space to the memory of all who served in the Great War would allow the conflict to be acknowledged in the heart of the nation's capital without requiring new construction.

What seemed like a sensible proposal was quickly challenged, however, from multiple directions. Representatives of the District of Columbia complained that the plan shortchanged local interests by intruding on a site dedicated to hometown veterans. The congressional delegation from Missouri wanted to protect the primacy of their own site in Kansas City (already home to the National World War I Museum and Memorial). In the end, Buckles's testimony was not enough to overcome these challenges, so the plan fell to political infighting.[2] The failure of Buckles's plea, despite the late-in-life celebrity that made him a desirable spokesperson, reflects the national failure to recognize the importance of what is arguably the central event of the twentieth century.[3]

Millions of people lost their lives in the carnage of the First World War—carnage that involved the destruction of empires, the creation of new nations, and the decimation of an entire generation. But how do we remember it? Buckles (who died in 2011 at the age of 110) was the last American who could claim to remember the war as a military veteran, but his celebrity derived more from his longevity than any burning public desire to think about the consequences of one of the most terrible conflicts in human history.[4] The centennial of the First World War, observed much more attentively in Europe, occasioned only minor interest in the United States, and the observances that did take place stood in striking contrast to the activities and publicity that surrounded the seventy-fifth anniversary of the World War II Allies' invasion of Normandy.[5] But that disparity suggests an answer to the question of how the Great War has come to be so marginalized in U.S. history. The First World War has been utterly overshadowed by its sequel.

The Second World War remains comparatively ubiquitous in popular culture, and there are undoubtedly good reasons for this. Primary among these, of course, is the fact that the Second World War, unlike its predecessor, achieved a clear and unconditional victory for the Allied powers. Almost as important is the notion that the later conflict has a more rewarding narrative arc for which victory makes a satisfying conclusion. In its most basic form, the World War II narrative depicts the forces of democracy and freedom, backed into a corner by the forces of pure evil, fighting back and emerging triumphant. The result of that triumph was the establishment of a new world order, a Pax Americana, that fulfilled Woodrow Wilson's World War I–era goal of making the world "safe for democracy." As Albert Auster put it, "World War II has become for Americans that mythic, Edenic moment when the entire nation bent itself to victory over evil and barbarism. The strength of the memory from World War II did not wane, even during the Cold War, the 'Forgotten War' in Korea, and the U.S. involvement in Vietnam. Thus World War II has become the indispensable symbol of American virtue and triumph. It can be brought forward to exalt American arms and the American spirit whenever contemporary events require it."[6] The success of that narrative is certainly no accident, and the persistence of World War II in the public consciousness has been especially evident on America's movie screens. Even a casual review of films made during the war years provides ample evidence of the concerted efforts of the Office of War Information and the American film industry to cement that narrative in the minds of the general populace as the war was still in progress. What is astonishing is the long reach of those efforts, which continued unabated for decades and remain potent nearly eighty years later.

If the Second World War remains the benchmark of triumphant American military superiority, however, what of its predecessor? What is the dominant narrative of the Great War, and how did it develop? As George Creel recounts in *How We Advertised America*, the usefulness of film in shaping public opinion was certainly taken into account by the World War I–era Committee on Public Information: "At the very outset, it was obvious that the motion picture had to be placed on the same plane of importance as the written and spoken word."[7] Movie stars such as Mary Pickford and Charlie Chaplin not only drew huge crowds at bond-selling rallies but also contributed short films to the war effort (*100% American* and *The Bond*, respectively). More important, both actors made feature films that used the war as narrative fodder, thus influencing the depiction of the war on-screen. The First World War is the first American conflict that was fully processed on film, not only by documentarians who photographed events for posterity but also by those working within the newly developed studio system to create fictional versions of the conflict. In the years following the armistice, those filmmakers came to include returning veterans with their own ideas about the depiction of the combat experience—ideas that frequently conflicted with established tropes for the portrayal of warfare on film. Those American filmmakers spent years modifying existing standards and working through a variety of narrative options before achieving a general consensus regarding a suitable approach to rendering the war on-screen. The development of that consensus, the changes it wrought on the depiction of war on American screens, and the ultimate result of that long process form the central concerns of this book.

Interpreting the impact and memory of a particular conflict is certainly not a new endeavor, and reams of literature have been produced assessing how individual generations deal with specific wars. Prior to the twentieth century, the primary outlets for this activity involved the higher arts—literature, painting, sculpture, and so forth. Matthew Brady and Alexander Gardner added photography to the list of available tools for shaping historical impressions of a conflict during the Civil War, and Eadweard Muybridge, with his post–Civil War government contracts for photographing military installations and activities (especially those related to the Modoc War) provided an early link to the new art of the motion picture.[8] The cultural products associated with these endeavors vary, but prior to the twentieth century, they tended to approach the experience of war through a traditional narrative that emphasized the positive virtues of military service. A young man leaves his home and family to take part in a military conflict. While his experience may entail hardship and loss, in the end he has matured into a better man, returning home to take his rightful place of authority with regard to romantic relationships, familial obligations, and social standing. This pattern can be seen throughout Western culture in works as old as Homer's *Odyssey* and continues with certain modifications until the mid-1920s.

The years between 1915 and 1934 saw a remaking of this narrative in an attempt to encompass the enormity of the First World War. Though often discussed in terms of the literary endeavors of such authors as Ernest

Hemingway, F. Scott Fitzgerald, and John Dos Passos or the rise of surrealism and expressionism in art, the move away from traditional approaches is no less important in the world of film. Frequently led by filmmakers with a direct experience of combat, popular film culture created a new and fully articulated vocabulary for addressing the impact of war on both individuals and society. Even more significantly, the rhetoric of these films argued strongly for an antiwar position, questioning every aspect of the wartime experience.

In the larger literature studying the conflict, three key historical works have paid particular attention to the memory of the Great War within and among the various nations that actively participated in the conflict. The most well known of these is Paul Fussell's groundbreaking and much-lauded *The Great War and Modern Memory*, which in many ways defines the terms of the discussion. Fussell, a veteran of the Second World War who was wounded in combat, argued that the First World War utterly transformed our views both of the experience of combat and of war itself. He was most interested in "the way the dynamics and iconography of the Great War have proved crucial political, rhetorical and artistic determinants on subsequent life."[9] By examining the British literature of the Great War, he traces the change from Victorian and Georgian rhetoric glorifying combat to the irony-studded musings and postwar recollections of those who experienced life in the trenches. In this view, the war led to a significant break with the past. This break, in turn, generated a "modern memory" that completely redefined the cultural approach to life itself—a new, modernist way of thinking that can be seen throughout the fabric of social and cultural life during and following the conflict.

Fifteen years after the publication of Fussell's work, George Mosse added to the discussion of the meaning of the Great War with his *Fallen Soldiers: Reshaping the Memory of the World Wars*. For Mosse, the war was not the radical break suggested by Fussell but part of a larger process of dealing with the aftermath of conflicts extending back to the Napoleonic Wars that manifests in various aspects of popular culture, cemetery design, and the construction of war monuments. Central to his argument is what he calls the "Myth of the War Experience," which is a central concern of veterans searching for meaning in their military service, though Mosse also suggests the importance of creating such a myth for political reasons: "Those concerned with the image and continuing appeal of the nation worked at constructing a myth which would draw the sting from death in war and emphasize the meaningfulness of the fighting and sacrifice. . . . The aim was to make an inherently unpalatable past acceptable, important not just for the purpose of consolation but above all for the justification of the nation in whose name the war had been fought."¹⁰ In this formulation, the First World War is less a turning point on the road to modernity than another step in a larger process that justifies the traditional standards forming the basis of nationalist conceptions of patriotism, public service, and general order.

For Jay Winter in his *Sites of Memory, Sites of Mourning: The Great War in European Cultural History*, the memory of the Great War involved neither the radical break suggested by Fussell nor the more specialized remembrance implied by Mosse. Rather, by examining the evidence of traditional expressions of grief seen in postwar art, literature, and war memorials, Winter demonstrates how communities sought continuity with the past by processing their impressions of the conflict through the application of existing tropes and forms. Winter argues that the war did not compel a radical break with tradition but instead "brought the search for an appropriate language of loss to the centre of cultural and political life" in which "older motifs took on new meanings and new forms." He tempers Fussell's more sweeping argument by suggesting that "the strength of what may be termed 'traditional' forms in social and cultural life, in art, poetry, and ritual, lay in their power to mediate bereavement. The cutting edge of 'modern memory,' its multi-faceted sense of dislocation, paradox, and the ironic, could express anger and despair, and did so in enduring ways; it was melancholic, but it could not heal."¹¹

The question of what is changed by the conflagration of the Great War and what remains the same is an important one, and all of these writers contributed nuances to the discussion. There are two shared assumptions, however, that weaken the argument in each instance. First is the dominant Eurocentric view of the conflict. While it is fair to assert that Europe shouldered the brunt of the war's miseries, the participation of more than four million American men and women is not inconsiderable and had a measurable impact on U.S. cultural, literary, and political life. Though it is unfair to criticize these works for not investigating issues that are, by definition, outside the scope of their subject, these writers did not address the question of how the war shaped American sensibilities and "modern memory." Fussell in particular is positively hostile to the notion of American literature comparing in any way to that of Great Britain and is dismissive of any literary endeavors that emerge outside of England.

This leads to the second shortcoming of these works, and the one that is the primary impetus of this study. None of these writers takes full account of the possibilities offered by cinema for understanding the attitudes and ideas of any nation regarding participation in the First World War. Not one to hedge his opinions, Fussell justifies his focus on English literature with the simple, spurious assertion that "in 1914 there was virtually no cinema."¹²

In his chapter "The Process of Trivialization," Mosse spends a few pages discussing film, but the depth of his general argument can be summarized in his assertion that "the end results in all nations were much the same: the war presented as melodrama, romance, or adventure."[13]

Winter is the most attentive to film generally, writing that "any account of the cultural codes through which mourning was expressed in the period of the Great War must explore this rich area of the history of popular culture. ... [F]ilms show well the imprint of the experience of mass death and mass bereavement on the cultural history of early twentieth-century Europe."[14] Despite this assertion, Winter's chapter on film is extremely limited. He attempts to compare the imagery of traditional religious posters to the spiritualist approach to the war taken by Abel Gance in his two versions of *J'accuse*. While this line of thinking is not without merit, it hardly does justice to the role of film in processing the wartime experience. In his more recent *Remembering War: The Great War between Memory and History in the Twentieth Century*, Winter is more circumspect about the use of film: "One of the unfortunate features of the memory boom is the tendency of commentators to term any and every narrative of past events as constituents of national memory or collective memory, understood as the shared property of the citizenry of a state. Nowhere is this more evident than in the case of film. Time and again the claim is made that the way cinema presents the past somehow passes in an unmediated manner into something termed memory."[15] Winter is absolutely correct that broad assertions of "memory" should be carefully regulated, for reasons discussed in chapter 1. The "memory" of one audience (those with firsthand knowledge of war, for example) may be entirely different from the "memory" evoked by that same film in their grandchildren. Despite increased pessimism, however, Winter's discussion of film in this regard is no more thorough: *Remembering War* focuses on a single film (Renoir's *La Grande Illusion*).

The subject of the Great War in film has not, of course, been entirely neglected. A variety of studies have focused on the depiction of the war on film either directly or as an influential aspect of another topic. The former category includes such works as Craig Campbell's *Reel America and World War I*, Peter C. Rollins and John E. O'Conner's *Hollywood's World War I: Motion Picture Images*, and Larry Ward's *The Motion Picture Goes to War: The U.S. Government Film Effort During World War I*. The latter category includes important works such as Kevin Brownlow's *The War, the West and the Wilderness*, Andrew Bergman's *We're In the Money: Depression America and Its Films*, Thomas Doherty's *Pre-Code Hollywood: Sex, Immorality and Insurrection in American Cinema, 1930–1934*, and Lea Jacobs's *The Decline of*

Sentiment: American Film in the 1920s. In addition, numerous studies have focused on the national cinematic output of the major combatant countries as it relates to their experience of the conflict.

This list demonstrates a particular lacuna in the discussion that, despite the opportunity presented by the centennial of the conflict, has not been adequately addressed. Given the worldwide influence of the American film industry following the conclusion of the conflict, there has been a limited amount of specific, thorough analysis primarily focused on the ways in which World War I is presented on American screens. The work of several previous scholars has provided a solid footing for addressing this topic, each approaching the subject from a slightly different perspective. Michael Isenberg supplied an early impetus for this volume with his *War on Film: The American Cinema and World War I, 1914–1941* as well as his article on *The Big Parade* in *Hollywood's World War I: Motion Picture Images*, helping to crystallize the difficulties of fixing the political stance of King Vidor's film. *War on Film* is less effective than might be hoped, however, especially given that when the book was published in 1981, Isenberg was forced to defend the idea of looking at films through a serious academic lens. Regardless, he outlined the parameters of the discussion in a way that pointed to further research.

In her *Reel Patriotism: The Movies and World War I*, Leslie Midkiff DeBauche offers the sort of research-oriented examination of World War I films that had previously been in short supply. DeBauche's central interest is the connection between the government and the film industry during the war, a relationship she examines via case studies of individual films made from 1916 to 1918. Her final chapter, however, skips forward nine years to focus on *Wings* while briefly discussing the treatment of the war in other significant films of the 1920s.

Andrew Kelly's *Cinema and the Great War*, though it also covers a variety of other national cinemas, thoughtfully considers many of the key American works that are discussed in this book, as does the most substantial work to emerge since the centennial observances, Michael Hammond's *The Great War in Hollywood Memory, 1918–1939*.

All of these scholars provide solid foundations on which to build, but much remains to be said regarding the way in which film depicts the First World War. The conflict does cause a rupture in the way that American filmmakers discuss wartime service, though this break is not as extreme as Fussell suggests, especially given that it does not persist for an extended period. My approach is perhaps more in sympathy with Winter's arguments, suggesting that this process takes place through a gradual manipulation of traditional standards that eventually alters the established narrative in which war is a grand and useful experience that molds callow boys into mature men. Throughout the 1920s, American filmmakers increasingly began to incorporate facets of the experience of Great War veterans that countered and undermined the accepted narrative tropes. This process reached its peak during the pre-Code era of the early 1930s, when the traditional narrative was briefly supplanted by an entirely new "disillusionment narrative" that questioned the premises of the traditional view of wartime service.

Though I open my argument with an examination of films commemorating the Civil War, I do so primarily because those films establish the primacy of a particular narrative model on-screen. It is essential to define this baseline to fully understand the ways in which that model is manipulated and transformed as a vehicle for filmed portrayals of the Great War (especially given that the two filmmakers I discuss most thoroughly, D. W. Griffith and Thomas Ince, specifically provide a bridge from narratives of the Civil War to narratives of the later conflict).

In addition, I intentionally focus on nondocumentary films looking back on the conflict. I do not attempt to analyze the many fascinating documentary and nondocumentary films made during the war, though a truly thorough history of those works would be welcomed.

Further, this volume does not take an exhaustive approach, attempting to include every American film that focuses on or mentions the Great War. Nor does the book address the recent spate of depictions of the First World War on-screen produced outside of the United States (a fact that speaks to the historical remembrance of the war in other combatant countries). These films include Sam Mendes's *1917* and Peter Jackson's *They Shall Not Grow Old* (both dedicated to the filmmakers' forbears who served in the war), François Ozon's *Frantz* (a loose remake of Lubitsch's *The Man I Killed*), and a recent version of *Journey's End* (directed by Saul Dibb).

Finally, I hesitate to refer to this as a traditional "genre" study. My qualms regarding the theoretical underpinnings of genre classification are reflected in essays by Andrew Tudor and Rick Altman that appear in Barry Keith Grant's *Film Genre Reader II*. As Tudor's "Genre" correctly suggests, despite the prevalence of generic terms such as *war picture* or *adventure film*, the use of the concept in academic studies is frequently problematic since "what is normally a thumbnail classification for everyday purposes is now being asked to carry rather more weight."[16] Though Altman's "A Semantic/Syntactic Approach to Film Genre" usefully attempts to give the notion critical clarity by suggesting a practical approach to function, the result is frequently an expanding thicket of ever-more-problematic division into ever smaller categories. I am not convinced that these difficulties can ever be entirely eliminated, so while the films discussed here share a topic and certain thematic elements, I prefer to think of what follows as the tracing of an attitude and narrative approach toward the Great War rather than as the birth and death of some sort of subgenre.

Chapter 1 reviews the properties of the traditional narrative, briefly examines its roots in literature, and traces its establishment as the standard filmic narrative. After discussing Stephen Crane's *The Red Badge of Courage* as a literary antecedent, I trace the ways in which the traditional narrative was used by early filmmakers such as Griffith and Ince in their films commemorating the fiftieth anniversary of the Civil War. These filmmakers then adapted and applied that narrative as their attention turned to the Great War. The success of this traditional formula extended well beyond the cessation of hostilities throughout much of the following decade.

Chapter 2 focuses on several major filmmakers who were also veterans and explores the ways in which they gradually transformed the traditional narrative. Their early efforts to come to grips with the experience of the war occurred in other media (a novel, a play, and a memoir), thereby allowing these creators the freedom to manipulate the established conventions in new ways. In films such as *The Big Parade*, *Journey's End*, and *Young Eagles*, Laurence Stallings, James Whale, and William Wellman brought their own perspectives to bear on the discussion of combat and its effects. By comparing their efforts across media, we can see that unlike earlier films that discussed warfare through a fifty-year-old lens, these men looked back after only a few years and found the traditional version in need of adjustment.

Chapter 3 examines some of the first films to break away from the accepted narrative conventions. These films included comedies and animated works that took advantage of the possibilities for exaggeration and hyperbole (both visual and narrative) offered by the comic form. Some of the earliest of these films were also made by men with military experience who were able to convey otherwise unacceptable images and truths under the cover of the "comic" label. Images of violence, combat conditions, and the general life of servicemen that would not have passed muster in a drama could be conveyed through satire or slapstick, thus paving the way for a discussion of such subjects in more serious works.

While most films examined in this study were produced in the context of the Hollywood studio system, chapter 4 examines the narrative tendencies of films produced outside of that system for a minority community that had its own perspective on the meaning of military service. African Americans were drafted in large numbers during the war, but their service was fraught with difficulties born of racist attitudes toward their abilities. At the same time, that service was a source of tremendous pride within African American communities across the country. The output of the makers of independent "race films" functions on a continuum that reflects both of these facts, as filmmakers tried to maneuver through the contradictory attitudes of the Black community toward wartime service.

Chapter 5 discusses another group for whom the First World War was a watershed moment. Women served throughout the conflict in a variety of capacities, and a small, but significant, group of films directly addressed their experiences. The changing depiction of these women and their roles in wartime narratives directly parallels the modifications to traditional narrative patterns taking place across the spectrum of filmmaking, and these unjustly neglected works are an important microcosm of my larger arguments.

Chapter 6 discusses the fullest development of the narrative scheme that supplanted the traditional model. This "disillusionment narrative" directly contradicted the many positive values upheld in the traditional approach as filmmakers reflected on the long-term aftermath of the conflict a decade later. The veterans depicted here saw none of the beneficial or positive results of war promised in the earlier narrative, instead finding themselves in an entirely new situation diametrically opposed to the conventional tradition.

Finally, chapter 7 discusses the ultimate results of the transformation and displacement of the traditional narrative. Political expediency, the enforcement of the Production Code, and the gathering signs of possible involvement in a future conflict combined to silence the more current view of warfare and its meaning. In the wake of the Second World War, the memory of the Great War was diminished as well as repurposed. Over the following decades, the positive, victorious narrative of the latter conflict was in part encouraged by the displacement of the negative aspects of war to stories of the prior struggle. The binary approach to the two defining events of the century continues to the present with the "Good War" remaining the on-screen opposite of the bad war that preceded it.

The eventual failure of the narrative transformations wrought by the First World War in no way lessen their significance. In fact, recent equivocal military experiences in Iraq and Afghanistan give them new weight. The memories of Great War veterans would likely resonate with survivors of those more recent conflicts. With that notion in mind, it becomes that much more important to carefully consider the ways in which the stories of that earlier conflict were and are conveyed on-screen.

Chapter One

THE CRADLE OF COURAGE

Warfare in American Film in the 1910s and 1920s

IN 1898 THE AMERICAN BATTLESHIP USS *MAINE* EXPLODED IN HAVANA Harbor, stoking martial sentiments that eventually led the United States to declare war on Spain. The resultant military adventures initiated American involvement in imperialism and pointed Theodore Roosevelt toward the White House. They also provided a sterling opportunity for fledgling filmmakers trying to establish the importance of a new medium. In his autobiographical account of the early years of the film industry, Albert Smith, cofounder of the Vitagraph Company, describes the effect of the *Maine* explosion on moviegoing audiences in 1898: "The *Maine* disaster opened a new cycle, the newsreel movie, and proved that a wave of patriotism can be as valuable to a picturemaker as a wave of passion."[1] As Smith goes on to recount, the films generated as part of that new cycle were sometimes authentic, sometimes outright fabrication, and almost always received by audiences with jingoistic enthusiasm. Discussing the reception given to a Vitagraph film of troops assembling for eventual transport to Cuba, Smith relates, "Public indignation over the *Maine* had taken on another form. Now the public was crying out its confidence in American strength; the spirit of patriotism was a rousing aria on every street corner. People were reaching out hungrily for something—anything—that would give them a chance to proclaim their patriotism. . . . [T]he audience saw their boys marching for the first time on any screen. They broke into a thunderous storm of shouting and foot stamping. . . . Requests for war movies poured in from the other theaters exhibiting our films."[2] Smith's adventures eventually took him to combat zones in both Cuba (during the Spanish-American War) and South Africa (to film the Boer War), and he was certainly not alone.[3]

As scholars such as Elizabeth Strebel, Liz Clarke, and Stephen Bottomore have detailed, the international film industry avidly recorded a wide variety of late nineteenth-century military conflicts, among them the

Spanish-American War, the Boer War, and the Boxer Rebellion.[4] Whether fabricated or authentic, however, most of these films considered their conflicts from the perspective of current events. Smith's use of the term *newsreel movie* indicates an important distinction that separates them from the films that will be discussed in the following pages. Though they laid a significant foundation for interpreting military conflict on-screen, their claims to documentary immediacy and authenticity (justified or not) place them in a different category. They are a filmic starting point, but this volume explores the development of a narrative standard more concerned with history and memory than reportage or jingoism. That narrative reflects cultural attitudes and necessities that changed drastically in the twenty years between the sinking of the *Maine* and the signing of the armistice ending the Great War, and one of the major turning points in the evolution of that narrative is the anniversary of the end of the American Civil War.

As the American film industry began to develop as a vehicle for narrative in the early years of the twentieth century, the voracious public appetite for new films encouraged a wholesale pilfering of stories from other cultural forms. The Vitagraph Company's "quality film" versions of plays such as Shakespeare's *Twelfth Night* or *Julius Caesar* and the Thanhouser Company's renditions of various English novels such as *Dr. Jekyll and Mr. Hyde*, *She*, and *The Vicar of Wakefield* demonstrate the range of literary topics that became fair game for translation to film. At the same time, filmmakers such as D. W. Griffith at Biograph Studios and Thomas Ince, under a variety of corporate banners, were developing new modes of production that streamlined these cultural borrowings and systematized the creation of new films on a regular schedule. Beyond their technical and organizational importance, however, these two filmmakers were crucial in cementing the standards that would apply to portrayal of combat and warfare on film from the early 1910s to the mid-1920s.

For both Griffith and Ince, their influence in creating those standards emerged from practical business considerations. The fiftieth anniversary of the end of the American Civil War prompted a reappraisal of that conflict that played out across a wide array of venues. In creating their own version of the Civil War, filmmakers drew on debates and perspectives that had already been expressed throughout American public life in textbooks, children's literature, fraternal societies, dime novels, monument programs, and romantic literature.[5] Filmmakers hoping to take commercial advantage of public interest in the conflict drew on those multifarious sources as well as the earlier "newsreel films" to create the model of a new type of war film—one that approached a given conflict from a reflective, historical vantage point rather than from a current, nationalistic perspective. At the most basic level, this model dictated new general parameters for the cinematic treatment of armed conflict, but it did so in a way that was particular to the needs of an audience looking back over fifty years. The gap between the end of the conflict and the exploitation of that event by the film industry took into account five decades' worth of arguments, assertions, and mythmaking by those who took part in the war and their descendants. The version of the Civil War that emerged on-screen was thus softened by both the romanticizing effects of time and a desire to show respect to a dwindling band of survivors of the war. Those needs were very different from the expectations of veterans of World War I, but the narrative requirements applied to the filmic valorization of the Civil War dictated the traditionalistic form that cinematic depictions of armed conflict would initially adopt when discussing the later conflict.

Thanks to the vagaries of film survival, Griffith and Biograph have become the primary example of many of the general tendencies of early cinema. A production schedule of two films per week encouraged the voracious consumption and regurgitation of material, and Griffith was constantly pressed for new topics. At the same time, he actively sought to collect, consolidate, and develop new techniques for conveying narrative information to his audience. In pursuit of this goal, he borrowed from both the popular and fine arts and frequently pushed the boundaries of accepted film conventions. As Sergei Eisenstein famously suggested in his "Dickens, Griffith and the Film Today," Griffith borrowed more than subject matter. His narrative style itself was an extension of formal tendencies that connect his melodramatic impulses directly to those of Charles Dickens, especially with regard to their shared style of "montage exposition." That the Russian filmmaker is most interested in the structural composition of Griffith's films is not a surprise given the importance of the American's editing on the development of montage theory. In terms of the use of that form, however, Griffith's films demonstrate a direct link between Victorian narrative sensibilities and more modern ideas, and this link in many ways makes him continuously relevant.

In seeking a suitable approach for their Civil War films, neither Griffith nor Ince would have been ignorant of the long-standing debates between veterans organizations and regional interests regarding the "true" history of the Civil War. Well into the early twentieth century, the Union veterans organization, the Grand Army of the Republic, continued an active program of "patriotic instruction," while the United Confederate Veterans promoted its version of history just as avidly.[6] Various Confederate groups stridently sought to guarantee that the textbooks used in American educational institutions reflected a version of Confederate motives and conduct that was acceptable to surviving veterans. For Southerners, this version of history included the importance of paternalistic relationships between masters and slaves, the primacy of states' rights in Southern secession and the nobility and chivalry of the Southern soldier defending his home and family. As James M. McPherson puts it, "The Lost Cause triumphed in the curriculum, if not on the battlefield."[7] At the same time, the community of American writers did not produce a major fictional narrative that captured the history and emotions of the conflict. As Edmund Wilson points out in the introduction to his study of war literature, the diarists and memoirists of the war fulfilled that function far more than authors of fiction.[8] It would, in fact, take thirty years for a novel to lay claim to being the ultimate representation of the Civil War. Stephen Crane's *The Red Badge of Courage*, published just as film technology was being introduced to the world, suggested a narrative template that filmmakers such as Griffith and Ince could also utilize as they depicted the American Civil War on-screen.

The Red Badge of Courage conveys the familiar story of a young man (Henry) who volunteers for military service, runs in panicked fear from his first combat experience, then redeems himself by his bravery later in battle. Most significant, however, is the way in which Crane defined a traditional approach to the depiction of warfare that could then be adapted as film was developing its own sense of narrative. Whether or not he knew it, Crane filled the comparative void left by a dearth of acclaimed Civil War fiction and laid the groundwork for transferring the standards of earlier war literature to the discourse of film. This is a complicated suggestion that can be broken down into three constituent elements.

First is the notion of verisimilitude as a key aspect of the narrative. Expectations of the audience with regard to what is "real" in the depiction of the conflict had to be met. Crane was obviously familiar with Civil War veterans and had heard stories at their knees, just as Griffith would remember of his own upbringing. This quality helps to give Crane's narrative a sense of authenticity that would be difficult to produce without a historical grounding. This does not, of course, suggest that a narrative must adhere entirely to the truth of a given situation, only that the narrative must convince an audience to believe in its reality.

Second, the traditional war narrative must teach larger moral lessons. A particular story might be told from a particular perspective, but the opinions expressed regarding the nature of war itself must resonate with prevailing values that are perceived as universal. This includes such qualities as courage, honor, and loyalty as well as a sense of the importance of the larger brotherhood of arms. Crane's approach to the lessons of war has an intrinsic appeal that relates to the experiences of any soldier and that resonated with both veterans and casual readers regardless of their political allegiance.

Finally, war is depicted as an opportunity for growth and maturation for key characters throughout the story. Lessons must be learned and processed as characters advance through the plot, and the final result of that progress is the growth of the individual. On balance, negatives are eventually balanced and exceeded by positives in terms of personal development. Despite being strikingly unsympathetic to the nature and opinions of its own protagonist as a character, the arc of Crane's story follows the traditional master plot of a youth who leaves for war, suffers to a greater or lesser degree, and becomes a mature man through his experiences. Though many scholars have been hesitant about the final lines of the book, given its general tone toward Henry throughout, there can be no question that the author reverts to the traditional form for his conclusion: "He felt a quiet manhood, nonassertive, but of sturdy and strong blood. He knew that he would no more quail before his guides wherever they should point. He had been to touch the great death, and found that, after all, it was but the great death. He was a man."[9]

In his *The Content of the Form*, Hayden White writes that "the authority of the historical narrative is the authority of reality itself; the historical account endows this reality with form and thereby makes it desirable by the imposition upon its processes of the formal coherency that only stories possess."[10] White speaks specifically of narrative history, but in his formulation, the line between historical narrative and fictional narrative is very thin. White further suggests that "the demand for closure in the historical story is a demand . . . for moral meaning, a demand that sequences of real events be assessed as to their significance as elements of a moral drama."[11] Speaking from the perspective of a historian, White suggests that the imposition of a moral is a clear component of the narrative representation of any historical event.

If, as White suggests, a moral is essential to a "true narrative" representation of a historical moment, Crane has placed his moral clearly on the last page. Despite the recounting of self-doubt, cowardice, animalistic passion, shame, and bravery that precedes these lines, the moral remains the traditional tale of a young man achieving maturity by grappling with mortality—both his own and that of his comrades and enemies on the battlefield. War is a trial as well as an opportunity. Though Crane's ability to balance competing approaches unconsciously leads him to set the stage for what is to follow, he does so in a way that maintains a hold on the traditional verities of narrative form.[12]

Despite moments that might suggest a more complicated intent, the conclusion of *The Red Badge of Courage* affirms the continued dominance of a traditional narrative. At the same time, Crane's prose style is frequently of a visual quality that relates well to the vocabulary of the newly emergent world of popular visual culture, further reinforcing the mass appeal of his work. Taken together, the three elements that dominate his approach to the story point the way for the films that will deal with the same subject in the next two decades and beyond. The model he created became an enormously influential prism through which to view warfare. That model dominated filmic depictions of the Civil War twenty years later and then defined the development of films dealing with armed conflict immediately following the First World War.

The influence of Crane's approach can be seen in the Civil War films made by Griffith during his Biograph years. Those films might simply be viewed as precursors of *The Birth of a Nation*, but their importance to both Griffith's own development of a narrative approach and (in part by virtue of his success) to the later general development of the "war film" has been less studied. In films such as *In the Border States*, *The House with Closed Shutters*, *The Fugitive*, *His Trust*, *His Trust Fulfilled* (all 1910), and *Swords and Hearts* (1911), Griffith establishes a pattern very similar to Crane's, wherein a "realistic" depiction of war consistently demonstrates universal narrative themes while producing a positive, moral outcome for central characters. This does not suggest that the horrors of war are entirely ignored. War-induced suffering and depredations afflict characters in each of these films, but in the final analysis, positive, moral lessons are always learned.

Griffith's sensibilities regarding war developed as an innate part of his upbringing in the postwar South. As he put it, "The stories told of my father, particularly by veterans who had fought under his command, were burned right into my memory."[13] Griffith's family tree included a great-grandfather who had fought in the American Revolution, a grandfather who had helped to defend Washington, DC, in the War of 1812, and a father who fought both in the Mexican War and for the Confederacy. As Richard Schickel details in his biography of the director, "Roaring Jake Griffith" served from October 1861 until a month after Lee's surrender at Appomattox Courthouse, achieving (according to family tradition) the rank of brigadier general.[14] Wounded in battle more than once (possibly as many as five times), the elder Griffith was a member of the unit that attempted to spirit Jefferson Davis out of the Confederacy after Lee's surrender. D. W. Griffith referred to his father as "my hero."[15] Despite the straitened circumstances suffered by the family following the conflict, stories of wartime glory were entertainment for young David, who recalled "listening to whittling oldsters by the horse trough before the general store fight the Civil War over again—with ever-increasing victories."[16]

Balanced with these tales of heroism, however, was a conviction to right the wrongs of history occasioned by northern dominance. "One could not find the sufferings of our family and our friends—the dreadful poverty and hardships during the war and for many years after—in the Yankee-written histories we read in school. From all this was born a burning determination to tell some day our side of the story to the world."[17] In other words, Griffith developed his political, historical, and narrative sensibilities in the same period during which veterans groups from both sides of the conflict were actively engaged in a struggle over the proper way to remember the war—and to define its larger meaning. The tone of his Biograph Civil War films, therefore, was defined not only by his family history and upbringing but also by larger cultural struggles to delineate the proper narrative model for America's bloodiest conflict and to define the meaning of war itself.

The significance of Griffith's personal development to the later evolution of the war film becomes even more apparent in light of the production trends of Civil War–themed films in the early to mid-1910s. In his *The Civil War in Motion Pictures: A Bibliography of Films Produced in the United States since 1897*, Paul Spehr lists a paltry seventeen films made with Civil War themes from 1897 to 1908. Beginning in 1909, however, the number escalated through the end of 1910 before exploding between 1911 and 1913. From thirty-one films in 1910, the number more than doubled to seventy-five in 1911, fell back to fifty-nine in 1912, skyrocketed to ninety-five in 1913, and then leveled off to thirty in 1914, twenty-five in 1915, and seventeen in 1916. It is reasonable to surmise that the various fiftieth-anniversary activities of those years led directly to the increased popularity of the topic on the screen and further to assume that the storm clouds of war in Europe led filmmakers to turn their attention to the new conflict once the celebrations of the Civil War had ended.

The importance of Griffith's contribution becomes clearer in light of the fact that between August 1909 (when he filmed *In Old Kentucky*) and the beginning of January 1911 (when both *His Trust* and *His Trust Fulfilled* were released to theaters), Griffith filmed and released seven films with Civil War subjects. Given that there were only thirty-two Civil War films in 1910, Griffith's contribution of nearly a quarter of the total cannot be overlooked.[18] Combining the measure of his productivity with the fact that these films were released before the explosion of works hoping to ride the coattails of anniversary observances, it becomes clear that the tone, style, and themes of Griffith's films set the bar for those that followed. This in no way suggests that Griffith was independently creating an entirely new form. Evelyn Ehrlich points out that these early Civil War narrative films borrowed many of their basic plot ideas from the romanticized drama and literature of the 1880s and 1890s without directly reproducing specific works.[19] Ehrlich identified specific narrative tropes that recur in early Civil War films, including the "loyal slave" plot, in which a dedicated Black servant saves his or her white masters from harm, and the "love/kindness across the lines" plot (what Ehrlich refers to as the "reconciliation plot"), in which friends, brothers, or lovers are opposed to each other yet reconcile before the conclusion of the narrative. Historian Scott Simmon notes that the director was manipulating the not entirely codified conventions of a "Southern" film genre while also suggesting the importance of "women's films" and various novelistic tropes popular in the South.[20] More important, in his *Stagestruck Filmmaker: D. W. Griffith and the American Theatre*, David Mayer discusses how thoroughly Griffith absorbed the established stage conventions for dealing with the topic of the Civil War. As Mayer suggests, these films function as an integral part of an ongoing argument, not as original attempts to deal with a radically new theme. In making these films, however, Griffith subtly alters the narrative focus of the stage melodramas, gradually moving from themes of community and reconciliation to the broader moral lessons learned by all participants (whether combatant or civilian) and finally to the way that those lessons affect individual characters. By 1911, as production of Civil War films soared, Griffith, in films such as *Swords and Hearts*, *The Battle*, and *The Informer*, had transformed older literary and stage conventions through his work and firmly fixed the primacy of verisimilitude, moralism, and personal growth as the key elements of a "war" film.

Like Griffith, producer Thomas Ince also adopted a narrative model that mirrored Crane's approach. Born into a family of actors, Ince was treading the boards as a young boy and eventually married Elinor Kershaw, an actress who was contracted to the Biograph Company. Through this connection he entered the world of film, traversing Biograph, IMP, and the New York Motion Picture Company before buying up land to make Westerns under his own banner. During the early 1910s, Ince directed, wrote, and supervised hundreds of films, most prominently Westerns that took full advantage of local resources. If he is remembered today, it is for two things. The first of these is his death in 1924 following a cruise on the yacht of William Randolph Hearst. Rumors and gossip almost immediately surrounded his demise and have continued to needlessly obfuscate the circumstances. In his authoritative biography of Ince, Brian Taves thoroughly demolishes the many falsehoods with a careful recounting of the nonscandalous truth.[21] Second, and more important, Ince was instrumental in the refinement of studio production methods for manufacturing films. Though not the first to utilize a shooting script or discrete production units, he was an enthusiastic proponent and practitioner of the industrialized system, which broke down the creation of a film into segments, assigning specific artisans to specific tasks.[22] These craftspersons worked from a shooting script carefully monitored and supervised by a powerful producer—Ince himself. This system not only allowed Ince to oversee (and take credit for) every aspect of the films released under his banner but also gave him absolute authority over the editorial content of the final product. This centralized control allowed Ince to contribute most effectively to the development of the war film in the early to mid-1910s.

Unlike Griffith, Ince was not compelled to right the wrongs imposed on a suffering Southern homeland. He had no story to set straight, and his Civil War films are more clearly a response to popular demand as the golden anniversary approached rather than an attempt to shape historical memory. However, in their own way, the Ince films affirm the same key elements that Griffith was utilizing to define the treatment of armed conflict. First, Ince was well aware of the virtues of verisimilitude, not only as a narrative strategy but also as an economic benefit. His many Westerns, made in authentic landscapes as the storied Western frontier was disappearing, employed genuine cowboys and Native Americans, many of whom had direct experience with the lifestyles they were depicting on-screen. Ince's most important star, William S. Hart, had Sioux playmates as a child and learned to speak their language, spent time with gold miners in the Dakotas, and participated in a cattle drive as a young man. His personal history led him to constantly insist on "realism" as an essential requirement of his screen persona.[23] This drive to verisimilitude would carry over to Ince's other productions and dovetails with Griffith's concern with believably depicting historical events on-screen. Second, Ince arguably adopted Griffith's "universalist" attitude toward warfare, emphasizing the commonality of experience for men at arms, and applied it to his own productions with a Civil War setting. This tendency was encouraged by the developing moralism of the Western, so the ways in which Ince may have adapted elements from the competing genre and applied them to a war setting is of particular interest. Finally, and most important, Ince encouraged the development of a morally redeemable protagonist. The traditional narrative involved the development of a youth into a mature man, but Ince's frequently demonstrated variant on this theme involved a moral maturation regardless of the age of the main character. In large measure, this thematic tendency was influenced by the financial success of the films made by Hart. What historian Jon Tuska has called Hart's "almost perverse moral fervor" made money, a fact that Ince would have been unwise to disregard.[24] Hart, who was well into middle age by the beginning of his film career, was hardly a callow youth. Frequently, however, he played the role of a criminal redeemed by his involvement in a local conflict. This notion carried enough resonance to affect the depiction of characters in other genres, especially with regard to the newly emergent portrayal of warfare on-screen.

Both Griffith and Ince held specific ideas regarding the purposes of their films. Griffith focused on the artistic development of film and the application of that art to both moral lessons that he believed were universally applicable and the believable presentation of a defensible version of the Old South. Ince concentrated on producing popular and marketable stories that gleaned their value from a realistic depiction of the fading Old West and the stark moral lessons that could be drawn against the background of America's national myth. These ideas met in the developing war film and defined the narrative parameters of such films for over a decade. Examining several of these films illustrates the practical application of these principles and demonstrates the fusion of these ideas to form the basis of a new genre. Before proceeding, however, it is useful to elaborate on the parameters of the elements that emerge as fundamental to the development of the war film.

The concept of verisimilitude bedevils the impact and understanding of any film based on historical events. Though the term encompasses a variety of possible meanings, at its root it suggests the basic believability of a narrative in a way that can be comprehended and processed by the spectator and that demonstrates a relationship to the "real" world. Within this basic meaning, however, several nuances are essential for understanding Civil War films and the way in which they set the standards for the films of the First World War (and beyond). Crucially, these films contained and reflected multiple "realities" that spoke to various audiences. The most important of these audiences were survivors of the period being depicted (both veteran and civilian). For this audience, verisimilitude would include not only the accurate physical depiction of the era in terms of costumes, sets, and props but also a reflection of their recollections of the feelings of the period itself. This does not imply that the film will reflect the *actual* reality of the period; rather, it will mirror the survivor's fifty-year-old recollections of the era, thus encompassing the intervening political and social struggles and the way that those events reshaped memories of the original events. The second "reality" is that of the next generation. This includes individuals such as Griffith and Ince who had no firsthand knowledge of the Civil War but who were deeply influenced by individuals (such as neighbors or parents) who had firsthand knowledge. The perspective of the members of this group is even further influenced by the politics of memory, so that someone like

Griffith might yearn to right wrongs that he had heard about at his father's knee but of which he had only secondary experience. The last audience is essentially everyone else—those for whom a conflict has been reduced to a set of key points and tropes. For this group, the mechanics of film grammar and performance outweigh other factors in determining the reception of a depiction of warfare on-screen.

The second important parameter for the definition of the war film is the notion of a "universal" moral perspective. The notion that moral lessons can be conveyed through art is certainly not unique to film. The particular form that this impulse assumes for Griffith and Ince, however, is specific to the medium and demonstrates an advance over the many stage melodramas that address this particular theme. Both of these men understood the uses of moral uplift and the importance of conveying messages across cultural and national divides. Griffith's impulses were demonstrably those of an early twentieth-century Progressive, and Ince's were certainly commercial. In both cases, however, the goal was to create a story that cut across sectional and class divisions, imparting a moral message that could be profitably processed by any member of the audience. Increasingly over time, qualities such as courage, self-sacrifice, and pity (to name only a few) take center stage over and above more divisive virtues such as love of country, self-preservation, and preservation of class. Foregrounding qualities with which few in the audience could disagree conveyed the values of war in a way that cut across, class, ethnic and racial lines.

Finally, this principle is extended by the use of stories that demonstrate "moral uplift" in characters in need of redemption. Such narratives not only argue that war and conflict may be viewed as redemptive experiences but also strongly tie into the American faith in starting over. At a time when millions of immigrants were still arriving on America's shores, the unmistakable message that even the worst coward or criminal could be made new by firmly facing life's trials is one of the themes that popularized the Western and did the same for films about warfare. Especially as the First World War commenced, the theme of military service as a redemptive way to acquire a "clean slate" and receive full membership in American society was repeated on a regular basis.[25]

These elements recur consistently throughout the Civil War films of Griffith and Ince but do not emerge wholly formed. In particular, Griffith's *The House with Closed Shutters*, *The Fugitive*, and *The Battle* and Ince's *The Drummer of the 8th* and *Granddad* all demonstrate the ways in which filmmakers experimented with and manipulated narrative elements that became crucial to the depiction of warfare on film. Taken together, these films defined a traditional approach to war narratives that was steeped in the values of the American Civil War but malleable enough to be adapted to the impending world war.

Filmed in June 1910 and released two months later, *The House with Closed Shutters* provides a useful starting point for tracing the development of Griffith's uses of a war narrative.[26] The story involves a cowardly soldier whose sister defends the family honor by taking his place on the battlefield, condemning him to years of shame-induced confinement behind the closed shutters of their ancestral home. Simmon has pointed out that "the motifs here—the dark family secret, the mysterious mansion, the long-suffering matriarch, the emotional extremes, the motivating force of honor, the sense of history as burden—all are now familiar elements of the Southern" genre.[27] Simmon places Griffith's approach to the Civil War in a larger context that looks back to Tolstoy and Dickens and forward to William Faulkner, suggesting a connection to the mode that would eventually be recognized as Southern Gothic. The film hints at the major concerns that developed later in the Civil War cycle but does not display those concerns in a fully mature state. The melodramatic tendencies of the narrative and the stagebound performance styles undercut any suggestion of verisimilitude. At the same time, Griffith is entirely willing to cast aside the notion of a universal audience with agreed-upon moral values in favor of particularly Southern sentiments. The prominence of visual elements such as the Confederate battle flag and the visage of General Lee as well as the thematic importance of family honor strike a definite Southern chord. Lastly, there is no question of personal redemption in this film. The only possible conclusion to the narrative is the eventual death of the main character and the attendant dishonor of the family.

With the release of *The Fugitive* later in 1910, Griffith demonstrated an advance in his approach to the problems of depicting war on-screen for a broad audience. The sympathies and style of the plot reflect a more complicated understanding of the desirability of verisimilitude, the tone is markedly more evenhanded, and the moral conclusions, though not absolutist, denote the possibility for individual growth.

The plot of *The Fugitive* involves a Union soldier who kills a Confederate pursuer before unwittingly asking the slain rebel's mother to conceal him in her home. The woman hides the Union soldier from pursuing Confederates even after she discovers that her son has been killed. Thinking of her enemy's mother, she sends him on his way after the danger has passed. The film concludes with shots of the Union soldier returning home after the war and the Confederate mother visited by her son's sweetheart and her new beau, then left alone to mourn.

The Fugitive immediately establishes a narrative tone of realism by the use of both performance and image. Rather than relying on melodramatic flourishes, the performances here are simple and unforced. This reflects Tom Gunning's assertion of Griffith's move from a "cinema of attractions" (depicting particular battles or "thrilling" events) to the rising dominance of the "narrator system" of a "cinema of narration" (concerned with the realistic portrayal of psychological motivations in the development of a protagonist) as well as the shift from a "theatrical" to a "verisimilar" performance mode discussed by Roberta Pearson in her *Eloquent Gestures: The Transformation of Performance Style in the Griffith Biograph Films*.[28]

At the same time, *The Fugitive* features striking exterior photography that Griffith uses to subtly increases the realistic values of his shots by removing them from a world of stagebound interiors. This quest for visual authenticity will take many forms over time, but in the visual construction of *The Fugitive*, Griffith is performing early experiments in how to manipulate his filmed images to generate an increased degree of verisimilitude.

This film also highlights Griffith's developing awareness of the need to appeal to mass audiences in a balanced way. *The Fugitive* is evenly split in its sympathies between North and South, and that division is apparent from the opening scenes. Intercut sequences between the Union and Confederate soldiers emphasize their similarity of attitude and experience regardless of allegiance as well as the universal traits and emotions shared by the men and their loved ones. *The Fugitive* ensures that the humanity of both sides is preserved and balanced in a rigorous counterpoint. The opening sequence shows the two soldiers as mirror images of one another in their attitudes, love lives, and family situations. This is even echoed visually in the fact that the homes of both are placed atop hills overlooking dramatic vistas. As the opponents meet on the battlefield, either of them could justifiably kill the other, and the narrative takes no sides in indicating a particular sympathy. When the Confederate's mother listens to the Union soldier's pleas for mercy, that balance reaches its fullest development and becomes a driving motivation in the plot. Recognizing the universal feelings of a mother for her son, the bereaved woman refuses to surrender her own boy's killer. This sense of narrative "objectivity" allows Griffith to fully emphasize the common aspects of the sufferings of war not only for his characters but also for his audience.

To argue that either of the surviving central characters in *The Fugitive* undergoes a redemptive change within the context of the plot is pushing the narrative too far. For the audience, however, such a change is in some ways implicit in the story. Audiences standing on opposite sides of the historical North/South division could feel empathy for either of the main characters (the Southern mother or the Union soldier), though neither experiences a true personal redemption. By implication then, *The Fugitive* functions as a "reconciliation" narrative, though neither character actually reconciles with the other during the events recounted in the plot. A reflective audience, therefore, looking back across five decades, could read the plot in a positive and redemptive way without Griffith delineating any events following those depicted on-screen that might contradict that interpretation. This ability of the narrative to be read in multiple ways by multiple audiences marks an important step toward the standards that would define the construction and function of later war films.

The last important step for Griffith in the movement from a specifically Civil War narrative to a more broadly significant war film is evident in his 1911 release, *The Battle*. The plot of this film straightforwardly recounts the wartime experiences of a single soldier and their impact on both his moral character and future. The opening scenes depict a raucous parting celebration for soldiers about to march to the front. A boy bids farewell to a girl, then joins the ranks of his fellows marching to battle. Once the conflict commences, the boy is stricken with fear and flees back to the girl's home. She laughs at him and sends him back into the fray; chastened, his resolve returns. Rejoining his unit, he volunteers to go for supplies when ammunition runs low, then personally leads a train of powder wagons back to the battlefield, where the supplies ensure that the enemy will be repulsed. At the same time, he has indirectly saved his sweetheart from harm, since her house had been commandeered as army headquarters. Victory assured, they embrace, and the film ends.

More than in any of his other Civil War films, Griffith here exploits the nature of film to provide the viewer with a verisimilar experience of wartime conditions. The narrative itself is pared down to essentials that could be transposed to any armed conflict, but the specific depiction of those moments would be familiar to members of the audience who had lived through the Civil War. The tender parting from a sweetheart, the colorful march of the departing troops, and the first fear of battle are all events that could be directly recalled by veterans of the conflict yet would also be passed down through decades of reminiscing about the past. Griffith's depiction of the actual fighting is carefully calibrated for maximum dramatic effect in a way that also takes full advantage of the filmmaker's ability to capture a particular point of view. There are only two camera positions for the front line: one with

The Battle, view from behind the entrenchments, peering toward the enemy.

The Battle, view up the defensive front line to the left.

the camera placed behind the entrenchments, peering over the shoulders of the combatants (toward the approaching enemy); and one looking up the line to the left (with the camera placed slightly behind and above the troop positions). Both shots anticipate perspectives that would soon become standard for the depiction of trench warfare, and both place the viewer in the position of a combatant in a defensive position. The camera never assumes the perspective of the approaching enemy, thus maintaining a clear narrative position for the audience.[29] At the same time, however, Griffith intercuts his increasingly standard "race to the rescue" and incorporates a broad variety of landscapes, thus ensuring a wide-ranging realism not previously available in depictions of warfare.

While displaying an elaborate reconstruction of battle tactics and conditions that might feel familiar to veterans of the conflict, Griffith also moves further in this film toward the universal perspective that began to emerge in *The Fugitive*. Unlike that film, which depicted characters from both sides of the conflict, *The Battle* focuses on a single perspective and a single soldier's experience. However, rather than highlight any element that might promote political or regional distinctions (such as the very Southern preoccupation with family honor that permeates *The House with Closed Shutters*), *The Battle* is carefully neutral with regard to such issues. Instead, it focuses on the personal experience of an individual, doing so in a way that would be familiar to veterans of either side. Though the main character is a Union soldier, wearing a Union uniform and marching with troops carrying a Union flag, absolutely nothing about the narrative would need to change if he were a Confederate. Consciously or unconsciously, Griffith has, in other words, accomplished the same task with this film that Crane accomplished with *The Red Badge of Courage*. By making the narrative one of a generic individual's personal experiences and emotions in combat, Griffith universalizes the film and enables it to communicate to audiences as a tale of war over and above the specific political and cultural assumptions surrounding a single conflict.

Griffith's last achievement with this film is his codification of the clearest form of the emerging traditional narrative on-screen. The protagonist begins the film as a callow and shallow youth concerned with the gaiety of his departure and the love of a girl. When faced with the first challenge to his bravado, he fails miserably. His humiliation as he cowers before his mocking sweetheart is the key moment of the film, since the mockery by a loved one impels his return to the field of conflict. Committed to improving himself, his voluntary bravery not only makes him romantically and socially fit but also earns him the approval of his commanding officer and singlehandedly turns the tide of the battle. This basic plot becomes the central organizational schema of a vast number of the films soon to be made about the First World War.

As Richard Abel points out in his chapter on Civil War films in *Americanizing the Movies and "Movie-Mad" Audiences, 1910–1914*, *The Battle* was widely acclaimed upon release and was enormously popular with audiences.[30] Even more important, he asserts that "trade press reviews tended to eliminate most references to the Civil War or to the North and South. Instead the film was described as an 'elaborate and realistic war picture' that depicted a story of youthful 'cowardice and subsequent redemption.'"[31] While the heroine of the film is arguably not developed enough as a character to be an object of audience sympathy, Abel quite rightly suggests that the hero's journey to redemption is the actual object of the narrative, superseding any regional, historical biases.[32] For Abel, this makes *The Battle* a central work that defines the use of the Civil War film as a nationalizing cultural tool that "for a brief period, . . . must have played a significant role in joining together disparate peoples in that 'imagined community' of reunion culture [and] in bringing a sense of 'lived experience' (however fictional) to the 'Civil War as unifier.'"[33] However, these films—and those of Griffith and Ince in particular—are even more important as the progenitors of basic narrative ideas that will define the form of the initial films dealing with the First World War.

Following in Griffith's footsteps, Ince's Broncho and Kay-Bee production companies undertook the regular production of Civil War films beginning in late 1912. Already well known for the production of Westerns, Ince mirrored that genre in his Civil War pictures with an increased focus on the redemption of a central male character, adding Griffith's pattern of ensuring a level of verisimilitude and maintaining a universal narrative approach amenable to various audiences.

In his 1913 *The Drummer of the 8th*, Ince is concerned less with narrative verisimilitude than with the exciting portrayal of scenes of battle. The sense of narrative "reality" is more a by-product of that intention than an intention in and of itself. Ince's productions were adept at making thorough use of both exterior scenery and all available manpower to create exciting action set pieces. The photography, blocking, and pyrotechnics of the battle scenes in *The Drummer of the 8th* confirm that skill while suggesting for the audience a visceral sense of combat. At the same time, Ince ensures a universalist balance by focusing the narrative on the story of a young boy following his brother into combat. As in *The Battle*, the exposition minimizes the importance of actual national sympathies. In fact, the initial scenes of this two-reel picture give no indication of which side is being depicted. The film could go either way until the actual moment of departure, when it becomes apparent that the brothers will fight for the Union. As in the Griffith film, the rest of the narrative could have remained unchanged if the uniforms were gray.

Ince's more important contribution to this narrative pattern is his application of the traditional narrative in which a young boy goes to war and becomes a man. While the relatively minor character of the mature older brother is restricted to a more conventional role as stalwart love interest, the immature younger son becomes the main protagonist. He is initially shown in the clothing of a child and, Tom Sawyer–like, climbs out a window with his drum, leaving a note for his parents scribbled on his school chalkboard.[34] Over the course of the film, he takes part in a battle, suffers the depredations of a prison camp, is wounded while escaping, discovers key intelligence, bravely returns that information to Union lines, and then dies after assuring his mother that he has "been slightly wounded" and that there is "no cause for worry." At every step of this narrative, young Billy acts as an increasingly mature adult, culminating in his final act of self-sacrifice. Crucially, his death does not invalidate the maturing effects of war but rather confirms them. Though the shocked response of the family to the appearance of Billy's coffin indicates Ince's ambivalence with regard to the final unhappy result of Billy's participation in the conflict, it does not lessen the narrative assertion that he has achieved a sense of maturity and purpose.

Ince's 1913 *Granddad* does not dwell on either issues of verisimilitude or moralism. However, the film is awash in redemptive moments, demonstrating the war's positive effects on no fewer than four of the characters. Mostly set in contemporary times, the story involves the relationship between a girl and her Union veteran grandfather, who happens to have a taste for the bottle. When the girl's father brings home a new teetotaling wife, the grandfather is made to feel unwelcome until he removes himself to the local poorhouse, thereby separating him not only from his immediate family but also from the fellow veterans at the old soldiers meeting house where he had frequently spent his time. After his departure, an armless Confederate veteran seeks out the grandfather to thank him for saving the veteran's life on the battlefield. Their eventual reunion in the company of fellow veterans as well as the penitent son, his wife, and the beloved granddaughter, comes just before the grandfather's death, and the film ends with shots of actual veterans commemorating Decoration Day at a cemetery.

With this film, Ince did not need to concern himself with a believable recreation of the issues or appearance of the Civil War. There is a brief flashback to battle, but the purpose of the scene is not to re-create a historical moment or convince the audience of the practical believability of the sequence. Similarly, the moralism of the entire film is pared down to a disapproving comment on the grandfather's drinking and the universal lesson of honoring one's elders. What is most important, however, is the complicated web of redemptive moments with which the narrative imparts that moral lesson.

Though the angelic granddaughter might seem to be the logical character around whom to focus the story, her beatific goodness and unwavering devotion actually marginalize her as something of a plot device. More significant are the ways in which each of the major adult characters—the grandfather, the son, the wife, and the Confederate veteran—undergo redemptive moments that significantly affect their respective characters in the eyes of the audience. Taken as matched generational pairings, the son and his wife provide the two characters with whom the audience might be expected to most closely empathize. Both intend well—the son by remarrying, the wife by trying to prevent the grandfather from drinking—but both see their intentions backfire. The son's masculinity and filial devotion are called into question by his acquiescence to his wife's wishes (and the practical result of those wishes). At the same time, the wife's ostensibly principled attitude toward her father-in-law's drinking is directly responsible for his departure, suffering, and eventual death. The older pair is portrayed more favorably, but neither is without flaws. The grandfather is not blameless in his drinking habit, and the Confederate has taken fifty years to express his gratitude. All of the characters, therefore, exhibit some characteristic worthy of change, and those changes result from interconnected causes that relate directly back to the events depicted in the wartime flashback.

The Confederate veteran's recounting of the grandfather's heroism and sacrifice is a key turning point in the narrative for all four of the main adult characters. By the simple act of telling the story, the Southern soldier repays a debt of gratitude, but by doing it in the particular context of the plot, he also supplies the impetus for the redemption of the other three characters. The grandfather's saving of a wounded enemy soldier and the capture and imprisonment that directly result from that act wipe away any blame that might accrue to the old Union soldier for his occasional dissolution. The viewer's knowledge of the grandfather's heroic past makes it imperative that the son reverse his easy acceptance of his father's self-sacrificing departure, and the old man's death surrounded by fellow veterans forces the wife to reconsider her uncharitable attitude. Ince cements all of these individual redemptions with the vérité footage of actual veterans and by implication extends the lessons learned by each of the characters to any potential viewer.

By this maneuver, Ince solidifies the last aspect of the narrative pattern that will come to define the depiction of the Great War for the next dozen years. The verisimilar depiction of battle, period, and place will provide immediate narrative excitement, while overarching moral lessons will guarantee that that audience is as broad as possible. Finally, individual moments of redemption for the main protagonists will personalize the way that war is experienced through film, drawing the audience further into the drama and implicitly suggesting that war, despite negative moments and with the passage of suitable time, can be viewed as an experience with positive effects both for the participants and for their descendants.

As they advanced to the production of feature-length films, Griffith and Ince continued to apply this narrative pattern to the creation of war films. Both men were involved with feature-length Civil War films—Griffith notoriously as the director of *The Birth of a Nation* and Ince as the producer and guiding hand of *The Coward*.[35] Though arguably employed to differing degrees, in each case the principles discussed with regard to the short films remain central to the features. Griffith's approach to verisimilitude in *Birth*, seen so clearly in battle scenes as well as the film's many historical reconstructions, led directly to the popular acceptance of Woodrow Wilson's (perhaps apocryphal) comment that watching the film was like watching "history writ with lightning."[36] Ince's utilization of the traditional narrative is the central theme of *The Coward*, in which a frightened Charles Ray becomes a Confederate hero. In both cases, universal lessons are taught, though those advocated by Griffith have increasingly been called into question. Most important, as the two filmmakers turned from the American Civil War to the new war in Europe as a source for narrative material, their depictions of the earlier conflict served as the model for their approach to the new circumstances, thus universalizing the narrative forms they had developed over the previous few years. In their most significant films dealing with the Great War, *Civilization* and *Hearts of the World*, Ince and Griffith transferred the established narrative pattern to their discussion of warfare in the present tense rather than the past.

The advent of war in Europe in 1914 remains the single most defining event of the twentieth century, not least in the art and business of filmmaking. The conflict decimated European film industries, enabling American companies to cement their dominance in world markets. At the same time, the decisive turn to feature-length films heralded by the artistic and financial success of *The Birth of a Nation* ensured that a particular level of narrative sophistication and visual storytelling would become the normative state around the world. Moreover, the newly emergent studios began to realize the extent of their ability to shape and mold public opinion. All of these trends are exemplified by the two feature-length films made by Ince and Griffith after the outbreak of European hostilities. The films seem at first glance to work at cross-purposes, with Ince producing the stridently antiwar *Civilization* and arguing against American involvement in the conflict and Griffith just as stridently advocating American intervention in *Hearts of the World*. A closer examination, however, reveals the ways in which the elements so dominant in the Civil War model functioned as a template for dealing with war in a general sense regardless of the films' political sympathies.

Civilization (1916) was released as Wilson campaigned for reelection in 1916 with the slogan "He Kept Us Out of War." Though allowances must be made for the alteration of the current surviving print by later hands, the film reflects the strident distaste for American involvement in the European conflict, and the narrative stakes out a position against war in general.[37] The story begins in a peaceful village in the nation of Nurma just as the people receive word that their conquest-hungry leader has decided to plunge them into war. The king tasks his chief inventor to use his new submarine to achieve naval dominance, but the inventor refuses to attack civilian shipping and causes the vessel to sink. In death, he is shown in a sort of Dante-like Hades, where Christ himself takes the inventor's place, returns to earth, and (with the help of an organization of pacifist women) shows the king the error of his ways. More significant than the plot, however, is the application of the narrative elements seen so recently in the Civil War pictures to the story of a new war.

Though ostensibly set in an imaginary kingdom, the Germanic nature of Nurma's society ably fulfills the requirement of verisimilitude. The costumes of the king and soldiers, the use of personal names such as Ferdinand (drawing an implicit connection to the assassination that instigated the war), and the blunt dramatic depiction of unrestricted submarine warfare provide the sense of an undeniable contemporary reality. At the same time, the notion of the resolutely militant army of pacifists, "standing shoulder to shoulder in the battle of Right against Might," acknowledges in one fell swoop the existence of an organized antiwar movement in America, the gathering strength of women suffragists, the visibility of the American Red Cross, and the legacy of nineteenth-century Christian missionary rhetoric emphasizing a "church militant." Though the surviving print was retitled in the early 1930s, it is striking that the surviving version of the film consistently uses the language of war to promote the struggle for peace. The pacifists are an "unseen army" who exhibit "courage" in the name of the "king of peace and brotherly love" while "obeying orders from a higher power" and collecting "recruits" to join in the "invasion of the capital." The film portrays the struggle for peace as a traditional warlike act and does so in a relatable and unironic way. At the same time, the graphic depictions of the terrors of actual combat were perceived as accurate and realistic renditions ripped from the headlines of the European war. This generated specific comment in the trade press. In *Photoplay*, for example, Julian Johnson wrote that Ince "has endeavored to approximate, as closely as possible, actual war conditions, and has not attempted to lend spurious aid to his argument by introducing incidents of doubtful authenticity."[38] Thus, Ince created a sense of the reality of his film not only as a depiction of the war seen and read about in newspapers but also as a portrayal of the strident quest for peace familiar to an American society not yet directly involved. This balancing act also implies the existence of a universal moral impulse to peace, which is further confirmed in the literal redemption of the kaiser-like ruler of Nurma initiated by Christ himself.

Two years later, with the United States now an active participant in the conflict, Griffith made his own contribution to the depiction of the First World War on-screen. *Hearts of the World* further confirmed the absorption of the narrative concerns of the Civil War films into the depiction of the current conflict, though in a more orthodox manner than Ince's preachment of peace. While Ince remained neutral in his depiction of a technically imaginary kingdom, Griffith is firmly in the realm of the reality of the conflict. The main characters are a young French girl (played by Lillian Gish) and her beloved (played by Robert "Bobby" Harron), the son of an expatriate American family. When war erupts, the boy enlists, the lovers are separated, and the Germans sweep through their home village, leaving carnage, brutality, and destruction in their wake. As always in a Griffith melodrama, they are reunited at the conclusion, with the boy defending the girl's honor until they are saved in the nick of time by advancing French troops.

The strident advance publicity showing Griffith touring trenches on the front lines in France provided him with a verisimilar authority before the film was even finished, and critics cemented that position in their reviews. "*Hearts of the World* gives a new realization of modern war," wrote Frederick James Smith in *Motion Picture Classic*. His comment that "Griffith, by permission of the Allied governments, obtained many scenes on the actual battlefields of Europe" was echoed by the reviewer for *Life* who wrote that "many of the war pictures . . . were taken at the actual front and under fire of the enemy's guns."[39] At the same time, the *Life* reviewer commented on a new addition to the "reality" of Griffith's film, imported from a year's worth of "Hate the Hun" propaganda films: Griffith "gives full scope to its patriotic inspiration of hatred for the Hun and Prussian methods of waging war."[40]

The absolute hatred of the enemy was a propagandistic commonplace in the films made during the First World War. (Any basic sampling of contemporary titles dealing with the war reveals the obvious use of the medium to encourage outrage against German militarism.) This attitude was certainly not the case for the Civil War films, but the perceived reality of the respective situations made what was less desirable in a post-facto drama acceptable in the portrayal of an ongoing conflict. The crucial point here is the perception of a "reality" being shown on the screen via the narrative.

As in their respective Civil War films, Griffith is less concerned than Ince with the narrative importance of personal redemption for his characters, though the Harron character certainly matures from boy to man and proves himself in battle. As is frequently the case, Griffith is interested in the universal nature of the wartime experience and the lessons to be drawn from it. His French town is a narrative reduction of any small community caught up in the maelstrom of war, and his characters are affected in a way that is easily relatable to any audience. As Johnson wrote in *Photoplay*, the plot is "subject matter which comes rousingly home to every man on earth who has not been mechanically deprived of his virility or born with his foot under the neck of an infallible monarch."[41] Johnson thus neatly encapsulates Griffith's particular version of a wartime "universal" moral, including all true men everywhere who are not the enemy.

Griffith and Ince's transferences of the narrative elements of their Civil War films to the exigencies of the depiction of the First World War are modulated by the simple fact that their films were made while the war was pending or in progress. These are certainly not narratives created as a means of processing the aftereffects of a conflict but rather works that fit neatly with Albert Smith's "newsreel films." That these films were fundamental in the creation and definition of a powerful traditional narrative, however, makes their treatment of these concerns an important transition for the way the same concepts would be applied to the on-screen narratives of the immediate postwar years.

The end of the First World War in 1918 did not, as is sometimes asserted, bring a complete end to the appearance of the conflict in feature films. Certainly, the propagandistic "Hate the Hun" pictures that proliferated during the war years were made immediately obsolete, and the overwhelming dominance of the topic in theaters was no longer the norm, but the subject was not completely banished from the screen in the first half of the 1920s. Films such as *The Cradle of Courage* (1920), *The Four Horsemen of the Apocalypse* (1921), and *His Master's Voice* (1925) further refined the extant narrative patterns that dictated the manner in which the war was discussed. By 1925, the release of *The Big Parade* initiated new ways of thinking about the conflict, but these new concerns did not sweep away the old patterns overnight. Films such as *The Patent Leather Kid* and *Wings* (both 1927) proved enormously popular exemplars of the traditional pattern, released just as new ways of thinking about World War I narratives were rising to prominence.

Lambert Hillyer's *The Cradle of Courage* in many ways demonstrates the fullest application of the concerns of the traditional Civil War narratives to a story of the Great War. This William S. Hart vehicle begins with documentary shots of actual troops marching through the streets of San Francisco, then advances to staged shots of a troopship disembarking soldiers into the arms of waiting loved ones. Among these men are "Sergeant 'Square' Kelly, ex-crook" (Hart's character) and "Jack Riley, son of a police lieutenant." These

This *Cradle of Courage* title card depicts both the relationship between two characters and the circumstances under which that relationship was formed.

intertitles, each immediately followed by a medium close-up of the relevant character, are further followed by an intertitle reading simply "Buddies." This single word is superimposed over a title painting of troops advancing together across a gloomy field filled with barbed wire under a sky full of exploding shells. Following a half dozen various "homecoming" shots, Riley introduces Kelly to his fully uniformed policeman father, followed by successive intertitles reading "Two who have met before" and "You were my boy's pal in France and that makes you my friend." Here then, in the first few minutes of the film, Hillyer and Hart (both of whom worked closely with Ince earlier in their careers) have established each of the key narrative elements. Vérité shots of parading troops and carefully calibrated homecoming scenes immediately ground the story in a believable contemporary reality familiar to any American civilian. At the same time, the "Buddies" title and construction of the homecoming sequence asserts the broader moral argument that all manner of men are made brothers by service in arms. Finally, the dichotomy between the "ex-crook" Kelly and his straight-arrow buddy Riley sets up an instantly recognizable dramatic situation that will see Hart pursuing a path to the redemption of his character's previous mistakes.

As in Hart's many Westerns, his character's resolve to do what is right is supported by the love of a good woman but challenged by a variety of external factors. Foremost among them is his own family (including his mother), who turn against him as a result of his move away from a life of crime. However, Kelly's resolve is informed by the moral lessons he learned on the battlefield. When he and his fellow soldiers are accused of being

"THE CRADLE OF COURAGE" MAKES GOOD ARMY HOOK-UP
This shows how Nathan, of Buffalo, worked the stunt for the Symphony, Binghamton, with the line, "The Cradle of Courage Is the U. S. Army, Join Now." This makes a real hook-up and can be used wherever the picture shows

The Binghamton, New York, Army recruiting station explicitly suggested that military service was in multiple senses *The Cradle of Courage*.

"yellow stool pigeons" as a result of his new convictions, Kelly fights a former criminal accomplice to defend the honor of the men with whom he served. We are told that this is "Part of the teaching of War's great Cradle of Courage—'fight clean.'" The war, therefore, has not only cemented his bravery but also reformed his character in a positive way. His wartime service has made him think differently about his fellow men and how he treats them. At the conclusion, Kelly, now a policeman, is shot in a gun battle with the former friend who has killed his brother. The film then spells out the benefits of war even more clearly with a title reading, "Out of the mill of war, grinding the stoop from his shoulders and the twists from his soul—Square Kelly to the world." The character, reformed by the universal lessons of combat, has been fully redeemed by his wartime experience. The concluding shots show that Kelly has not only done what is right but has also won the girl and earned a rapprochement with his previously obstreperous criminal mother. The final shot is of a bugler sounding a call on a now-quiet battlefield, leaving the audience to consider the particular events of the narrative as well as the ways in which the war may have performed the same positive transformation on other returning servicemen.

The traditional lessons of the narrative were spelled out in a brief story, "Army Can Hook in with Bill Hart in 'The Cradle,'" in the November 1920 issue of *Moving Picture World*. Albert S. Nathan, a Buffalo-based Paramount employee, explicitly connected the film's run at the Symphony Theater in Binghamton with military recruitment, persuading the theater operators "to advertise that 'The Cradle of Courage is the U.S. Army.' Then the Symphony paid back by dwelling upon the army angle of the story in its own posters."[42] *Motion Picture World* reminded readers that "Hart joins the army and makes a man of himself in this story, and it works in particularly well for the recruiting sergeants." An accompanying photo shows an advertising poster for the film prominently displayed over the door of the Binghamton recruiting station, and the caption reminds publicists everywhere that "this makes a real hook-up and can be used wherever the picture shows."[43] The connection of military service with positive character reform is thus made crystal clear as an element of advertising hucksterism.

Arguably the most important and certainly one of the most profitable of the early 1920s World War I films was Rex Ingram's *The Four Horsemen of the Apocalypse*. Based on a popular novel by Vicente Blasco Ibáñez, the story concerns a family of expatriates living in Argentina. When the head of the family dies, he fails to secure passage of the estate to his favored grandson, Julio. Instead, the husbands of his two daughters return to their native countries (France and Germany) with their respective families, setting up a conflict that will culminate on the battlefields of Europe. Like *The Cradle of Courage*, the film adheres to the pattern of narrative concerns set down in the Civil War pictures. Unlike its predecessor, however, Ingram recalibrates those concerns to meet the dramatic needs of the preexisting novel as well as to suit the emergent dialogue regarding the personal moral and ethical standards against which his star and lead character would be measured.

Four Horsemen is never unduly concerned with the generation of a sense of narrative verisimilitude. The film is not intended to be truly believable or relatable to the audience in the same way as Griffith's and Hillyer's films. The best-selling novel lent itself to an interpretation that emphasized the epicness and exoticism of the story, foregoing a sense of believability in favor of more sweeping dramatics. As Thomas Slater argues, screenwriter June Mathis was "drawing on her familiarity with romantic melodrama and adaptation rather than realism, either physical or psychological, or the actual experience of the war."[44] The war itself is a real enough presence, but the true attraction of the story is that of the errant grandson, played by rising star

Rudolph Valentino. As Gaylyn Studlar points out in *This Mad Masquerade: Stardom and Masculinity in the Jazz Age*, the casting of Valentino represented a newly emergent and unsettling type of masculinity and provided an important verisimilitude of character. The film "works to make Valentino's deviant masculine type acceptable to a wide audience within a xenophobic and nativist culture."[45] The Italian actor's previous career as a dancer not only emphasized his problematic sexuality but also provided him with instant credibility as the spoiled and oversexed son of a corrupt and wealthy French family. While earlier films that used the war as a narrative element had assumed a circumstantial connection between their audience and their story, here the viewer is asked to understand a character type.

This approach to the character of Julio Desnoyers precludes the empathy that might previously have been a key method of conveying both the believability and the moral of the narrative. The depiction of the moral qualities of the Julio character is unremittingly negative, and the moral concerns of the film are consequently depicted in a starkly one-sided manner. Julio is a wastrel and spendthrift, interested in presenting himself in vaguely sexual terms as a dancer and pursuing a career in art to facilitate his dissolution. As Studlar points out, he "displays the suave duplicity associated with the lascivious pan-European seducer."[46] The central relationship of the film is his affair with a married woman (Alice Terry) who is not only adulterous but betraying a brave husband wounded in combat while Julio scoffs at military service. Valentino therefore becomes emblematic of an entire morally bankrupt system and a severe test of the notion that redemption through wartime experience is possible.

As the film advances and Julio descends to a level of apparently irredeemable moral turpitude, the narrative seems altogether to preclude the notion of redemption. Confronted with his lover's combat-blinded husband, Julio is concerned only with his own happiness. Her commitment to atoning for her adultery, however, leads him to reconsider. She attributes her resolve directly to the war, saying, "Life is not what we thought. Had it not been for the war, we might have realized our dream. But now, my destiny beside him is marked out forever." Duty, inspired by wartime sacrifice, has led her to forgo their previous amorality, and now the recognition of her priorities leads Julio to reassess his position. Rather than question her constancy to him or assume a return to conventional moral norms, he declares, "How could I dare hope for your love? I have been a coward!" and resolves to join the army and fight. Though it could be argued that the transformative power of their love has led him down this new path, it is also clear that Julio seeks redemption for his cowardice and that it can only be achieved through the experience of service at arms. His moral failings are exemplified by his failure to do his part, and his decision to fight trumps the catalog of deficiencies he has accumulated throughout the narrative to this point. When we see Julio after four years in the trenches, his physical appearance and demeanor have utterly changed. Valentino's days-old growth of beard erases the effeminate urbanity that previously defined his character, and his heavy coat adds bulk to his otherwise willowy frame. Here is a man who *looks* like a soldier, and an intertitle confirms that the transformation of his character is more than simply physical: "He is a different Julio! One hears everywhere of his unselfishness and his bravery." This is further affirmed by his distribution of a care package from home to his fellow soldiers and by his own assertion that he is "content—very content." The death he will soon meet in the trenches in no way lessens his transformation but instead confirms the value of war in redeeming his past indiscretions. As a final affirmation of his character, the now chaste and pure love he feels for his previous mistress is validated further by his spectral visit to encourage her to remain with the husband who needs her care. The war has not only corrected the deficiencies of Julio's character but also allowed him to be a guiding light to those who survive him.[47]

Perhaps the most unusual manifestation of the traditional model in a World War I film is to be found in the independent production *His Master's Voice* (1925).[48] The star of this feature-length film is "Thunder, the Marvel Dog," and the film announces its moral concerns in the first intertitle of the story proper, following a shot of Thunder with a young pup (identified as his son, Flash). "Thunder had seen Life, had faced Death, made sacrifices and won glory, and now, in peaceful retirement, taught his son the qualities essential to good dogs—courage, love, loyalty." Thunder is thus the narrator of the "gallant tale" of "how he had brought up his Master" to appreciate the importance of these virtues. The story that follows shows Thunder by the side of his timid and cowardly master (Bob) as the boy is humiliated by the town bully and denigrated by his own uncle. Thunder has "plans to take care of his Master's interests" and does so as best he can. When Bob is drafted (his uncle declaring it "the best thing that could have happened to him"), his mother tells him to "think of the glory of it" as Bob expresses his fears. As the representatives of the draft board come for Bob, Thunder is asked if he'd like to enlist in the Red Cross, and the dog answers in the affirmative by leaping up, ready for action. The next scene shows Thunder "helping" on an ambulance in France and then stumbling upon Bob cowering in an abandoned farmhouse. "His hopes for his Master blasted, pity burned in Thunder's heart. Something must be done!" The dog literally grabs Bob's collar in his mouth and begins to pull him back to the trenches. Once there, Thunder is everywhere. He delivers water, rescues a wounded soldier in no-man's-land (to the cheers of both Germans and Americans), and follows Bob on a dangerous mission to rig an explosive charge. Fending off German attackers, the dog ensures that Bob can reach the cut detonation wire. Inspired by Thunder's example, Bob makes a valiant effort, but when his wounded master's strength fails him, Thunder himself connects the wires that cause the detonation and ensure a successful attack. In recognition of their efforts, both Bob and Thunder are decorated for "great courage and exceptional bravery." Bob returns home a changed man, now able to assert himself and proud heir to the mantle of service previously held by Civil War veterans. The film doubly emphasizes this relationship by intercutting shots of returning doughboys with aged Civil War vets who have gathered to greet the newly discharged soldiers.

As in *Four Horsemen*, verisimilitude is not the primary concern of this narrative. While that earlier film was more concerned with emphasizing the dangerous elements of Valentino's sexuality, his shaky grasp of masculinity, and the extreme defects of character that could be corrected by military service, *His Master's Voice* concentrates on the natural moral lessons to be taught by war. The remarkable use of a dog as both narrator and moral exemplar demonstrates not only the malleability of these narrative concerns but in some sense their inevitability. The "courage, love and loyalty" shown by Thunder are a part of the natural order of things, and as Thunder tells us in his own "words," Bob is made a better man by following this natural example.

Released within months of *His Master's Voice*, King Vidor's 1925 film *The Big Parade* began a process of reassessing the usefulness of the traditional model as a way of depicting and understanding the experience of combat on-screen. That reconsideration did not immediately undercut the viability of the earlier narrative pattern, however, and in the latter half of the 1920s, two very successful films demonstrate the continued prominence of the established traditional model as a new narrative emerged to challenge the older pattern for dominance. In 1927, both *The Patent Leather Kid* and *Wings* resolutely displayed the positive merits of combat, becoming major box office hits.

First National's *The Patent Leather Kid* starred Richard Barthelmess as a cocky young boxer forced to face up to his own cowardice when he is drafted into the army. The death of a friend as they advance against an enemy position inspires the Kid to a feat of bravery that guarantees the success of the attack, though he is severely wounded. The final shot of the film shows the recuperating boxer being tended to by the girl he loves and saluting the flag he had previously spurned, both outcomes the result of his redemptive transformation through combat.

William Wellman's *Wings* is in many ways the ultimate expression of the traditional Civil War film narrative standards applied to the First World War. The film was a huge financial success for Paramount and received an Oscar as Most Outstanding Production (later revised into the first Best Picture award). It featured star players Richard Arlen and Buddy Rogers as high school rivals who find friendship on the battlefield and Jobyna Ralston and Clara Bow as love interests. It also featured a version of the Great War that fit comfortably within the narrative standards promoted in the first half of the 1920s. The film's verisimilar approach emphasizes not the experience of the soldier on the ground but—in a nation giddy over Charles Lindbergh's solo flight over the Atlantic just a few months before the film's release—the more rarefied experience of the chivalric "knights of the air." One of the key selling points touted in the souvenir book sold at screenings is the romanticization of technology—both in aviation and in film, where it could capture dramatic moments with impressive accuracy. The story has "the great adventure of the sky as its background," and the heroic underpinnings of that perspective are further reinforced by the dedication page, which specifically links the film not only "to those young warriors of the sky whose wings are folded about them forever" but also to Lindbergh himself.[49] The authenticity of the film as a reflection of the combat experience might be questionable, but its sense of believability would have been immediately endorsed by aviation-enthusiast parents and their aviation-obsessed children reading the various heroic "Air Service Boys" adventures of Charles Beach.

That "believable" version of the war unquestionably promoted a moral world in which chivalry was the dominant code. Throughout the film, members of the German air force are depicted as the kind of men who deliver messages to warn of fallen heroes or refuse to fire on planes with jammed weapons. The universal camaraderie of combat is shared by all who take part, and rules of proper behavior are paramount. Bravery, patriotic enthusiasm, and a sense of fair play are the primary attributes of the men who fly, echoing the same lessons earlier learned by Hart in the trenches or taught by Thunder the dog.

Finally, *Wings* unquestionably promotes the usefulness of war as a redemptive and maturing proving ground. By enlisting, Jack pursues a "path of glory mounting to the stars." At the conclusion of the war, he is hailed as a conquering hero and as "a man returning where a boy had gone away." Even more important, however, is the way in which participation in the war provides its own absolution. Despite the fact that Jack has mistakenly shot

The cover of the *Wings* souvenir book emphasizes the excitement and drama of aerial combat.

down his best friend, Dave, as he tried to fly across enemy lines, the dying man forgives Jack, telling him that it was not his fault. When Jack returns home, Dave's mother tells him, "I—I wanted to hate you, John, but I can't. It wasn't your fault. It was—war!" Finally, as he confesses a supposed drunken sexual indiscretion to the woman who loves him (actually a nonindiscretion with her that resulted in her being sent home from the ambulance corps), she tells him, "I can't blame—anyone—for anything! What happens from now on is all that matters." Thus the war has not only brought about Jack's maturation from boy to man but has neatly redeemed any errors of judgment he may have committed while undergoing the process. The death of his friend does not lesson his position in the community or his own moral standing and is

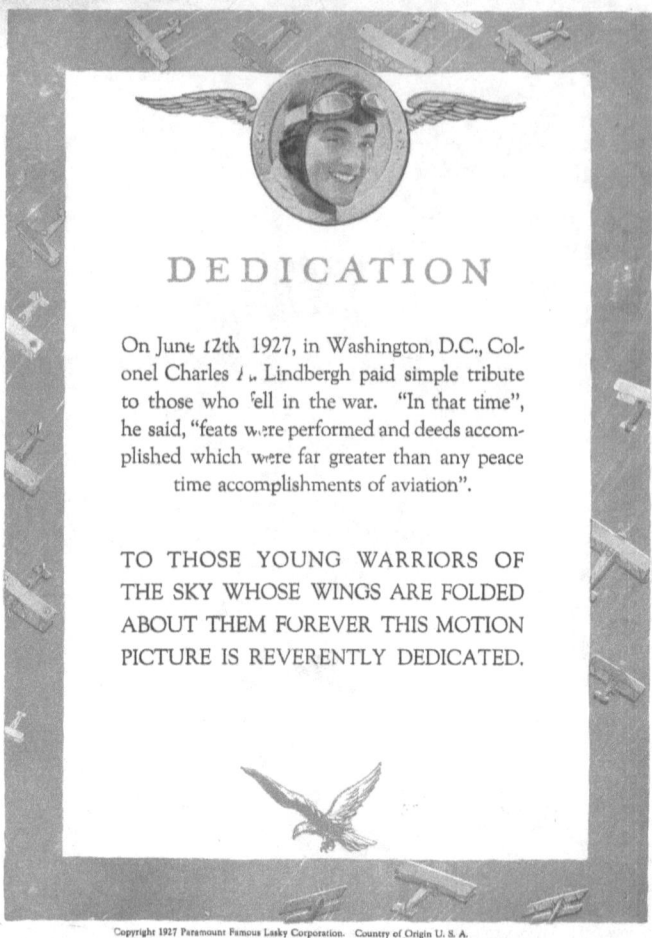

The *Wings* souvenir book dedication page implicitly connects the heroics of Charles Lindbergh to the heroism of World War I aviators.

entirely forgiven. The war has worked its magic, and the film can end with the hero contentedly kissing the woman he loves.

In these World War I films, the narrative conclusions regarding the usefulness and benefits of participation in combat do not differ markedly from those seen in *The House with Closed Shutters*, *The Coward*, or any of the other Civil War films. Those earlier films are crucial antecedents to a narrative that depicts combat as a useful means of encouraging personal growth both as an individual and as a member of society. Courage, bravery, loyalty, devotion—these are virtues refined in the crucible of war that make the participants better men. Though friends may die, fears may be exposed, or conflicts may have other unfortunate aspects, the ultimate result will be a redemptive maturation within an established moral framework. Presented with enough of a sense of verisimilitude to avoid violating the memories of those who experienced the war years firsthand, the narratives of these films used the same basic elements to repeatedly affirm this perspective. Just as veterans of the Civil War could read *The Red Badge of Courage* or patronize Griffith's or Ince's anniversary films to reinforce their sense of the place of the Civil War in their own lives, it was assumed that the same prevailing pattern of narrative concerns would continue to function for veterans of the Great War. As the 1920s progressed, however, it increasingly became apparent that this was not the case. In both literature and film, the narrative approach to the First World War was first questioned and then reshaped to suit the more immediate needs of veterans processing and reflecting on events of the more recent past.

Chapter Two

COMBAT, LITERATURE, AND FILM

Combat Veterans and the Production of Narratives
of Wartime Service, 1925–1930

IN THE MID-1920S, THE UNITED STATES BEGAN IN EARNEST TO COME TO GRIPS with the Great War and its effects. Veterans flooded bookstores and libraries with memoirs and unit histories, and a vast selection of novels and short stories set during the war were published and/or translated into English. In works such as *The Great Gatsby*, *A Farewell to Arms*, *Soldier's Pay*, and *Three Soldiers*, writers F. Scott Fitzgerald, Ernest Hemingway, William Faulkner, and John Dos Passos struggled to comprehend the meaning of the conflict and its impact on an entire generation of young men. Taken together, these works defined—and continue to define—what came to be known as the Lost Generation. As Keith Gandal points out in his *The Gun and the Pen: Hemingway, Fitzgerald, Faulkner, and the Fiction of Mobilization*, however, there is a masked irony to the success of these novels. While defining a mood and tone that continues to shape our view of the war, many of these men were not directly involved in the conflict as combatants:

> The "quintessential" male American modernist novelists were motivated, in their celebrated postwar literary works, not so much, as the usual story goes, by their experiences of the horrors of World War I but rather by their inability in fact to have those experiences. The famous sense of woundedness, diminishment, and loss in these works, the sense of mourning for fallen worlds . . . stems, not principally from the disillusionment or the alienation from traditional values brought on by the crisis of the Great War or the failure of civilization it represented . . . but instead from personal rejection from the U.S. Army.[1]

Gandal's argument does not account for those who experienced some aspect of combat, such as volunteering for an ambulance corps or receiving training without being sent overseas, but he makes a useful point regarding the formation of notions of military service. Those impressions are not always the result of actual combat but may sometimes emerge from established ideas surrounding the idea of military experience. Notions of military service created during the anniversary of the American Civil War were influential in forming the narrative patterns that prevailed in film depictions of warfare through the mid-1920s. The disjunction between those traditional notions of combat and the actual experience of soldiering created an intellectual foment that those who served were forced to confront in their later literary efforts.

While these authors pursued their postwar literary endeavors, other men were also processing their responses to the Great War. Like the purveyors of literary postwar modernism, these men had to find new ways of expressing themselves that radically modified an established schema of narrative tropes, but they had to perform this task within a very different artistic context. Filmmakers such as Raoul Walsh, Howard Hawks, James Whale, and William Wellman teamed with writers such as Laurence Stallings, John Monk Saunders, and Erich Maria Remarque to create their own versions of the wartime experience. Unlike their literary contemporaries, however, many of these men had direct exposure to combat conditions. Though that exposure varied, the combined effect of their service fundamentally altered the depiction of the war on-screen. The fact that Stallings, Whale, and Remarque served in the trenches during major battles, that Walsh edited raw footage of battle for propaganda purposes, that Saunders and Hawks trained flyers for combat, and that Wellman actually flew combat missions deeply influenced their treatment of the war as a narrative subject. Their work brought about a wholly new approach to the dramatic portrayal of conflict rooted in their firsthand experiences. However, because that approach took initial root outside of the conventions of filmmaking, it is vital to examine how new ideas were made manifest in relation to one another as these filmmakers grappled with the transition from page to screen. The success of their efforts led to the development of a new narrative that displaced the traditional model established by D. W. Griffith and Thomas Ince as the standard during the industry's previous forays into depicting combat.

Though all of these men contributed in one degree or another to the reformulation of the depiction of the Great War on-screen, the key players in the process were the three men with the most direct combat experience. Stallings, Whale, and Wellman all served as active-duty combatants during the conflict, and all suffered emotional and physical hardships as a result of their service. Stallings fought as an infantryman at Belleau Wood, and his wounds eventually forced the amputation of his leg. Whale served a year in the trenches in France before being captured and spending more than a year as a German prisoner of war. Wellman flew with the Lafayette Flying Corps and was decorated and shot down; he was also widowed by a German artillery attack. In each case, these men's artistic proclivities dictated not only the manner in which they would enter the world of filmmaking but also the way in which their view of the war would manifest in their work. Stallings's literary tendencies (especially as seen in his thinly veiled autobiographical novel *Plumes*) made him a direct precursor to Hemingway and Faulkner and deeply influenced the eventual form and impact of *The Big Parade* and *What Price Glory?*[2] Whale's predilection toward the theater created a direct correspondence between his staging of *Journey's End* in London and his later films *Journey's End* and *Hell's Angels*. Wellman's wartime memoir and his early interest in Hollywood (and his fortunate connection with Douglas Fairbanks) shaped his depiction of combat in works such as *Wings*, *Legion of the Condemned*, and *Young Eagles*. Crucially, unlike the "quintessential" writers discussed by Gandal, these three men felt no deficiency regarding their participation in the First World War. Each had done his duty and suffered for it. By combining their particular artistic strengths and their personal military experiences through the medium of film, they formulated responses to the war that found full expression in the cultural mainstream and altered the prevailing patterns for the depiction of combat on-screen.

Throughout the first half of the 1920s, filmmakers' prevailing approach to the First World War differed little from the attitudes of filmmakers who had memorialized the American Civil War in the mid-1910s. War narratives routinely exalted traditional virtues such as courage, bravery and devotion and portrayed war as the ultimate method of molding immature, untested men into fully formed, responsible members of society. In literature, however, the postwar spate of dry regimental histories and simplified fictional representations began to give way in the mid-1920s to literary works informed by experience and featuring a strikingly different tone. The divide between filmed and written perspectives gradually converged on a thematically unified portrayal of the effects and experience of war, displacing the older narrative model and replacing it with a new approach combining an incisive literary critique of combat with the discursive and artistic potential of American popular cinema. In the vanguard of this change was Stallings, a veteran of the U.S. Marine Corps.

Laurence Tucker Stallings was born in Macon, Georgia, in November 1894. His family had deep Southern roots, and two of his paternal great-uncles were killed fighting for the Confederacy. As a boy, he was reputedly fascinated with heroic tales of the Civil War, and held Confederate Memorial Day as equivalent (if not superior to) the Fourth of July. In 1912, he enrolled at North Carolina's Wake Forest University, where he majored in classical studies and biology, played football, edited the literary magazine, and met his first wife, Helen Poteat, the daughter of the university president. After college, he found a job as a reporter and joined the Marine Corps reserve, receiving an assignment to active duty in July 1917. In 1918, he sailed for France as a second lieutenant and saw heavy action at Chateau-Thierry, leading the first wave of attack at Belleau Wood. In late June, "Stallings went after a machine gun nest that had to be wiped out. . . . A bullet caught him in the right leg and ripped off his kneecap. He went down, but he threw the grenade anyway and wiped out the entire nest." When he recovered consciousness in a hospital, Stallings refused to allow the leg to be amputated, so doctors inserted bone grafts in an effort to salvage the appendage. Stallings was decorated for heroism and returned home, marrying and continuing his work as a reporter. In 1922, a bad fall on ice forced the amputation of his leg. After his release from the hospital, Stallings traveled to Europe with his wife and began work on his novel *Plumes*.[3]

This biographical information is necessary for understanding Stallings's later work. *Plumes* basically recounts the details of Stallings's life as the background of the main character, Richard Plume, with three crucial differences between the reality and the fiction. First, the second chapter of the novel recounts an entirely fictional history of the Plume family in America from 1685 to 1912. (Stallings came from a long line of Baptist ministers, and neither of his grandfathers fought in the Civil War.) The tone of the chapter establishes the heroic tradition of the past but also mocks that tradition. Representatives of each successive generation are maimed in combat, though their stories are passed down from father to son in a manner that minimizes the anguish of their wounds and maximizes their commitment to service. Each injury is worn as a badge of honor, and sons are expected to take up the torch when it is passed to them. Stallings (especially in the context of what is to follow) thus explicitly criticizes the heroic tales of his youth that fostered his eagerness to enlist.

Second, Stallings repositioned his marriage from after the war to before it. When Helen Poteat married Stallings, she was well aware that she was marrying a man who was ravaged by injuries received in combat. Despite his anguish about the effects of his condition and any burden it might place on his wife, Stallings could console himself with the fact that she had some idea of the problems she might face. In the novel, Richard's wounds are made that much more grievous by the fact that he marries Esme before shipping out. Unless Esme accepts divorce, she will be forced to remain with Richard as he deals with the agony of his injuries. Though these agonies are described at great length (there is much talk of the scars on the leg, the many operations, the painfulness of the leg brace), one of the most painful aspects of the wound in Richard's eyes is the fact that his wife must share these problems with him, and he blames himself for her situation.

The last variation between fiction and reality has a direct bearing on the postwar perception of combat in the popular mind. Stallings was wounded in circumstances that would generally be considered heroic. He was leading his men in an attack, successfully completed his mission despite his own wounds, and was decorated for his actions. Essentially none of this is included in *Plumes*. The circumstances of Richard's wounding are recounted in a brief but intense flashback that is just a few pages long. Notions of heroism are entirely removed from the scene. Instead, there is an emphasis on the physical pain of the wound, the pain of responsibility, and the pain caused to his wife. Describing the wound to Richard's leg, Stallings writes,

> For an hour he had held his eyes away from [his knee]—the lean white cords, like E strings on a bass fiddle, and the Turkey red matting of what had been a white gauze tourniquet. It couldn't be bleeding again. There was no more blood in him to flow through that damned gaping hollow of his thigh. The blood had crawled up his spine and in the back of his hair. He could feel it stiffening upon his neck. . . .
>
> . . . The foot was turned exactly around, its heel and toe reversed, and was swarming with gnats. . . . The right kneecap was still glistening white, despite the low light from the west, as it hung by its ligaments over the jagged opening of his stained breeches.[4]

There is no glory here, only the carefully described agony of a devastating injury. Even more important, the wounded Richard speaks directly to the impulses and influences that have brought him to this point:

> Richard Plume, center of the universe, had life stolen from him. Stolen, by God, by all those scoundrels who were not there upon the ground with him. The God-damned scoundrelly orators were not there—were not with him. . . .
>
> . . . [B]ack home thousands of loose-lipped sons-of-bitches were talking pompously of supreme sacrifices made pompously. What a fool to have given [his wife] up for them. . . .
>
> . . . Why did he want to make his world safe? A world of blacked boots is safe for democracy anyway.[5]

There is absolutely nothing glorious or redemptive about Richard's injury. Instead, it is a senseless sacrifice made at the behest of misguided ideals and impulses that will destroy both him and those he loves. In the end, *Plumes* indicates that the lessons of Richard's (and Stallings's) life speak to the senselessness of all war and to the Great War in particular.

Each of these changes implicitly criticizes both the war and the cultural imperatives that left Stallings utterly unprepared for the reality of combat. The novel itself constitutes an attempt by the writer to come to grips with this conflict between the heroic ideals inculcated during his youth and the facts of his wartime experience. The oppositions between heroic romance and bitter recrimination and war as pageantry or slaughter, proving ground or personal hell are exactly the same concerns that drove the late-1920s transition to a new narrative model for the depiction of war in film. Though unjustly forgotten, *Plumes* essentially initiated this process in both literature and film.

Though Europe had produced a number of important fictional works critical of the war by the early 1920s, the American literary establishment lagged behind. Henri Barbusse's *Under Fire*, Ernst Jünger's *Storm of Steel*, and Rebecca West's *Return of the Soldier* all appeared before 1920, and each touched on elements of the war that Stallings would address. With the possible exception of Dos Passos's *Three Soldiers*, however, no earlier American work so devastatingly critiqued the war, and certainly none could do so from the relatively unassailable perspective of a decorated veteran. (As recounted in Townsend Ludington's biography of Dos Passos, he, like so many members of the Lost Generation, was a noncombatant ambulance driver, thoroughly embittered by his service, and harbored radical political views).[6] The success of *Plumes* provided Stallings with immediate cultural capital that he used to good effect in his position as a columnist for the *New York World*. It also brought him into contact with a variety of leading literary lights, including the members of the Algonquin Round Table (of which he was a charter member) and a fellow writer on the staff of the *World*, Maxwell Anderson. Collaboration with Anderson led to the writing and production of Stallings's other key literary success of 1924, the drama *What Price Glory?* Like his novel, this coauthored play (Stallings's hand is most evident in the bitter second act) was a critical and financial success that not only allowed Anderson to quit the paper and move on to a successful career as a playwright but also led Hollywood to take an avid interest in both properties and their common author.

Sometime in 1924, a reliable up-and-coming MGM director with a penchant for philosophy pitched a proposition to producer Irving Thalberg. Weary of making "ephemeral films," King Vidor wanted to develop a story around one of three topics: steel, wheat, or war.[7] Thalberg preferred the last of these options. As Scott Simmon and Raymond Durgnat point out, the success of Anderson and Stallings's "stage version of 'What Price Glory' . . . prompted Irving Thalberg to gamble on Vidor's subject—so long as Stallings himself was involved."[8] Though no major films dealing primarily with the war had been made in Hollywood since the armistice, Stallings's successful literary career thus provided the impetus for the creation of the first of many subsequent war films of the 1920s, *The Big Parade* (1925).

When Vidor, Stallings, and Thalberg set out to create a film dealing with the Great War, they faced two conflicting impulses. The first was to accurately reflect the embittered tone of Stallings's novels (and those of his literary contemporaries). The second was to hearken back to the heroic ideal of the Civil War past seen so frequently in the traditional narrative model. Their failure to adequately justify these two contradictory approaches is the opening maneuver in a ten-year process to create a new narrative vocabulary for discussing war and combat. This new model had to provide an adequate means of conveying the "reality" of war for returning veterans in the face of an accepted, standardized, and entrenched cultural construct that ran counter to that "reality."

Vidor had no specific plot in mind for his "war" film but "only an approach. I wanted it to be the story of a young American who was neither overpatriotic nor a pacifist, but who went to war and reacted normally to all the things that happened to him. . . . The average American is not overly in favor of [war], nor abnormally belligerent against it. He simply goes along for the ride and tries to make the most of each situation as it happens."[9] This statement in and of itself introduces the kind of narrative ambivalence that is seen in the final film. Vidor's frequently stated desire for "realism" is inherently undermined by his optimistic suggestion that the average American soldier would "make the most of each situation as it happens," especially when such situations are as harsh and unforgiving as those described by Stallings in his novel.

Apparently happy to receive a generous paycheck and to experience the Hollywood social scene, Stallings quickly produced a five-page story outline, partially reproduced in Durgnat and Simmon's volume. As those authors attest, the writer's initial treatment featured a lighter tone, more in keeping with his earlier short story "The Big Parade" published in the *New Republic* in September 1924. In that work, a lieutenant is forced to choose a single one of his tightly knit group of nine surviving trench veterans to remain behind while the others join in a military parade in Paris. As in *Plumes* and

What Price Glory?, Stallings carefully navigates the tonal disjunctions of war-weary veterans forced to engage in absurd acts—in this case a comical show of strength for a clueless French public. The story embodies a complex mix of emotional cues, but a lightness of touch is imparted to the lieutenant's very real fears that the man who remains behind will be killed before the rest of the unit returns. The culmination of this balancing act occurs at the conclusion of the story. The man left behind has taken advantage of the situation and deserted. His conscience-stricken superior officer last sees him boarding a railcar headed away from the front accompanied by a pretty girl. The implied brotherly bond of the veterans therefore falls to the wayside as the troubled lieutenant returns to the trenches with the remaining eight men.

This same facility for contrasting the serious and the comic and for manipulating traditional tropes is seen in Stallings's description of Jim Apperson in his first story draft for the film. Jim is "the model son, generous, filled with guts, handsome, careful, mannerly, unrestrained," but he has also "attended five colleges in succession, carrying nothing with him but his suitcase," is "completely irresponsible," and "hasn't a grain of respect for family traditions."[10] The description itself recalls earlier treatments of war in film and points in the direction of yet another version of the traditional narrative. In Stallings's hands, this might have developed in a manner as double-edged as "The Big Parade" or the theatrical script for *What Price Glory?*, but for the Hollywood filmmakers it provided an initial template that could easily be folded into traditional narrative patterns. Even so, Vidor "wanted more" than the bare outline.[11] When Stallings announced his intention to return to New York, Vidor, along with writer Harry Behn, bought tickets for the same train and kept the celebrated soldier talking about his own wartime experiences during the whole cross-country trip. The outline and the reminiscences, by their nature covering ground also covered in the autobiographical *Plumes*, formed the screenplay of *The Big Parade*.[12]

An examination of the resultant film reveals the tensions between portraying war as a heroic adventure and Vidor's declared intention to create a "realistic" portrait of the common soldier. As in *Plumes*, a large number of details and events correspond to Stallings's personal biography. Prior to the war, Jim Apperson (played by John Gilbert) is engaged but not married. When the war begins, he is swept up in the tide of patriotism and volunteers for army service. Like Stallings, Apperson is sent to France, where he takes part in the first attack wave at Belleau Wood. He is wounded in the leg while attacking a German machine-gun nest, and he eventually loses the leg. Uncomfortable at home, he does not remain with his family after being mustered out of the service. These surface similarities, however, do not lessen the pull toward romanticism displayed in the film. Even the presentation of these bare facts is colored by the portrayal of war as a heroic/chivalric endeavor.

A recognition of the dual nature of the narrative is apparent in contemporary reviews of the film, not just in the film itself. An anonymous reviewer for *Photoplay*, for example, referred to the film as "war . . . from the mud-splashed perspective of a cootie-bitten private . . . war as war actually is, with soldiers and women playing their parts bravely as plain human beings." While failing to acknowledge that plain human beings might quite reasonably be something less than brave in wartime situations, this review also summarized the story with the broadly romantic description of the main characters as "a French maiden, an American doughboy and his two modern musketeers."[13] In his review for *Life* magazine, Robert Sherwood (a veteran himself) exhibited the same conflicted approach. He significantly overcredits Stallings (whom Sherwood must have known as a fellow member of the Algonquin Round Table) for his story involvement and for "choosing King Vidor as director and John Gilbert and Renée Adorée as stars" and then claims that Vidor has, "made war scenes that actually resemble war" and depicted soldiers who are "recognizable and real." At the same time, however, Sherwood acknowledges that "the picture itself is essentially a love story—and a supremely stirring one at that."[14]

The conflicted nature of the film's stance is further highlighted by the contrast between an interview featured in the souvenir book for the film and a *New York Times* report on the film's production. The *Times* story emphasizes the care taken to make the film as authentic as possible, cataloging meticulous efforts to ensure that every detail is correct "on account of the familiarity of the war to millions."[15] In the interview, however, Vidor emphasizes his desire to highlight the humanity of those involved in the conflict: "Now War is a very human thing, and in the ten years' perspective the human values take predominance, and the rest shrinks into insignificance. . . . The human comedy emerges alongside the terrific tragedy. . . . You get the true poetry, romance and atmosphere of it in the ten year view from the date of its origin. You realize not only the deep personal feeling but also the queer sentimentality."[16] The use of terms such as *poetry* and *romance* is reinforced in an unattributed blurb on the second page of the program that characterizes the film as a "brave tale of the humors and thrills of War days . . . told honestly" and the war itself as "the grandest lark of history."[17] The disjunctions between depicting authenticity and portraying the war as a "lark" are difficult to bring into alignment. Even the images featured in studio publicity frequently seem to straddle the line between romance and reality, awkwardly

This advertising herald for *The Big Parade* highlights the awkward juxtaposition of darker martial imagery and conventional romance.

juxtaposing darker-themed illustrations with romantic motifs. Vidor later obliquely acknowledged the dichotomy by arguing that he now found *The Big Parade* "mild" in terms of any "anti-war lesson" and asserting only that he was making a "more realistic thing."[18]

Though these conflicted comments indicate the beginnings of new thinking about the depiction of the war, *The Big Parade* fits neatly into traditional narrative patterns. Nearly every biographical aspect has been altered to increase the positive virtues of wartime service. Initially seen in a barber's chair receiving a shave, Jim responds indignantly to a question about his future employment: "Me . . . work? I should say not!" His initial introduction to the audience is as one of the "rich men's sons," and his condition is directly contrasted with the working-class occupations of the men he will soon befriend in the service (one a bartender, the other a construction worker). The enthusiasm his fiancée (Justyn) exhibits for the declaration of hostilities ("Aren't you thrilled we're going to war?") directly contrasts with Mrs. Apperson's anguished reserve on hearing the news, thereby painting the young Justyn as an empty-headed child. Jim's immediate reaction to his mother's fears that he will enlist is to say, "I have enough war on my hands... with Dad," which is not the response of a mature, responsible adult. Even his enlistment is shown as the result of a youthful, patriotic impulse rather than any measured consideration. All of these elements combine to portray Jim as an immature and callow youth made even softer by the hazards of wealth.

Every subsequent episode of Jim's involvement in the war demonstrates the positive effects of military service on his transition into adulthood. In basic training, Jim comes into contact with members of the working class and learns the meaning of honest labor (whether marching around France or shoveling manure). His billeting in a village behind the lines gives him the opportunity to romance Melisande, a French farm girl, thus achieving a degree of separation from Justyn, the object of his youthful infatuation ("As long as Jim could remember he had been in love with Justyn"). Even when not directly contributing to his maturation from youth to manhood, Jim's actions are romanticized opportunities to build character. Jim is wounded in combat not as he leads an authorized attack on an enemy position but because of his emotionally "heroic" reaction to the death of his close friend in no-man's-land. As Slim lies dying and a senior officer warns Jim that he has orders to be quiet, Apperson cries out, "Orders! Orders! Who the hell is fighting this war—men or orders? . . . I came to fight—not to wait and rot in a lousy hole while they murder my pal!" Following this outburst, Jim charges alone from the shell hole in which he has taken shelter, demonstrating the same bravado seen in the soldiers of innumerable previous films set during the Civil War. Even his painful return home on crutches and one leg is treated less as a life-altering wound than as a life-changing opportunity to return to France to be reunited with his true love. Thus, at every step, the war provides prospects for a positive outcome. Vidor's claims of "realism" are anchored firmly in conventional expectations to such a degree that even moments sometimes interpreted as antiwar (such as Jim's outburst in the shell hole) lead to actions and results that continually move the protagonist along a path of maturation and improvement. The contrast between this approach and that of *Plumes* could hardly be more marked. Every action in the novel advances toward the ultimate destruction of the main character as a responsible and self-reliant man. Because of the war, Richard eventually loses not only his physical ability to walk but also his ability to support his family and his capacity to love. Despite moments in the narrative that could have been—but are not—portrayed as crushing, Jim Apperson emerges stronger as the result of his experience. Clearly then, in spite of claims that the film is both depicting war accurately and making an outright antiwar statement, the process of converting Stallings's stories to the Hollywood screen has removed their harsher elements, forcing them to conform to an established standard for the portrayal of war in film. Despite its inability to move too radically from the established model, however, *The Big Parade* initiated a further discussion of the war that increasingly permitted filmmakers the license to contest the conventional approach to a war narrative.

Stallings's selection as a scenario writer for *The Big Parade* was inspired by the enormous success of *What Price Glory?*. Though perhaps not as bleak in outlook as *Plumes*, the play is far from being as broadly comic or lighthearted as is sometimes suggested. This false memory of the written work is largely influenced by the 1926 film adaptation directed by Raoul Walsh. Despite assurances in the souvenir program that "'What Price Glory' the film remains a perpetual record of 'What Price Glory,' the drama" and that "William Fox has adhered faithfully to the play in its transcription to the screen," the film altered a number of key elements from the play.[19] These alterations reflect the disjuncture between the previously dominant narrative and the beginnings of a new "disillusionment narrative" much closer to the tone of the contemporary literature of the First World War. The resultant amalgamation of contrasting dramatic tones within the film reflects the awkwardness of this shift and highlights strategies used by the filmmakers to reconcile the extremes of these two narrative styles.

Stallings and Anderson's play follows two professional soldiers, Captain Flagg and Sergeant Quirt, during a part of their tour of duty in the trenches in France. The narrative of the play is straightforward, but the methods it uses to convey its points are fairly complex. The play is divided into three acts, with the first and third taking place behind the lines and the second taking place in the cellar of a building on the front lines. In the first act, Flagg and Quirt are brought together when Quirt is assigned to replace Flagg's recently killed top sergeant. They begin to compete almost immediately for the affections of a local farm girl (Charmaine) and receive orders to advance to the front. In the second act, the two soldiers lead their men in battle and comfort the physically and psychologically wounded in the shelter of the cellar. The third act sees them return to their original locale, where they continue to compete for Charmaine (this time with cards and a pistol) before being recalled to the front. The play ends with Quirt running after Flagg, protesting that he should not be left behind as the troops move back up to the lines.

When first performed, the play immediately caused a sensation for a variety of reasons. Primary among these were the inclusion of much saltier language than contemporary audiences were used to, the perception of a realistic attitude toward and depiction of the war, and, most important, its many moments of humor.[20] Read today, the language is almost unremarkable, except that it is not the cultured writing of the drawing room comedies and dramas in vogue at the time. Liberal use of the words *damn* and *bitch* as well as lines such as, "This horny pelican is going aboard the skip's old hooker every night" were guaranteed to raise eyebrows.[21] This contributes as well, of course, to the perceived "realism" of the work, which is most straightforwardly apparent in the second act, which was written mostly by Stallings.[22] Several monologues discuss conditions at the front, and one green lieutenant comes close to cracking from the psychological strain. His long diatribe against the war includes a description of a dying German sniper begging for help as he hangs from a tree in no-man's-land (comparable to a similar description in *Plumes*). In addition, casualty figures are discussed, and several characters are severely wounded (with their deaths implied in several cases).

Arguably more important than these elements, however, is the calculated use of humor within the context of the narrative. In both "The Big Parade" and his story draft for the film of the same name, Stallings used humor incisively as a tool for navigating his feelings regarding the ultimate meaning of the war. Even *Plumes* is not without moments of wry levity. *What Price Glory?* continues this pattern of using humor as commentary. Stallings and Anderson point up the absurdity of war as a game by positioning their two protagonists at each other's throats throughout. Quirt and Flagg are loud, boisterous characters who have soldiered for years and have encountered each other before. Their competition over Charmaine, a young woman depicted as little better than a prostitute, reflects a longer struggle over women that has played out between the two of them at stations across the globe. At the same time, it provides a counterpoint to the more deadly game in which they find themselves engaged. Their dislike for each other is counterbalanced by their mutual respect, and their competition is a comment on the drive that makes them good soldiers even in the face of the chaos of the trenches.

Their rivalry is depicted in ways that can be considered humorous, but the "comedy" (the word is inappropriate without conditions) is of a particular kind. It works within the context of men living on the edge and experiencing the absurdity of war but never tips over into a cruder farce. The comedy is tinged with tragedy rather than being funny. Paul Fussell comments on the irony-weighted recollections of Great War veterans and how they used small, absurd moments or details to process their general recollections of the combat experience. One doughboy, for example, recalled the absurdity of "grand-looking cavalrymen, ready mounted to follow the breakthrough," on the first day of the Battle of the Somme. Another vividly recalled the deaths of five officers because of the image of one man's pet terrier lying next to the remnants in the trench.[23] The stage version of *What Price Glory?* uses its "humor" in exactly the same way to portray the horrors of war. In the first act, when Captain Flagg gets drunk on leave, the scene could be read as a moment for slapstick. Stallings and Anderson allow for that possibility but implicitly intend that the audience not dwell merely on the image of the drunken officer but reflect on the circumstances that lead him to get drunk. Even more pointed is the moment in the first act when a general arrives to issue orders for a raid across enemy lines.

> THE GENERAL: And Flagg, some Yankee Doodle back in Hoboken sends you some posters with his compliments.
> FLAGG: Posters? What for?
> THE GENERAL: To post behind the German lines—sent to all companies of this brigade.
> FLAGG: My God! What are we advertising? Camels?
> THE GENERAL: Oh no! It's intelligence work. Explaining our mission over here to the German soldier. There are three hundred posters. Send a small detail through the German lines some night and tack 'em up all over the place.[24]

Read incorrectly, this is farce, and some audiences may have accepted it in that spirit. As Fussell suggests, however, veterans would view such an exchange in a very different light. Assigning men to tack up posters behind enemy lines is not so very far from gaily dressed cavalrymen charging into machine-gun fire—which is itself only a half-step from the whole notion of trench warfare. Though applying a more subtle style to two-thirds of its length (and recognizing that the use of humor is tempered by the straightforwardly embittered second act), the implicit disillusionment of this play is just as cutting as that of *Plumes*. The competitive game playing, cursing, and absurd comic ironies may superficially make the play more palatable for an audience than the bitter acidity of the novel, but they are all part of a method that makes the work no less powerful in its condemnation of war as a destroyer of men.

In 1926, when Fox Film Corporation released its screen adaptation of *What Price Glory?* it faced some of the same issues that had faced Vidor and

Stallings when creating *The Big Parade*. Like Vidor, Walsh had to address the question of choosing between the accepted film standards of a romanticized traditional narrative and attempting to transfer the bitterness of the play to the screen. In this instance, the decision is further complicated by the question of fidelity to the original text of a successful and well-known stage drama, concurrently leavened (potentially) by the play's use of humor to comment on the wartime narrative. The result is a curious hybrid of narrative intentions achieved primarily by alterations and additions to the original text, a complete (though perhaps calculated) misreading of the tone of humor in the play, and, most important, the creation of a dual structure that allows elements of both the traditional and emerging narrative approaches to coexist in the same film.

The film version of *What Price Glory?* includes basically all of the narrative high points of the stage play. The plot content of the first and third acts is almost entirely retained, and the second act, while simplified, remains essentially the same. The film consistently differs from the written text in three ways, however. First, and most superficially, the titles of the silent film contain much less harsh language than that used on the stage. Legend has it that many audience members (used to reading lips from years of silent film viewing) objected to the language of the actors as they performed, but the objectionable elements generally do not make their way to the intertitles themselves. Second, the film alters a number of characters to conform to established film conventions. Charmaine, for example, is a lovestruck girl rather than a calculating wanton: "Thrilled by war in her front yard—fascinated by the men who stop at her smile on the way to die." Rather than an object of contention for two men engaged in constant competition, she becomes a fully fledged (if not entirely respectable) love interest. Unlike her stage counterpart, who settles her affections on whichever soldier is nearest, this character eventually expresses her true love for Sergeant Quirt. In addition, a number of other characters are fleshed out or altered (Corporals Kiper and Lipinsky are demoted to private and become comic relief). Finally, the scope of the film is expanded to include scenes that are only suggested in the play. Heroic images of combat, with troops bravely advancing in the face of enemy fire, are an expected part of the war narrative tradition and are included here (the play shows no combat at all). Earlier encounters of the two main characters in China and the Philippines, which are only mentioned in the play, are shown at length in the film as a sort of prologue. Flagg and Quirt are seen brawling over prostitutes in both places, with Quirt emerging as the victor in both instances. Each of these changes alters the bitterness of the stage drama by adding an element of adventure and romance, and each becomes a component of the two major changes that dichotomize the narrative along the separate tracks of the standard traditional approach and the emerging narrative of disillusionment.

The first of these larger changes involves the interpretation of the humor of the stage play. Stallings and Anderson used humor in a very calculated and particular way in their text, emphasizing the absurdity of events rather than their comic elements and portraying the quarrels of the two officers as a release from war rather than suggesting that they form a comic team. The film disposes of these distinctions almost entirely. Flagg, for example, is introduced as someone "soldiering for wages—loving and fighting for fun." He is immediately set up as a boisterous character, both by his introductory intertitle and by his initial actions (which involve a quarrel with a prostitute's pet monkey). The same is true of Privates Kiper and Lipinsky, who acted as impartial commentators in the play but in the film function merely as comic relief. Throughout, the competition between Flagg and Quirt is treated as rough fun; it is not in any meaningful way an outlet for the horrors of war. The effect, of course, is a strong pull in the direction of the traditional narrative, demonstrating that war is an entertaining (if occasionally deadly) proving ground for true manhood. This turns the carefully modulated absurdist tone of the play into one of knockabout fun, which was by no means the intent of the writers.

The filmmakers may not have been entirely unaware of this problem and presumably hoped to address it through their second major alteration to the mechanics of the stage drama. This alteration is a calculated division between the two types of narrative, emblematically represented by two types of soldiers. In this scheme, the qualities of the traditional narrative are attached to the draftees, most of whom either are not mentioned by name in the play or barely exist as characters. The burden of the disillusionment narrative is assumed by the professional soldiers (mostly officers, such as Flagg and Quirt), who, despite their romanticized elements, are given moments of deep pessimism regarding both the particular circumstances of the First World War and the nature of war generally. This dual narrative strategy results in an awkward ideological mix, with conflicting messages emerging from both narratives as they uncomfortably attempt to work together to create a coherent whole.

The traditional aspects of the film graft established tropes of the form onto the framework of the original story. Aside from the additions regarding the professional officers, stock draftee characters are brought into the narrative and placed in standard situations that lead to predictable results. For the most part, these soldiers are recognizable only by the most simplistic

The sensitive artist with his mother from *What Price Glory?*

traits (the sensitive artist, the henpecked husband, and so forth), and their experience of war is shown to consist of situations familiar to any soldier in any conflict (mail call, mess, the heroic departure of troops for the front, and the like). Similar scenes can be viewed in war films going back to the early 1910s (in some cases even earlier, such as Edison films showing assembled troops moving inland after landing in Cuba). Though these characters tend to be generic, a few are granted sketchy backstories. The young artist, for example is briefly shown painting by a river as his mother approaches. This shot immediately establishes both his sensitivity and his immaturity, thus also establishing his need to make the painful transition to manhood. In the context of the film, that transition can have only two results: death (as in the case of the young artist) or recognition by the professionals for a job well done (and a successful shift to maturity). Following action on the front lines, Flagg tells his men, "They sent in babies to baptize in blood and fire. You've gone through it and—from one old soldier to another I'm as proud of you as America should be!" There could hardly be a more literal demonstration of the function of these troops as emblems and subjects of a narrative that emphasizes the usefulness of war as a path to maturation.

Such draftee characters are counterbalanced by specific instances of a parallel disillusionment narrative, all of which involve the unit's professional officers. These moments are distributed throughout the running time but often specifically utilize the intertitles to starkly comment on the nature and effects of war. So, for example, on his return from combat, one soldier writes in his diary, "Back again after the first terrible experience under fire. We lost all but eighty. The horror of it haunts me—the stench of the dead—the blood—the maddening rumble of the guns." This language resembles that seen in contemporary war literature, but the full effect of such moments is limited when they are intermingled with conventional narratives. Though the expression of such sentiments indicates that the film is attempting to turn toward a new narrative model, the difficulty of full conversion is emphasized by the film's treatment of act 2.

Though the film narrative reflects that of the play fairly faithfully, the one major exception is the abridgement of the events that take place in the cellar on the front lines. Rather than being a staging area from which several raids are undertaken, the cellar in the film is a respite from the battle and a dressing station for the wounded. This scene features the clearest condemnations of war in the longest two monologues of the play (one by Quirt and the other by an anguished lieutenant). The film completely excises Quirt's monologue but retains a shortened version of the lieutenant's words. Entire lines are essentially transferred directly from the text of the play to the intertitles of the film: "My men look at me like whipped dogs," the officer says before continuing, "Flagg! I'm going to take my boys out of the muck and blood. And I'll kill you if you stand in my way."[25] The film, however, adds a line in which the lieutenant refers to his soldiers as "white faced boys with the stink of the dead in their nostrils." They key word here is *boys*, which emphasizes—even amid the most harsh, bitter, and disillusioned scene of either the play or film—the uneasy junction created between the two types of narrative.

On its release, Walsh's *What Price Glory?* was both critically well received and a financial success. However, it is also an important bridge between the dominance of traditional narrative expectations and the nascent new approach emphasizing disillusionment with the wartime experience. Though the attempt to combine the two forms is not entirely successful, the film constitutes an effort to move in that direction and paves the way for large numbers of works in the early 1930s that would dispose of the traditional model completely.

In her *Decline of Sentiment*, Lea Jacobs argues that both *The Big Parade* and *What Price Glory?* may be read as "male adventure" tales that are part of a pattern of declining sentimentality seen throughout the film industry of the 1920s: "These two films . . . represented a sharp break with previous films about the War and stood apart from more traditional representations of male heroism and honor."[26] At the same time, however, she concedes that "as the [films] retreated from . . . areas of difficulty, or made compromises with the theatrical original [in the case of *What Price Glory?*], they became relatively more sentimental."[27] Though Jacobs is correct in asserting that both films represent advances in the realistic and unsentimental depictions of the war, the problematic nature of the term *sentiment* weakens the argument. She sometimes, for example, reads humorous incidents as *more* sentimental than might be the case. To cite one instance, she finds Karl Dane and Tom O'Brien as Jim Apperson's friends in *The Big Parade* "too much like a vaudeville team to carry a serious film."[28] Though their humor may seem low from a modern perspective, her extensive quotations from Sherwood's review of the film fail to include his claim that the two characters are "rough and blasphemous but typical crusaders of the A.E.F."[29] Jacobs applies the same malleability to her discussion of other films, suggesting that the scenes of the Paris leave in *Wings* are "quite tame and sweet" (despite the insinuations of drunken sexual shenanigans that run throughout the sequence) and asserting that "in tone and theme both *Journey's End* and *The Dawn Patrol* are indebted to the play *What Price Glory*" (though the nature of that indebtedness remains undefined).[30] This is not to suggest that Jacobs is mistaken in asserting that something interesting is going on here, but the boundaries and the mechanism of that change are not fully articulated. These two films opened the door to a larger modification of the traditional treatment of the war narrative on-screen. As other filmmaking combat veterans created their own war narratives, they grappled with the inadequacy of the old model. Over time, this process led to a continued deemphasis on heroism of any kind and an increasing sense of combat not as a proving ground for an individual but as an inexorable mechanism that mundanely wore down men of all nationalities in its own questionable service. War gradually came to be seen as an unstoppable force that imposed a similar, universal experience on all of those unfortunate enough to take part. In the case of a filmmaker and former infantryman such as James Whale, this viewpoint fostered attempts to depict a vision of warfare that enabled him to completely dispense with the accepted standards of the traditional narrative and to dispose of the notion of military service as heroic. For William Wellman, steeped in the public romanticism of service among the Knights of the Air, this emerging new notion of the war and its meaning tempered the traditional approach with a sense of the larger, universal realities of combat. In both cases as well as throughout the industry, the sentimentality discussed by Jacobs would be transformed not merely by the vagaries of taste but also by individuals bringing their own experiences to bear on situations and stories that allowed the creation of an entirely new way of dealing with war as a subject.

Like Stallings, Whale experienced war from the frontline trenches. A quiet young man who hoped to teach art, Whale was apolitical and did not enlist on the outbreak of hostilities. Instead, he spent a year as a volunteer camp worker for the YMCA. In 1915, presumably assuming that he would be conscripted, Whale enlisted as an officer cadet, and he was commissioned a second lieutenant in the summer of the following year. Over the next eighteen months, Whale saw frontline fighting in the waning days of the First Battle of the Somme, at Arras, and in the 1917 Flanders campaign, during which he was captured while leading a raid on a German pillbox. He spent the remainder of the war in a prison camp.[31] Aside from developing an abiding hatred of all things German, Whale made generally constructive use of his time, especially with regard to the amateur theatrical productions staged by the prisoners. These efforts not only provided relief from the tedium of imprisonment but gave Whale a taste for the theater that would guide his postwar career. Inspired to pursue work in the London theatrical world, he eventually became involved in the staging of a play by a fellow veteran in London in the late 1920s, an event that led not only to fame in England but to direct involvement in the American film industry.

Written by R. C. Sherriff, an ex-infantryman who had been wounded in combat, *Journey's End* tells the simple story of a group of officers stationed in a frontline trench in March 1918 and awaiting the start of a major German offensive. Young Second Lieutenant Raleigh reports to his new position eager to begin his career as a soldier, his enthusiasm stemming in part from his knowledge that he will be under the command of Captain Stanhope, his sister's fiancée and a friend of the family. (Raleigh has pulled strings to ensure the assignment.) Stanhope is less than thrilled regarding his new subordinate, at least in part because he has tried to put all civilian life behind him as a way of dealing with the stress of combat. He also liberally uses alcohol as a respite from the horrors of the trenches and as "liquid courage," a fact that shames him and that he would like to keep from the woman. Over the play's three acts, Sherriff manipulates conventional expectations by playing the character and attitudes of Raleigh, an exemplar of the traditional narrative, against those of Stanhope, who demonstrates the beginnings of the emergent narrative of disillusionment. Stanhope's harsh efforts to temper the boy's naivete appear cruel and sadistic, especially in the face of Raleigh's romantic attitudes regarding both his friend and their mutual situation. The final result of this contrapuntal treatment of the two men occurs in the waning moments of the play when Raleigh is brought into the officers dugout struck through the spine by a piece of shrapnel. He innocently believes, "I'll be better if I get up and walk about. It happened once before—I got kicked in just the same place at football; it—it soon wore off."[32] He is, of course, mistaken, as the wound is mortal. He dies in the arms of his friend and superior officer, who allows himself a moment of tenderness before heading out into the trenches to meet the German attack. The drama ends with a lone candle blown out by an explosion as the entire dugout collapses.

According to James Curtis, Whale was initially unenthusiastic about the play, which was slated to run for only two performances, but his experiences as a veteran made him ideally suited to the material. Matthew Norgate, a representative of the Incorporated Stage Society, which staged the play, later recalled that he "went to [Whale] partly on the strength of my knowledge that he had himself been in the trenches."[33] As Sherriff recalled, Whale at first "didn't seem very enthusiastic about 'Journey's End.' . . . He said little about the play beyond the comment that certain scenes were too sentimental and would have to be brought down to earth or cut out."[34] The director warmed to the material, however, both designing the set and casting struggling young actors such as Maurice Evans, Laurence Olivier (for the initial run), and Colin Clive (as Olivier's replacement after the initial engagement). At least in part because of the director's commitment to minimizing sentiment, the play was applauded as a work that "displayed the whole agony of war in the trenches," that allowed veterans to tell civilians that war was "Exactly like that," and that the *Evening Standard* compared to the work of Homer in having room for both "personal humors and . . . impersonal tragedy."[35] With backing secured thanks to the initial positive reviews, the two-day engagement turned into a two-year run at a first-class London theater during which the play garnered great acclaim. When the show moved to New York in 1930, it carried Whale with it.

Whale's trip to Broadway occurred at a pivotal moment in film history. Since the birth of the talkies, Hollywood producers had been trolling New York for directors, actors, and plays that were deemed suitable for the new technology. At the same time, the advent of sound in film encouraged a move to a more realistic treatment of various topics, including the First World War. As a successful recent stage drama dealing with a topic enjoying a resurgence of popularity in both literature and film, *Journey's End* was therefore perfectly placed to bridge the differences in the treatment of combat across the stage, literature, and film. After a brief apprentice period, Whale began to cross that bridge with his first two films—*Hell's Angels* and *Journey's End*—both of which dealt directly with the First World War.

The troubled production history of *Hell's Angels* has entered the realm of Hollywood lore (and been recounted for more public consumption in the form of Martin Scorsese's *The Aviator*), but Whale's role in that history is less well known. After production began as a silent film, producer Howard Hughes essentially rebooted *Hell's Angels* when it became clear that sound technology was transforming the film industry. Fresh from stage success in London and New York as well as a brief period observing Hollywood production methods (including uncredited involvement as a dialogue director on the film *The Love Doctor*), Whale was brought in to stage and direct dialogue scenes in the aviation epic. Dissatisfied with the script, Whale encouraged Hughes to hire Joseph Moncure March (author of "The Wild Party") for rewrites and then conferred with and encouraged March as he worked. Though the initial inspiration for the film was the success of Wellman's *Wings*, the final work displays an attitude toward the war that stands in marked contrast to its predecessor.

The basic story of *Hell's Angels* involves two brothers—Roy, a straight arrow played by James Hall, and Monty, a layabout played by Ben Lyon—and the no-good woman who comes between them (Greta Nissen in the silent version, Jean Harlow in the final release). Though the tortured production history makes the assignment of overarching story elements problematic, the evidence of the film itself indicates the contradictions permeating the entire industry regarding the treatment of the war. Following the model laid out in a traditional narrative, the immature, "worthless" brother might be expected to see the error of his slack attitude and return to a "good" woman by the conclusion of the story, chastened and socially acceptable. Instead, Whale and March completely invert expectations in three key ways. First, there is no "good" woman. Harlow is depicted as sexually opportunistic, promiscuous, and faithless, and that characterization never changes. Despite the "good" brother's infatuation with her (and his self-delusion regarding her character), it is clear to the audience that she is certainly not a girl to come home to at the conclusion of the conflict.[36]

Second, as in the text of the stage version of *Journey's End*, a definite sense of the unheroic circumstances and universal futility of the entire war is allowed to permeate the narrative. This is perhaps most pronounced in a scene at the pilots' mess hall, with Lyon's Monty holding forth with a long, detailed defense of his apparent cowardice. The moment completely disavows war as an activity promoting maturity and heroism, demonstrating that at best the film is conflicted regarding the utility of armed combat. Unwilling to assume his responsibilities on night patrol, even after (or perhaps especially given) the death of a comrade who had taken his place the previous night, Monty leaps up from the dining table and proclaims,

> I'm not yellow! I can see things as they are, that's all, and I'm sick of this rotten business! You fools, why do you let them kill you like this? What are you fighting for? Patriotism... duty... are you mad? Can't you see they're just words? Words coined by politicians and profiteers to trick you into fighting for them! What's a word compared with life ... the only life you've got? I'll give you a word... murder! That's what this dirty rotten politicians' war is! Murder! You know it as well as I do! Yellow, am I? You're the ones that are yellow! I've got guts to say what I think! You're afraid to say it! So afraid to be called yellow, you'd rather be killed first! You fools! You poor stupid fools!

These sentiments markedly contradict the tone of earlier conventional narratives and give clearer definition to the same feelings expressed by *The Big Parade*'s Jim Apperson in the outburst that follows the death of his friend Slim. They would also be entirely at home in the stage version of *Journey's End*, where (in lines omitted from the film version) Osborne and Trotter specifically refer to orders to execute a raid on German lines as "murder" not once but twice.[37]

Finally, the conflicted view of Monty expressed throughout the film indicates the growing complexity of issues surrounding involvement in the war. Though he essentially enlists on a whim and is depicted as the irresponsible and selfish sibling, he does care about his brother. Even his womanizing is not entirely irredeemable, as it provides him with the clarity to immediately see the Harlow character as unworthy of Roy's affections. His mess-hall diatribe functions as a defense against accusations of cowardice but is also immediately countered by his volunteering for a suicidal mission at his brother's side. That mission results in the ultimate repudiation of war as a valuable cauldron for personal development when both brothers are captured by the Germans (after achieving the mission's goals). Faced with death, Monty is willing to reveal sensitive information in exchange for his life. Rather than talk him out of doing so with appeals to courage, duty, or honor, however, Roy uses a ruse to obtain a pistol from the Germans and then shoots his brother. Monty tells him not to cry, since "it was the only thing you could do," but death—while it might protect Monty from yet another transgression—is certainly not the preferred pathway to redemption.

The uncomfortable melding of two diametrically opposed narrative patterns marks *Hell's Angels* as another significant turning point in the transition to a new narrative of disillusionment and demonstrates the influence of Whale's unsentimental approach to war from the beginning of his involvement in filmmaking. It cannot, however, be read in isolation. In part as a consequence of the vagaries of its production, *Hell's Angels* was not released until after Whale's most significant statement on the nature of combat, his film version of *Journey's End*. Unlike the grand, Hughes-produced opus, *Journey's End* had no ties to the established narrative patterns of popular film and made no concessions to the earlier forms. Rather, it directly reflected the sentiments of its writer and director regarding their wartime experiences and, like the stage version, was free to dispense with any notion of war as a heroic or useful enterprise. Though Whale modified his material in several ways while transferring it from stage to screen, he remained true to the underlying attitudes reflected in the play. He thus presented something notably different from most preceding films and capitalized on the inroads made earlier by Stallings's work and influence.

As James Shelley Hamilton pointed out in his review of *Journey's End* for *Cinema* magazine, Whale "has not done anything revolutionary or even novel in technique—in fact the production may easily be made a theme for argument among those who like to discuss the relative merits of stage and screen."[38] Even a cursory viewing of the film bears this out in terms of visual style and set design, with most of the story taking place (as in the play) in a single dugout, shot simply. In terms of the text as well, Whale (working again with March) made no grand additions to the story, resisting any urge to embellish the play by inserting flashbacks or an on-screen love interest.[39] Given the directness of the transposition of the story to the screen, then, the few changes Whale made assume an added importance, especially given that (with one exception) the majority of them consist of deletions from the original text.

The one additive change to the film is apparent from the first shot and prefigures the theme of Whale's other alterations. Whale had discussed "opening up" the material in interviews, and the initial sequence of the film provides a tour of the battlefield as it traces the progress of a relief column through no-man's-land. Ironically for a play that features such a small cast of characters in a confined space, Whale uses this sequence to reduce specific details regarding any individual or their situation, initially denying viewers any sense of a protagonist. While leaving the viewer adrift in terms of the characters, he also moderates the class-consciousness of a story told almost exclusively from the perspective of officers. The easy, grumbling banter of the

Tommies as they move to their position contrasts with the stiffer formalities of the officers and highlights the presence of both types of soldiers on the battlefield in a way that the original text did not. At the same time, the barren bleakness of the landscape and the constant rumble of shellfire give a visual notion of a setting only insinuated in the play. This pattern continues periodically throughout the film, with certain dialogue exchanges reset from the comparatively sheltered dugout to the harsher, more dangerous, but more egalitarian setting of the trenches. Those trenches implicitly universalize the entire story, since it is there that the officers and men are on equal footing. Even more, the same effect can be seen in the brief but intense scenes of combat, where not only is death indiscriminate in claiming victims but it is also difficult to distinguish any of the combatants as characters. The soldiers are visually equal targets for death on the battlefield.

In and of themselves, these scenes might simply be construed as an opportunity to add action or expand the parameters of the setting, but this argument is given more authority by an examination of Whale's deletions when transferring the play to the screen. As with the addition of battlefield exteriors, those deletions consistently reduce any opportunity to confer traditional heroic status on the characters while making the tragic, disillusioned circumstances of the combatants broadly relatable to the largest possible audience.

Three types of material are consistently removed from the screen version of *Journey's End*. First, nearly every mention of the technical details of combat has been systematically deleted. The first few minutes of the play include mention of "Minnies," "a Lewis gun," and "Mills bombs" as well as the disposition of troops in the trenches and sleeping arrangements for the officers. Such material has almost always been removed from the film.[40] While this might be seen as an attempt to simply pare down the more arcane mundanities of the story, that argument loses authority given that the film itself is so concerned with the accumulation of those everyday pedestrian details of life at the front. While those details create a specificity of circumstance relatable to Sherriff, Whale, and their fellow veterans, they also make the text less accessible to a nonveteran viewer. Their removal broadens the appeal and message of the film for a general audience. While we may recognize the troops as specifically British, in other words, the point is not belabored in a way that might prove distracting for a non-English or nonmilitary viewer.

Similarly, Whale consistently reduces details that would be specific to English social and cultural life. Raleigh's use of social connections to ensure his appointment is minimized in the film, as is most discussion of Stanhope's standing as a student. At the same time, talk of gardening and archaeology in specific locations in the English countryside is almost entirely removed, along with extended conversations regarding English football.[41] These deletions not only universalize the cast as representatives of a greater mass of soldiery but also narrow the focus of the drama by disallowing the very brief moments that provided relief from the sheer grimness of the overall narrative.

Finally, like Stallings and Anderson in *What Price Glory?* Sherriff included a vaguely bumbling colonel who serves as a veiled criticism both of the senior staff generally and specifically of their thoughtlessly wasteful use of their troops. Among the reproachable aspects of this character is his regular suggestion that officers will earn the British Military Cross for heroically following the suicidal dictates of their superiors. For the film, Whale diligently removed any reference to medals or awards and with it any suggestion that traditionally rewarded heroism is a factor in the characters' actions. He also modulated the depiction of the colonel himself, making him less the doddering object of satiric barbs and more a fellow functionary in the larger bureaucracy of warfare.

In making these changes, Whale did more than simply streamline an existing play for adaptation to the screen. He had two major effects on the depiction of the Great War in film that can repeatedly be seen in its successors. First, he successfully adapted one of the harshest depictions of the Great War ever created—one that was widely perceived as reflecting the true "reality" of combat—from the stage to the screen, distilling that grimness even further through his deletions from the original text. Prior to *Journey's End*, vestiges of the traditional approach persisted in filmed narratives of the First World War, but Whale's film dispensed with that romanticized view by bringing Sherriff's play to the screen in an unadulterated rendition. At the same time, Whale contributed to the ongoing shift in the parameters of the war film from narratives that portrayed war as an entrée into fully mature participation in a society to stories that showed war as a universal tragedy. Though war films would still be told from a particular national perspective, it became increasingly common to see films in which the horrors of war were shared among fighting men of all nationalities regardless of their political allegiances. This perspective had tentatively been seen in a few earlier films such as Rowland Lee's *Barbed Wire* and John Ford's *Four Sons*, but in the period following the release of *Journey's End*, the prevalence of this view became more pronounced in works such as Lewis Milestone's screen version of *All Quiet on the Western Front*, Ernst Lubitsch's *Broken Lullaby*, William Dieterle's *The Last Flight*, and fellow veteran Wellman's *Young Eagles*.

Wellman's *Wings* is one of the primary expressions of the traditional narrative in relation to the First World War. However, his public attitudes toward the war and his direct involvement in combat make him a test case for the development and general spread of new ways of thinking about the conflict in the late 1920s and early 1930s. Notions of the comparative nobility of the war in the air are present in much of Wellman's work (including *Wings*), but they exist alongside a general conception of combat and the enemy that is modulated over time. This reflects Wellman's development from an adventure-seeking volunteer to a reflective veteran, but (especially given the success of *Wings*) it also makes him an exemplar of the industry-wide shift in attitude toward the war.

In 1917, bored with his employment options and impatient with schooling, twenty-one-year-old William Wellman had been desperate to join the fight. An airplane ride had made him an aviation enthusiast, and he saw his involvement in the war as both an opportunity to learn a skill and an outlet for his restless spirit: "America's entry into the war was imminent, and being an adventurous young man, I had to get into it. I wanted to fly!"[42] Rebuffed by the U.S. Naval Aviation Service for his lack of education, Wellman signed up with other volunteers for service in a unit of American expatriate ambulance drivers, having "been told by friends that once overseas in the ambulance service, the American volunteer had two choices at his disposal. He could either stay in the ambulance service or he could join the French Foreign Legion and in turn be trained for the French Flying Corps." The young volunteer never served in the ambulance corps, transferring to the Lafayette Flying Corps on the day of his arrival in France.[43]

Immediately following the war, Wellman's enthusiasm saw an early outlet in a written memoir, *Go Get 'Em!*, but it also remained apparent in interviews and in his films for the rest of his life. He made a definite mark as an aviator, credited with shooting down five enemy planes, but his public testimonials to the romance of flying had an even greater initial impact on the shaping of public memory regarding the First World War. Though his career remains underassessed, one of the key points of general agreement is the importance of autobiographical elements throughout the Wellman filmography. According to Todd McCarthy, "What does seem to have mattered was for Wellman to have a gut feeling for the material at hand."[44] As Frank Thompson writes, "Wellman's personal involvement in his projects often went far beyond merely injecting the films with his own sensibilities; Wellman could well have been the most blatantly autobiographical director of the era. Many aspects of his private life found their way into his work, especially his days as a flyer in World War I."[45] Given its success and later reputation, *Wings* is the primary example of this tendency, and at least part of the continuing interest in that film is its embrace of the traditional narrative. In quick succession, however, Wellman made two other films dealing with the war, *Legion of the Condemned* and *Young Eagles*. While these works continue to be dismissed as "cheaters" made to cash in on the success of their predecessor, a closer look at the surviving evidence suggests that they display a noteworthy evolution of Wellman's views regarding his wartime experiences.

Released in 1928, *Legion of the Condemned* was unmistakably an attempt by Paramount to profit from the success of *Wings*. Starring rising talents Gary Cooper (who had played a memorable bit part in the earlier picture) and Fay Wray, the film also reunited Wellman with *Wings* writer John Monk Saunders.[46] Designed to make maximum use of leftover aerial footage from its predecessor and not intended (from the perspective of studio executives) to break new ground in any way, the film did well both critically and at the box office.[47] *New York Times* reviewer Mordaunt Hall's comments are fairly dismissive, though he acknowledges that "judging by the demonstrative approval of the audience at one juncture, [the film] was more than moderately successful."[48] The film is impossible to completely assess at this point, given that no print seems to survive. Remaining stills, reviews, and the novelization of the script, however, make it possible to at least consider its position as the central part of Wellman's unofficial World War I air combat trilogy.

As related in Eustice Hale Ball's version of Saunders's screenplay, the story involves Gale Price, a dashing young correspondent for "a more or less obscure Western paper" who falls in love with a society girl at an embassy ball in Washington, DC, in 1916.[49] On the night he intends to propose to Christine, he finds her " . . . *not even resisting the vulgar embrace of the duel-marked Baron!*"[50] He then declares that there is "no such thing as love in this world" and decides to go "Hun hunting."[51] Ostensibly drained of the will to live, Price joins the Legion of the Condemned, an international squadron of aviators described as "blood hunters who jested at death even as they scorned life," men who "were not calculating to save their miserable lives for the end of the war."[52] Not only did Hall's review comment on the film's depiction of this desperation, but David O. Selznick remembered it years later as a model of efficient screen storytelling: "The opening of [Wellman's] *Legion of the Condemned* I've many times quoted as one of the most brilliant uses of film to tell a story that I've ever seen. He told the story of four individual men in, I think, less than one minute each."[53] As related by Hall, each minute-long montage revealed that a woman lay at the root of the trouble for each airman, making Gale one among many hoping to die after losing faith in both life and love.[54]

After varied adventures, it is predictably revealed that Christine was in fact acting as an espionage agent for the United States and that her dalliance with the German officer was for the purposes of gathering intelligence. Gale's

A Paramount Picture.   "TO A BRAVE AND SPEEDY DEATH!"   *The Legion of the Condemned.*

The members of the Legion of the Condemned have chosen death as a suitable solution to the problems they face in life.

faith in mankind (and in love) restored, he joins her on a secret mission, but when they are captured, his friends in the squadron redeem their souls by rescuing Gale and Christine as they are standing before a German firing squad, an effort that costs some of the men their lives.

Wellman's film retains elements of the traditional narrative, and a comparison of the novelization and Wellman's memoir reveals a strikingly similar use of language as well as a common reliance on familiar negative tropes regarding the German enemy. In *Go Get 'Em!*, Wellman describes his reaction to a German bombing raid: "There kept ringing the shrieks and cries of strong men driven mad, of weak women and innocent children shattered and burned. If there had been something of mere excitement-craving in my earlier desire to fly for France, it was that night wiped out utterly. . . . Before I went to sleep I made a silent vow that I would do my little best to avenge a few of the one hundred and fifty noncombatants who had been the victims of Boche bombs that night."[55] Similarly, he relates seeing a French pilot's body riddled with bullets after safely making an emergency landing: "You can imagine the black rage that filled us at this sight, so indicative of the most inexcusable vindictive brutality."[56] This anecdote in no way tempers his description of his excitement at strafing a German airfield: "The battle madness still had me in its grip, and pointing my plane still further earthward, I turned my gun on the trenches. The pilot dropped. Then, only eight

A Paramount Picture.   *The Legion of the Condemned.*
THE FLYERS DETERMINE ON THE RECKLESS ATTEMPT TO SNATCH CHRISTINE AND GALE FROM THE ENEMY.

The pilots portrayed in *Legion of the Condemned* were far from callow youths.

yards above the ground, and with motors going at full speed, Tom and I flew across the field, shooting at everything in sight, and pouring our bullets into the open ends of the hangers."[57] These comparisons between memoir and novel, along with the lifelong pattern of autobiographical content in his films, suggest that Wellman's general attitude toward warfare, at least as far as a public position is concerned, might reasonably parallel that expressed in his work. Despite more traditional moments, however, there are important indications throughout his informal aviation trilogy that suggest that Wellman's attitude toward the war was changing. As it had for both Stallings and Whale, that change involved an increasingly universalized understanding of the experience of combat and a reformulation of the nature of the enemy. Though we can only speculate about *Legion of the Condemned*, several differences between it and its predecessor can be reasonably asserted based on the available evidence.

First, though the men who serve in the Legion of the Condemned have lost faith in society, their maturity and heroism are never in question. Surviving images from the film show almost all the members of the Legion as older men, far past the age of the traditional hero of a war narrative. At twenty-seven, Cooper himself was older than most of the fliers who trained and fought with Wellman (who was only twenty-one when he volunteered). Unlike the initially immature main characters in *Wings*, these men have lived

A Paramount Picture.   *The Legion of the Condemned.*
GALE PRICE JOINS THAT BAND OF GALLANT LOST SOULS,
"THE LEGION OF THE CONDEMNED."

Gary Cooper as Gale Price in *Legion of the Condemned*.

lives that have led them to this juncture and are not themselves responsible for their fates. Rather, society has betrayed them, and they have made their own decisions about how to come to grips with that fact.

Second, unlike the young flyers in *Wings* who anticipate returning home to the women they love, the members of the squadron expect combat to lead only to death. The battlefield offers not maturation but immolation, tempered by the hope that through their own deaths these men can restore integrity to themselves (specifically) and to the human race (generally). Rather than anticipate the possibility of death as an undesirable outcome of combat, these men seek it as a primary goal.

Finally, unlike *Wings* or *Go Get 'Em!*, the novelization of *Legion* demonstrates the beginnings of a level of universalized feelings for soldiers across national lines of the conflict. The international nature of the squadron immediately points in this direction, featuring representatives from France, England, the U.S. South and West, and Argentina. The novelization goes further, however, suggesting that German soldiers might warrant inclusion in the brotherhood of men at arms. There are several examples of this phenomenon, but the most effective is a passage in which the squadron commander reads a letter taken from a dead German officer and muses, "This doubtless amiable captain had no personal vendetta against [Allied spy] Byron Dashwood; the two would have been friends under other circumstances and drunk to each other's good health and prosperity! And yet imperial greed and the conquer-lust of a small group of militarists and industrialists had compelled the one to order the slaying of the other—to lose his own life within the week at the hands of an avenging squad of raiders!"[58] Here, again, the enemy begins to be shown as a small cog in a larger machine, blameless in and of himself for the war and certainly not to be hated for playing his part. Though there is no way of knowing if such sentiments were reflected in the finished film, their inclusion in the novelization suggests that they were perhaps hinted at in the screenplay or in what appeared on-screen.

Though not conclusive, these points indicate that like Whale, Wellman was beginning to reconceptualize his notions regarding the nature of combat. This new formulation consistently moved away from the vitriolic rhetoric of the late 1910s but at the same time departed further and further from the notions of war embraced by the romanticized traditional narrative. The argument receives additional support from an examination of the last part of the filmmaker's unofficial war trilogy, 1930's *Young Eagles*.

As a third chance for Paramount to profit from unused *Wings* aerial footage, *Young Eagles* might be expected to be something less than innovative—and in many ways, that is entirely true. Featuring Buddy Rogers (who had also starred in *Wings*) in the lead role along with up-and-comer Jean Arthur (in one of the most wooden performances of her career), the story itself is set entirely in France and is essentially recycled from apparently unused portions of *Legion of the Condemned*. Rogers is infatuated with a local woman (the film elides the question of whether she is a prostitute), and after being denied leave to visit her, he shoots down a top German ace (played by Paul Lukas) to earn a three-day pass. To loosen the tongue of the proper German officer, Rogers is forced to take him along to Paris, where it is somehow expected that drunken revels will produce useful intelligence regarding enemy plans. When all parties meet up (in what may or may not be a bordello), Lukas and Arthur run away together to Germany, leaving Rogers tied up and embarrassed. Only after Lukas shoots down Rogers in battle and the armistice is signed does Arthur express her preference for the American over the German. Summarized this way, the story appears trite, and it many ways it is. However, the tale has a number of interesting aspects that make it a provocative culmination to Wellman's developing conception of the war and its meaning.

First, though the film delicately dances around the issue, Arthur's character may easily be read as an available whore, yet again departing from the stereotype of femininity that typically dominates in the traditional narrative. Rogers has no girl at home and has no interest or desire in proving his manhood for her benefit. In fact, his initial eagerness to engage in combat is shown to primarily revolve around sexual opportunism. He therefore fights for none of the accepted, traditional reasons but essentially for the sake of hedonism.

Second, and more important, the German enemy is shown as literally just another one of the boys. Despite his aristocratic bearing and vaguely courtly manner, the Lukas character is entirely comfortable with the American, and they become fast friends. Lukas apologizes to the insensible Rogers while removing his uniform for use in escaping and refers to him several times as *kamerad*. Later in the film, the German officer, acting in concert with Rogers's commander and standing next to the American pilot's hospital bed as he is readied for surgery, tries to impart to him the will to live.

Finally, the film not only displays these attitudes but also repeatedly makes them explicit not only as part of the script but also visually. In the most significant example, the sequences showing each man shot down by the other use nearly identical images, framing the victor's aircraft with the inverted fuselage of the loser. In both cases, the defeated pilot is hanging upside down in the cockpit, unable to extricate himself without the assistance of his opponent. The photography draws a clear equivalency between the two men. This suggestion that the men are not personal enemies but are fighting only because of the dictates of nationalism is displayed in the script itself on several occasions. After the armistice, Rogers says to Lukas, "Give me your trigger finger. We're through shooting at each other. It's not legal anymore." In effect, this depicts their combat as a friendly competition between equals sanctioned by their respective governments. The parallelism between the two functions as a key element of the romantic plot. It is suggested that Arthur has been sexually involved with both men and could therefore freely choose either as the recipient of her favors at the conclusion of the film. When she selects the convalescing Rogers over Lukas, the loser of the romantic competition salutes the winner with a simple "C'est la guerre," suggesting that even in the realm of sexual conquest, the men pursued the same goal, competed as equals, and bear no ill will toward one another.

By virtue of their wartime service, all three of the filmmakers discussed in this chapter possessed unique views of the meaning of combat and the motivations and character of those who fight. Unlike many other members of the Lost Generation, these men had gone off to war and had experienced significant losses as a result. The amputation of Stallings's leg eventually contributed to his death. For the rest of his life, Whale remained reluctant to discuss his years in the trenches or in prison. And although Wellman was initially the most traditional in his approach to the subject, he ironically suffered the most from his service: not only did he suffer physical injuries that troubled him for the rest of his life, but unbeknownst to even his family until only a few years before his death, he married in France but was widowed less than a month later by a German bombing raid.[59] These men's involvement in filmmaking offered a very public forum for discussing the war and for gauging its effect. Because their initial endeavors along these lines were in other fields (Stallings's novel, Whale's direction of a stage play, Wellman's written memoir), each man had the opportunity to begin to develop his ideas about the war away from the conventional narrative standards of Hollywood filmmaking. Thus, each approached the war from the dual outsider perspectives of having served and having considered the impact of the war without the pressure to conform to the prevailing narrative. The results were not unadulterated ruminations on combat, but each of these filmmakers joined fellow veterans in contributing to the industry's larger reassessment of the war, and playing particularly important roles in that regard.

All three returned to the war as a subject of their later works. Stallings edited *The First World War: A Photographic History* in 1933, wrote the narration for a 1934 documentary by the same title, and then wrote a history of the American Expeditionary Force, *The Doughboys: The Story of the AEF, 1917–1918*, published in 1963. Christine Gerblinger argues that Whale's horror of the trenches informed his treatment of death in his 1931 version of *Frankenstein*, and he also filmed a version of Erich Maria Remarque's German "homecoming" story, *The Road Back*, in 1937.[60] Wellman returned to the subject several times, including sequences of World War I combat in *Heroes for Sale* and *Men with Wings* before famously ending his career after studio meddling forced him to add a happy ending to his very personal *Lafayette Escadrille* (in which William Wellman Jr. plays his father as a young man). None of these works, however, had the impact of those created between 1925 and 1930.

In his "The Greatness and Continuing Significance of *All Quiet on the Western Front*," Andrew Kelly argues that the film "was a leap forward for cinema in critically addressing war and peace issues. Here the Great War is seen as it was: a brutal waste. No film up to then had shown this."[61] Partly by virtue of receiving a Best Picture Academy Award, Milestone's 1930 film has remained the known quantity to which people point when making such claims. However, the films discussed in this chapter were made and released before Milestone's work, and each of them covers aspects of the war that Kelly (and others) credit *All Quiet* as being the first to seriously address. Despite its reputation, *All Quiet* was simply part of a larger process that began well before its production and continued for several years after its release. Unlike most of the other films discussed here, its position as a sound film that won the industry's highest honor prevented it from either being pronounced technologically inferior or entirely suppressed as politically dangerous under the rules of the Production Code. *All Quiet* remained in circulation and available, inflating its importance in relation to the larger process of narrative change and minimizing the role of its many contemporaries.

In their credited film works of the late 1920s, Stallings, Whale, and Wellman contributed to the ongoing reassessment of the First World War and its meaning. They gradually redefined the prevailing narrative standard away from conventional expectations and toward new ways of thinking about armed conflict that stressed the unheroic, painful, and universal nature of participation in the Great War. By doing so they not only offered a version of the war more in tune with the experience and feelings of fellow veterans but also opened the door to new possibilities for depicting the conflict. Moving away from established narrative conventions encouraged the general adoption of new standards for representing the physical violence of war on film. At the same time, the tendency of these filmmakers to portray war as a more universal experience opened the door for underrepresented groups to generate competing narratives of their own. Finally, these men also set the stage for an examination of the larger effects of the conflict on veterans as they attempted to return to their homes and reintegrate into society.

Chapter Three

COMEDIES, CARTOONS, AND CARNAGE

World War I in American Comic Short Films

IN THE LATE 1920S, AS VETERANS OF THE GREAT WAR BEGAN TO INFLUENCE the depiction of armed conflict in dramatic features, they were not alone. As William Wellman, James Whale, and Laurence Stallings manipulated the standards of the traditional narrative, another group of filmmakers were developing their own alternative vocabulary for discussing the conflict. The depiction of the war favored by this group drew on the earlier narrative but approached the subject in a manner that granted them additional leeway. They used this freedom both to expand the terminology for discussing warfare and to create a narrative that further encouraged the dissolution of traditional standards. Like their more dramatically minded counterparts, Otto Messmer, Walt Disney, and Buster Keaton also had firsthand knowledge of the battlefields of France, and their cartoons and comedies directly contributed to the popular conception of the First World War. These filmmakers initially undertook their innovations in the context of short film production, but like their predecessors D. W. Griffith and Thomas Ince, they brought these new ideas with them when they transitioned to feature-length films.

Unlike dramatic features, the nature of the production and exhibition of short "gag" comedies made it essential to convey story and character material to the audience in the most concise and efficient manner possible. Short production schedules and high production volume encouraged a reliance on audience familiarity with conventions, but it also *dis*couraged the kind of deliberate pre-production that inhibits on-set innovation. The comics and animators who created this work were thus positioned to exploit a creative tension between established narrative ideas and visual tropes and a new, developing vocabulary for depicting the realities and unpleasantness of combat that more accurately reflected the experiences of those who had taken an active part in the First World War. At the same time, thanks to the established comic practice of borrowing from the work of others, a successful new convention could be circulated quickly and persist for years.

The suggestion that comedy can help to leaven the horrors of war is neither new nor radical. In his influential *The Great War and Modern Memory*, Paul Fussell specifically discusses the use of irony by the combatants themselves. In one instance, he quotes the memoirist Philip Gibbs's comment that "the more revolting it was . . . the more [people] shouted with laughter."[1] Fussell also cites a passage from the memoir of a private who was tasked with heating water for the officers but forbidden from using any of the available wood to build a fire. Reflecting on the incident several years later, the private acknowledged that the supreme irony of his conflicting orders kept the incident prominent in his memories of the war.[2]

Though these cases quietly suggest the disturbing reality of war, they also exemplify the usefulness of comedy in processing the absurdity and waste of combat. It is not hard to imagine Charlie Chaplin, Buster Keaton, or Harold Lloyd using the latter anecdote as grounds for a comic sequence. Comedy did in fact afford a useful means for processing some of the more horrible and grotesque aspects of combat for the general public. For filmmakers of the 1920s and early 1930s, both live-action and animated comedy provided a useful way of bridging the gaps between memory, reality, and perception. Examining the history of particular comic ideas from 1918 to 1938 facilitates tracing the introduction of new—deeply serious—narrative, visual, and aural concepts in popular film via comic origins and examining the gradual acceptance of those ideas as general tropes of the depiction of combat.

The use of short cartoons and comedies to comment on the First World War predates by several years the U.S. involvement in the conflict. In 1915, J. R. Bray's character Colonel Heeza Liar spent time at the front, in the trenches, and dealing with a zeppelin.[3] In 1916, Charles Bowers's Mutt and Jeff were seen at outposts and in the trenches, and in 1917 Earl Hurd's Bobby Bumps volunteered and had run-ins with a tank and a submarine.[4] Live-action comedy stars such as Flora Finch (*Strictly Neutral*, 1915), Mack Swain and Chester Conklin (*Saved by Wireless*, 1915), Sydney Chaplin (*A Submarine Pirate*, 1915), Lloyd Hamilton and Bud Duncan (*Ham Agrees with Sherman*, 1916), and Harold Lloyd (*Luke's Preparedness Preparations*, 1916; *Luke Joins the Navy*, 1916), all made films dealing with war-related themes before the United States had declared war. Most of these films have not survived, but those that do often treat the war as only a peripheral means of generating a plot. In *A Submarine Pirate*, for example, the "Mysterious Inventor" and "His Accomplice" are never identified by any nationality, and their secretive scheme involves command of a "pirate submarine" with a decidedly Prussian military bearing. In 1915, uniformed men patrolling the sea in a submarine and looking for ships to attack could hardly fail to evoke the actions of the German navy. However, while the film pointedly shows "panic stricken passengers" being rescued by a convenient U.S. Navy gunboat (and uses stock footage of actual sailors firing naval guns), references to the war are oblique. Hamilton and Duncan's *Sauerkraut Symphony* (1916) is similarly vague, though here the title is surely a direct reference to nationality, even if the crazed union agitator who attempts to blow up the sauerkraut factory is something less than a comment on German politics.

Perhaps the most relevant of these pre-armistice films are those made by Lloyd and Charlie Chaplin, who are still counted among the greatest comics of all time. Lloyd made at least four short comedies involving military themes, including *Luke's Preparedness Preparations*, *Luke Joins the Navy*, *Kicking the Germ Out of Germany* (1918), and *A Sammy in Siberia* (1919). Only *Luke Joins the Navy* and *A Sammy in Siberia* appear to have survived, but plot summaries are available for the other films. Chaplin made two films dealing with the war, *The Bond* (1918) and *Shoulder Arms* (1918), both of which survive. *The Bond* was a one-reel short made to encourage the sale of bonds and is essentially plotless, but the three-reel *Shoulder Arms* remains probably the best known of any of the comedies dealing with the First World War.

When these films were made, Lloyd had not yet distinguished himself from the general mass of comics grinding away making one- and two-reelers, so his narrative choices are arguably less influenced by any concern with his comic persona than with striking a balance between the topical and the humorous. In *Luke Joins the Navy*, Lloyd's Luke (a precursor to the more well-known Glasses character) enlists as a way to prove his manhood, thus falling neatly in line with established narrative conventions regarding military service. The one-reel film opens with Luke tending to a general store and flirting with a customer (Bebe Daniels). The girl is accosted by a bully, but Luke is unable to help, ceding that responsibility to a sailor who enters the store. When Daniels leaves with her rescuer, a disconsolate Luke is comforted by his friend Snub Pollard, who has just fled the home of his own overbearing mother. The film thus neatly encapsulates the primary benefits of military service demonstrated in earlier Civil War films. Enlisting will affirm the masculinity of both characters by teaching Luke to defend himself and forcing Pollard to achieve a level of maturity. Inspired by a recruiting poster, they enlist, and what follows are rather generic attempts to utilize a naval ship (and attendant servicemen/extras) as a comic prop while engaging in various slapstick hijinks. Story is not primary in the construction of this film, and the incomplete print available leaves the conclusion of Luke's romance an open question (though Pollard is shown escaping from the clutches of his overbearing mother with the help of other sailors). The war itself is never mentioned, and the film's main usefulness as a comment on the impending conflict is as an advertisement for the benefits of military service.

A Sammy in Siberia similarly relies on the conventional narrative formula as Lloyd's character (first seen relaxing on a Siberian snowbank) finds the courage to fight off rampaging Bolsheviks to protect an attractive Russian peasant girl and her family. The film is most interesting for touching on the oft-forgotten postwar U.S. involvement in Russia; otherwise, it carries over the simplistic wartime narrative pattern, replacing one malevolent enemy/comic foil with another.

Though Lloyd's other two service/war shorts no longer exist, plot summaries suggest that they followed prevailing trends with regard to their subject. *Luke's Preparedness Preparations*, made a year before the United States entered the war, portrayed Luke organizing and drilling a home guard unit, providing an opportunity for the expected physical knockabout complications. *Kicking the Germ Out of Germany*, however, showed the Glasses character fighting in the trenches and dreaming of rescuing a comely Red Cross volunteer from the clutches of a comic kaiser. This would seem to reflect the standard wartime use of certain tropes (the Red Cross nurse, the soldier as resourceful innocent abroad, and a caricatured version of German soldiery) to tell a propagandistic tale of Allied victory.[5]

The example of Lloyd's films thus demonstrates the same narrative approach for dealing with the war that can be seen throughout the film industry's dramatic features. Military service is initially promoted as a means of achieving maturity, leading to predictable results such as the vanquishing of a tormentor, emancipation from social or familial shackles, and (almost always) success in romance. During the war, this narrative was adjusted to promote a more propagandistic view of the enemy, and following the armistice, it remained the primary structure for discussing the war, even in a comedy. The formula was so successful that Lloyd returned to it in 1921 as a basis for his first feature, *A Sailor-Made Man*, in which a wealthy, spoiled Harold decides that he wishes to marry attractive socialite Mildred Davis. Her father demands that Harold prove his manhood before the match can be made, and Lloyd's character responds by joining the navy. He eventually rescues Mildred, kidnapped by a maharajah in an exotic port of call, thus proving his masculine credentials and winning the girl. As in most other immediate post-armistice films with a military theme, there is not even an oblique reference to the horrors (or even the rigors) of war, though the cooperation of the navy ensures that military vessels provide suitably realistic backdrops for the very standard story. Despite his four previous efforts and the intervention of several years, Lloyd falls back on the typical formula and does nothing to develop the view of the military beyond established themes and expected tropes.

Two years before Lloyd's feature, another comedian had in fact suggested new possibilities for portraying the war on film. Chaplin's *Shoulder Arms* remains one of the best-known World War I films made contemporary with the event itself. Released only a few weeks before the signing of the armistice, Chaplin employed his trademark pathos in telling the story of a recruit's training, time in the trenches, and participation in a secret mission behind enemy lines. Stung by accusations of shirking his duty, the comedian was walking a fine line with his choice of topic. Partly due to his fame and partly due to the wealth he accumulated as a result of that fame, Chaplin had been accused of ignoring his responsibilities by not returning to England to enlist.[6] Although he actively participated in Liberty Bond activities with such stars as Mary Pickford and Douglas Fairbanks, the suggestion of shirking resonated in some quarters and made the war a potentially problematic subject for Chaplin.[7] Indeed, biographer David Robinson reports that the comedian lost confidence in the film before it was released and that only Fairbanks's enthusiastically positive reaction to a private screening saved it from being scrapped altogether.[8] Chaplin not only persevered but also decisively broke from the established narrative convention for the depiction of warfare.

The film has frequently been cited for its realistic depiction of life in the trenches, and Chaplin himself implicitly made this assertion by prefacing the 1959 *Chaplin Revue* version with "authentic" footage of trench life from the Imperial War College. What the film pointedly does not do, however (contra Robinson's spoken introduction to the most recent home video release of the film) is depict any of the carnage or blood of combat. Most of the violence that is shown is pitched at the level of Chaplin's earlier slapstick comedies (such as Chaplin disguised as a tree and knocking out German soldiers with his limbs or a portly German infantryman getting stuck in a drain through which Chaplin had escaped) rather than as any comment or reflection of wartime conditions. More important, the true contribution of the film to the depiction of the war is an outgrowth of the actor's established comic character. Chaplin's comic persona largely precludes the application of most of the conventions of the traditional narrative. His Tramp character has no family obligations and generally begins any film without romantic connections. At the same time, he has no need for the kind of battlefield lessons that will make him a better citizen since, by definition, he functions as a solitary being with no social responsibilities. Chaplin manipulated this fact in some of his most successful work, and his tentative development of relationships with the little orphan in *The Kid* or the blind girl in *City Lights* provide those films with much of their emotional impact. With *Shoulder Arms*, Chaplin specifically excluded the possibility of such connections by eliminating an early sequence showing his character as a husband and father prior to being drafted.[9] Including those scenes would have provided the unnamed protagonist with a motivation to fight, but removing them makes him a man alone, standing very much outside the accepted patterns of a traditional war story.

Chaplin retreated from the radicalism of his approach by framing his story as a dream, thus not precluding a conventional family life for his doughboy protagonist. The notion of soldiers as disconnected from society and its obligations, however, became increasingly prominent during the late 1920s and early 1930s in more dramatic films. Frank Borzage's *Lucky Star* (1929) and William Dieterle's *The Last Flight* (1931) featured characters who chose to break from the expected framework and live in complete isolation following their combat experiences. For these characters, separation from families and romantic entanglements is the only rational response to the horrors of combat. Their experiences have not matured them or made them ready to assume new roles in society. Instead, the war has brought them closer to the isolated ideal of Chaplin's comic persona, as they exist in a world for which they are not entirely suited and are more comfortable following their own notions of engagement with society rather than those required by social norms.

While the new narrative convention suggested by Chaplin rose to prominence nearly a decade after *Shoulder Arms*, other comic filmmakers were having a more immediate impact on the visual depiction of the war. For these men, the rigorously physical world of slapstick comedy and the surreal unreality of cartoons created new options for the display of physical violence on-screen. The most prominent of these possibilities involved the depiction of mass casualties and the portrayal of dismemberment, and in both cases the path to new conventions was opened by one of the most popular movie stars of the 1920s, Felix the Cat.

In 1922's *Felix Turns the Tide*, Felix nobly elects to do his duty when confronted with the news that rats have started a war on cats. Parting from his close friend and employer (the local butcher) and bidding farewell to his girlfriend (who promises to be true), our hero marches off to the recruiting station and joins the army. Up to that point the film is fairly conventional, but an intertitle reading "The battle rages" announces a decidedly unconventional second act. This section begins with a simply drawn but expansive depiction of a battlefield featuring multiple reinforced positions. Over several days, lines of charging cats are repeatedly blown away by entrenched artillery. At

Cat corpses in no-man's-land from *Felix Turns the Tide*.

The devastation of war as depicted in *Felix Turns the Tide*.

the same time, a mouse in an observation balloon uses a cannon to violently blow cats out of trenches, leaving their dead bodies scattered over no-man's-land. Firing himself from an artillery piece, Felix reaches the balloon, kills the mouse, and drops the body to the ground, where it lies out in the open and on display to enrage the army of mice. Returning to his own lines, Felix is dismayed to find that his army has been decimated. The filmmakers show us a shot of mounds of cat corpses, then reinforce the effect with another shot that follows an admonition from an on-screen character to "Look again."

"Look again" from *Felix Turns the Tide*.

Though the allowable level of violence in films prior to the sound era is frequently underestimated, this entire sequence is striking for its sheer gruesomeness. Fully understanding what is going on here requires considering the primary filmmaker himself.

Though the Felix the Cat cartoons were produced and sold by Pat Sullivan, a combative impresario, the key creative force behind the character and films was Otto Messmer, the young, New Jersey–born son of German immigrants. Messmer had quietly built up a career as a cartoonist and animator beginning in the mid-1910s, but that career was put on hold when he was drafted into the army in 1917. As animation historian John Canemaker reports in his definitive study of Felix the Cat, "Messmer witnessed his share of horrors. He recalled speaking with a buddy in the trenches one moment, then turning to discover a bullet hole had pierced the man's head. Then there was a German sniper shot out of a tree, who conversed with Messmer in German as he lay dying. The man showed the American soldiers pictures of his wife and children, and offered them cigarettes and candies."[10] Following his discharge in 1919, Messmer teamed up again with Sullivan and created the character of Felix.

It is difficult to believe that Messmer's horrific experiences in the trenches did not dictate his treatment of war in *Felix Turns the Tide*, made a little more than three years after his return from Europe. Indeed, in *Before Mickey: The Animated Film, 1898–1928*, historian Donald Crafton specifically cites Messmer's identification with the character as a key to Felix's popularity:

"Messmer injected his animal creation not only with his statements and ideas but with his whole self, breaking down the distinction between animator and animated."[11] Perhaps most significant, however, such images, which refer back to the Great War, were comfortably placed on the screen only a few years later. Graphic depictions of actual combat remained anathema in 1922, but by showing armies of rats and cats (and the eventual reinforcement of the feline army with soldiers who are literally sausages ready-made for the slaughterhouse of frontline battle), the material could both maintain its horrific integrity and be made acceptable for a general audience. Several more years passed before any dramatic feature film depicted the rigors of combat in such uncompromising visual terms, and even a film such as *The Big Parade*, released two years later, does not match Messmer's depiction of combat as an unforgiving meat grinder.

Messmer's influence on the visual portrayal of war demonstrably did not remain an isolated example. Another young animator created his own cartoons recognizably set on the battlefields of the First World War. Walt Disney had lied about his age to volunteer as a Red Cross ambulance driver, and though he did not arrive in France until after the armistice was signed, he served as an ambulance driver during the occupation.[12] The connection between the work of Disney and that of Messmer can be seen not only in the repetition of certain gags and in the general tone of Disney's Oswald the Lucky Rabbit cartoon *Great Guns!* (1927) but also through the direct personal link of the common distributor of their films, Margaret Winkler.

An explicit Disney-Messmer connection may be seen well before the birth of the Oswald character, in Disney's earlier Alice comedies. As Russell Merritt and J. B. Kaufman point out in their definitive study of Disney's silent films, "more than one witness has confirmed" that the invention of the main cartoon character of those films, Julius the cat, was originally suggested by Winkler.[13] As a distributor of the work of the Fleischer Brothers, the Felix the Cat cartoons, and early films by Disney, Winkler played a crucial role in the history of animation. Her association with Disney began just as her role as the distributor of the Felix the Cat films was coming to an acrimonious end. The suggestion that Julius "grow[s] more imitative of Otto Messmer's Felix the Cat as he goes along" supports the idea that Winkler (and her husband and business partner, Charles Mintz) were using Disney's work as leverage in their arguments with Sullivan.[14] In 1926, Disney's *Alice's Little Parade* freely cribbed from *Felix Turns the Tide*, placing Julius on the front lines of a war against an aggressive army of mice. Though the Alice comedy is a less developed work than the later Oswald cartoon, the basic plot as well as multiple gags provide a clear connecting link between *Felix Turns the*

Recruitment as depicted in *Great Guns!*

Recruitment as depicted in *Felix Turns the Tide*.

Tide and *Great Guns!* As Merritt and Kaufman point out, Disney "constantly repeated himself . . . working safely within the prescribed limits of comic animation defined by others," including Messmer.[15] Crafton argues that "the 'Oswald' plots were sometimes modeled on Messmer's films," specifically mentioning Disney's Oswald war film as a direct remake of *Felix Turns the Tide*.[16] With *Great Guns!*, Disney not only refers back to Messmer's earlier effort but also contributes to an increasingly active filmic conversation regarding the depiction of the Great War.

Hand-to-hand combat in *Great Guns!*

Great Guns! begins with an announcement of war essentially lifted from King Vidor's *The Big Parade* (1925). As a newsboy shouts word of a declaration of war, bells and whistles sound to mobilize the populace, just as they had in a similar sequence in the live-action film several years earlier. Animal citizenry respond en masse and are shown marching through a tent marked *Recruiting Office*. Going in, they are a disorganized collection of disparate civilians, but they emerge from the other side as regimented soldiers. This gag, which is only the sixth shot of the film, is lifted wholesale from *Felix Turns the Tide*, clearly indicating that the Disney animators recalled the earlier film and had no qualms about borrowing (they had previously borrowed the same gag in *Alice's Little Parade*).[17] Oswald, like Felix, is shown saying goodbye to his girlfriend, and their parting kiss dissolves to a shot of Oswald kissing her picture while sitting in a flooded trench. Several shots of combat recall the earlier cartoon, especially a scene of opposing trenches from which soldiers emerge to shoot each other. Rather than bodies scattered in no-man's-land, however, the casualties here fall back into the fortifications. This reticence to show corpses is interesting given what occurs seconds later. In hand-to-hand combat with a mouse opponent, Oswald literally knocks off the creature's head, though a blow to the body forcibly reattaches it.

Approached by an enemy general, Oswald flees under fire, but he is saved by his encounter with a friendly elephant, whom he enlists as an artillery piece. Firing cannonballs from the elephant's trunk provides an effective counter to the enemy advance until a returning volley enters the elephant's body, ricochets throughout the torso, and then explodes, leaving only four

Artillery failure in *Great Guns!*

disconnected feet and a tail (which Oswald has been using as a firing mechanism). The four disembodied feet flee the scene of their own accord, followed by the tail. Left without his weapon, Oswald temporarily defends himself by batting away cannonballs with his ears, but eventually one find its mark and the rabbit disintegrates into a pile of refuse. Waving a Red Cross flag, Oswald's girlfriend literally sweeps the pieces into a basket, takes them to a medical station, places them in a cocktail shaker and pours out a reconstituted Oswald.[18] Their kiss provides the fade-out to a happy ending.

With *Great Guns!*, Walt Disney gives his audience a "Disney Version" of the Great War which stands at odds with his later reputation. Though the depiction of violence is a staple of comedy, this cartoon is poised at an interesting moment, looking back to Messmer's version of his firsthand experiences, but also positioned as an early marker of the complete re-assessment of the Great War which would occur in the American popular cinema over the next few years. In presenting his version of frontline combat, Disney does not shirk from the depiction of fairly intense violence and the damage it might do to individual characters. In fact, he is demonstrably ahead of the curve.

One prime example of this is the film's casual use of a dismemberment gag where a character in combat believes he has lost (or in the case of animated films, actually does lose) a limb. Harry Langdon introduced a version of this combat-focused gag in his *All Night Long* (1924). In that film, the joke involves Harry being buried up to his neck in a mound of dirt following an explosion. Two legs stick out awkwardly and impossibly from the mound, and the comedian believes that they are his until his attempts to extricate

Harry Langdon (parts of him) in *All Night Long*.

himself reveal a second soldier buried upside down in the dirt. The fact that this situation is presented as a joke takes on added meaning when we consider that Langdon's gag precedes by a year the revelation of John Gilbert's lost limb at the end of *The Big Parade* (a moment that can still elicit gasps from audiences).[19] Disney's version comically inverts the usual course of events by presenting the feet of the elephant as the sentient survivors of the dismemberment, but his treatment remains one of the earliest and most violent iterations of this particular trope.

Variations of this dismemberment gag recurred in several films over the next fifteen years. Comedians such as Wheeler and Woolsey in their *Half Shot at Sunrise* (1930), Keaton in *Doughboys* (1930), and Laurel and Hardy in *Block-Heads* (1938) developed versions of this material, applying it in ways particular to their own characters.

In *Half Shot at Sunrise*, Bert Wheeler and Robert Woolsey portray their usual, slightly risqué selves, spending large swaths of the film attempting to shirk responsibility, woo women, and thumb their noses at authority. Throughout most of the extremely scattered narrative, they engage in shenanigans familiar to their fans, which take place behind the front lines in a shenanigan-friendly Paris. As Ed Watz points out in his definitive study of the team, however, the film makes an extremely jarring shift away from comedy when the duo are placed on an actual battlefield. Bert and Bob are carrying papers that have to be transmitted to an officer in a forward trench. When the communication trench is destroyed, Bob volunteers Bert for the mission. The scene is played straight, amid an authentic-looking battlefield

The dismemberment gag as seen in *Half Shot at Sunrise*.

landscape. Wheeler later remembered that there were "bombs going off . . . and the stuff was breaking and bursting all around us."[20] As Bert makes his way through no-man's-land, a bomb explodes, obscuring him from view. Bob heads out to look for his friend and finds a moaning head and a disembodied arm protruding from the ground. Bert claims that he can "feel nothing" when Bob takes his hand, but pulling on the appendage reveals an entirely different body buried in the dirt. The arm actually belongs to a military policeman who has been pursuing the duo throughout the film, and the scene ends with the pair being chased back into a friendly dugout, from which the sounds of a fight are heard.

Though this version of the dismemberment gag is less visceral than Langdon's, its appearance here reinforces two key points. First, the joke demonstrates the tendency of material to repeat through appropriation by others. An uncredited Roscoe "Fatty" Arbuckle worked as a gagman on *Half Shot*, and it is reasonable to suggest that he was familiar with Langdon's work. Though Langdon's career began in 1924, just as Arbuckle was dealing with the fallout of the Virginia Rappe scandal, which ended his on-screen career, Arbuckle continued to direct in Hollywood under a pseudonym, and he would have been conversant with the work of other film comedians. At this point it is impossible to know exactly which gags were contributed by whom, but Wheeler later attested that Arbuckle "put a lot of great things in our pictures himself." Watz suggests that the "improved visual humor" of certain Wheeler and Woolsey features (beginning with *Half Shot*) is directly attributable to Arbuckle's influence, and gags of this type are primary to that assertion. (Watz also specifically suggests the earlier Langdon film as a source for the dismemberment gag featured here.)[21]

The second key point is the importance of the gag in a film that was widely seen and financially successful.[22] As in the earlier examples, the audience for this film was presumably accepting of the (temporary) suggestion that one of the protagonists had been blown to pieces. Though the suggestion may not have been entirely comfortable, two other examples demonstrate a gentler variant of the dismemberment gag in other films of the 1930s.

Both Keaton's *Doughboys* and Laurel and Hardy's *Block-Heads* also feature versions of the dismemberment gag. In each case, the impact is softened when compared to Langdon's original version, but both also serve to demonstrate that the violent physical effects of combat did not go unmentioned. In *Doughboys*, Keaton and Sally Eilers are caught in a barrage on the battlefield that leaves them covered in rubble. In this film, the gag is a clear descendant of the earlier version, though shorn of the most horrific physical implications. More interesting is a European promotional painting for the film that depicts Keaton as a gangly, broken-looking body tangled in barbed wire. The implications are less disturbing than earlier forms, but there is a clear suggestion of a painful physical result caused by combat.

The latest iteration of this particular gag appears in *Block-Heads*. Before a 1918 attack, Stan is ordered to remain at his post, guarding the soon-to-be-vacated trench. He dutifully does so for twenty years. Ollie receives word that Stan has finally returned to the United States and goes to meet him at a soldiers' home. This sets up a macabre version of the dismemberment gag when Stan folds his leg under himself while sitting in a wheelchair, leading to series of lesser gags revolving around the presumption that Stan is a wounded invalid.

In these instances, physical devastation is not only shown as a natural part of the war experience but is used as the foundation of the humor. The audience must have a basic understanding of the horrific physical effects of combat for the gags to have any meaning. In his *Classical Film Violence: Designing and Regulating Brutality in Hollywood Cinema, 1930–1968*, historian Stephen Prince discusses the difficulties of depicting the effects of physical violence on-screen and elaborates on the systems used to avoid censorship in the era of classical filmmaking. He specifically emphasizes a strategy that utilizes the "poetically oblique expression" of violence, concealing the worst effects by strategically placing them off-screen.[23] Though the films discussed here predate the era with which Prince is most concerned, the evidence of these animated films and comedies suggests that filmmakers in the 1920s and 1930s initially took a more direct approach. Without the visual depiction of the physical effects of violence, the basic premise of the gag is incomprehensible to the audience. The viewer must not only process the horrific implications of disembodiment but feel relief at the fact that such an injury did not occur. Disney understood this fact when depicting such injuries in *Great Guns!*, just as Messmer had earlier recognized that "real" mass killing could be referenced on-screen if properly cushioned by the unreality of animation.

Both dismemberment and violent death are highlighted in perhaps the most brutal animated depiction of World War I on-screen, *Bosko the Doughboy*. As with the perpetuation of the dismemberment gag, this film provides a key example of the extension and use of newly developing tropes of violence and demonstrates the longevity and spread of such material throughout a segment of the industry. Made by Hugh Harman in 1932, *Bosko the Doughboy* literally begins with a bang. Rather than fading away, the opening credits literally explode. What immediately follows is not an introduction of the main character but various shots of absolute chaos. A skyrocket explodes above a twisted landscape of mangled barbed wire, a hail of bullets and shells flies across the screen, debris rains from the sky, and the shadowy silhouettes of soldiers carrying rifles race across the bottom of the image. The first living being to appear is operating a smoking machine gun that (with a smile at the audience), he turns to shoot directly at the camera. After a brief interlude to show an artillery piece in its death throes, there is a shot of a shell hole ringed by barbed wire. Soldiers race past as artillery strikes, throwing up dirt and debris. Suddenly, an ostrich infantryman comes into view over the far side of the landscape. A shell goes right through his body, leaving a large round hole where his stomach should be. He pushes his long neck through the wound in disbelief before saluting the audience and falling into the watery puddle inside the shell hole. This is followed by a shot of a marching band of eight soldiers who are struck by a shell, instantly vaporizing five of the troops and leaving only three to reenact Archibald MacNeal Willard's painting *The Spirit of '76*.

This introduction constitutes almost 20 percent of the film, before Bosko himself even makes an appearance. Though the intent is assumed to be humorous, the implications are horrific, and the visual depiction of violence is stark. Even more significant is the fact that these examples are seen throughout the film. The literal obliteration of a soldier via explosion, for example, is repeated when a bugler is incinerated while calling troops to go over the top.

In addition, at least three variants of the dismemberment gag appear. Aside from the unfortunate ostrich, a dachshund is quite graphically cut down to size when his entire midsection is cut away by machine-gun fire,

The explosive opening moments of *Bosko the Doughboy*.

The unfortunate ostrich in *Bosko the Doughboy*.

and when a hippo has a shell shot directly into his mouth, Bosko unzips the animal to remove the explosive.

Though the violence of the imagery is unmatched, the actual inventiveness of the gags in the film is fairly limited—they are largely borrowings from earlier cartoons. For example, the violent explosions and the image of a body draped over the limb of a tree may be seen in *Felix Turns the Tide*, and a shell destroying Bosko's photograph of his girlfriend as well as the artillery round ricocheting through the body of the hippo are rooted in *Great Guns!* Hugh

The bugler meets his fate in *Bosko the Doughboy*.

A dachshund is dismembered in *Bosko the Doughboy*.

Harman, the director who created Bosko in the late 1920s. used the character as the foundation of a new cartoon series after he and his working partner, Rudolf Ising (who had also collaborated with Disney), were dismissed from Universal. Both men began their careers with Disney, worked on the Oswald cartoons, and would have been familiar with the Felix cartoons that so frequently provided inspiration for Oswald's antics.[24] In many ways, therefore, *Bosko the Doughboy* is simply a reworking of its predecessors, but the level of violence is magnified to a degree that far exceeds that of either of the earlier

Battlefield surgery in *Bosko the Doughboy*.

efforts. The film may thus be read as an indication of the success of those works in paving the way for new illustrated depictions of screen violence. Visual ideas put forward by men with firsthand experience of the battlefield, such as Messmer and Disney, are fully integrated into a new, graphic (in multiple senses of the word) conception of the battlefield generated by men without such experience (such as Harman and Ising). That influence can be directly traced through the visual evidence of the films themselves.

As these new visual ideas became increasingly common in the late 1920s and early 1930s, an additional weapon was added to the filmmaking arsenal. The introduction of sound redefined the notion of realism on the screen, and comic filmmakers were at the forefront of experimentation with this new technology. As with the introduction of innovative visual ideas, comic films and cartoons were fundamental in the creation of aural tropes that helped to shape the depiction of the World War I experience for moviegoing audiences. The goal of provoking laughter under the harsh narrative situations presented by combat is a delicate balancing act, but doing so in the face of the realism of sound forced new approaches to basic assumptions regarding the use of music and dialogue, just as they had with graphic depictions of combat.

In his *Film, a Sound Art*, Michel Chion situates animated cartoons in the early history of sound films. Given that silent films and early sound processes frequently employed unsynchronized sound and sound effects, Chion suggests that the synchronization of sound and image was a key benefit of the new technologies that led to the sound revolution of the mid- to late 1920s: "The proof that this synchronism of sound and image in the brand new sound film was still something magical, an enchanted encounter between two entities that produced the spark of life, can be observed in some of the very first musical animated cartoons of the 1930's."[25] Though he privileges the synchronicity of cartoons featuring musical performances, he also explicitly connects sound cartoons with live-action films by suggesting that "in the early years of sound we find more than one example of live-action cinema attempting to approximate the freedom of these visual effects and with music that tries to free the image from its realist obligations."[26] Music is frequently superseded by other types of sound in films dealing with the Great War, though Chion glancingly addresses this point as well by suggesting that "a particular kind of rhythmic noise symbolizes the energy of the early sound cinema.... In the many films about the Great War there are symphonies of explosions and detonations."[27] Though the use of these sounds of the battlefield is important, it emerges from a much longer tradition of sound effects use in silent film. As Stephen Bottomore points out, the appropriateness and proper application of sound effects in theaters was actively debated throughout the silent period, especially in the early 1910s: "The theoretical debate over sound effects—and especially about how, when, or whether to use them—not only was extremely interesting, but may well have laid the foundation for an aesthetic governing sound effects practice in later periods of cinema."[28] Though the use of effects diminished throughout the 1920s, they continued to be frequently employed during battle scenes in war films such as *Wings* and *What Price Glory?* While sound effects were occasionally used in interesting ways in comic films (the gunshots and shellfire of *Bosko the Doughboy* fulfill the promise of Chion's "rhythmic noise," and Keaton's use of the sounds of a gas mask in *Doughboys* is particularly terrifying), effects are not the only application of sound technology that straddles animation and live-action films. Chion suggests that "once the talking film really found its bearings and unplugged its ears, the realist tendency seems to have prevailed; audible ordinary speech and real voices became the rule (sometimes brutally so). But in fact it was not quite so simple; the tension between naturalist speech and melodrama often persisted."[29] In fact, the use of sound in live-action comedies, intertwining with lessons sometimes learned from animation, expanded the use of the new technology by freely manipulating developing aural conventions. Experiments with aural tropes involving the sounds of the combat experience are a constant theme throughout the comedies and cartoons dealing with the Great War in ways that relate to more serious dramas dealing with the same subject.

Historians have noted the importance of musical performance to the introduction and acceptance of sound technology. In *A Song in the Dark:*

The Birth of the Musical Film, Richard Barrios privileges musical films made from 1929 to 1932 as "the testing ground upon which sound film proved itself, an agent for the exhaustive trials and tests . . . that turned sound from a freak gimmick to a standard-bearer."[30] Less noticed, however, is the importance of musical numbers outside of the actual musical genre, including performances featured in films about the Great War. The relationship between cartoons and comedy provided a natural entrée for music as it moved from animated film to live action. These interludes not only functioned as breaks within grimmer narratives but also used music to evoke audience nostalgia for experiences and events receding into the past.

Both of the animated World War I cartoons starring Bosko feature musical performances by the lead character. In *Bosko the Doughboy*, Bosko dances his way across the wooden flooring of a waterlogged trench with a harmonica-playing horse (and fellow soldier). In *The Dumb Patrol*, he performs on a piano in a bombed-out French house as a way to woo a French girl (who responds with a dance performance). In both cases, though the use of a background score is constant, the narrative comes to a halt for the sake of the musical performances, and the interludes end with a return to the unpleasantness of the battlefield. *Bosko the Doughboy* segues from the trench dance to scenes of lice attacking a sleeping soldier, while *The Dumb Patrol*'s piano performance concludes when an enemy aerial bombardment transforms the piano into a harp (before a second bomb destroys it completely). Both cases demonstrate the way in which animated films are free of Chion's "realist obligations," but live-action comedies initially attempted to use musical performance in a similar way.

In 1932, Laurel and Hardy's *Pack Up Your Troubles* began with an extended sequence of the duo being drafted, in training, and on the battlefield. Borrowing from the successful approach of animated cartoons (and the earlier technique of silent film accompaniment), the entire running time is blanketed with a musical score. Though there are no performance interludes, the comic style of the nondescript underscore provides a jarring contrast to the harshness of the subject matter. Narrative events such as the news of the death of a comrade, an enemy bombardment, and an over-the-top attack on German trenches are all insistently accompanied by jaunty tunes that purport to emphasize the scenes' comic intent. Using music to emphasize the humorous over the serious might certainly be seen as a valid choice for an established comedy team during the transition to sound. Whereas cartoons are shielded by their unreality, however, even comic live-action films are not entirely free of Chion's realist obligations. The music is frequently at odds with the images, striking an awkward tone and making this use of sound uncomfortable. As with live-action dramas, *Pack Up Your Troubles* suggests that new methods must be found to integrate music into screen comedy. Even techniques that had worked for silent films or that might work in some contemporary instances (such as animated films) demanded modification to suit the changing requirements of integrating sound, picture, and narrative subject.

Though a constant comic underscore proved problematic, another integration technique was available for comic films. Wheeler and Woolsey's *Half Shot at Sunrise* does not feature a constant underscore but instead includes isolated musical numbers that, much like the trench dance and piano interlude in the Bosko cartoons, provide temporary relief from larger narrative concerns. The film's plot involves the comic team evading pursuing authorities and then seeking to prove their worthiness on the battlefield. While eluding the police, Bert pauses several times in the middle of a chase to serenade Dorothy Lee. Later, when asked to deliver a message to the front, Bob is convinced to brave the trenches during a musical number that immediately precedes the harrowing final reel. The comic duo's vaudeville roots may have predisposed them to the strategic insertion of such musical interludes, but the general subject matter (especially in the concluding reel) certainly calls into question the function of those interludes in the treatment of an otherwise serious subject. In both of these cases, the uncomfortable juxtaposition of conflicting tones is just as obvious as in the Laurel and Hardy film. The musical interludes may provide a break within a harsher narrative, but the extreme changes in the tenor of the film from one scene to the next demonstrate the difficulty of using sound in a comic way while dealing with the subject of combat.

Though those difficulties confuse attempts to use sound in certain comic films, they are resolved with more success by filmmakers who treat music not as a constant comic presence (as in a cartoon) or as an element in awkward opposition to a more "realistic" situation or setting (as in a musical) but as a natural function of wartime experience. In other words, comic filmmakers mirrored the work of their more dramatic counterparts, realizing the need to forge a new relationship of sound and image particular to their subject matter. This realization built on the standard modes of musical performance in silent film, where well-known songs or pieces of traditional music would be performed to evoke emotional reactions from the audience. However, the delicate question of how wartime experience might clash with fictional depictions of combat made the introduction of music more problematic. In the case of the Great War, comic filmmakers realized that music could continue to perform an important function not by being directly comic, as in an animated film, but rather by evoking nostalgic moments codified as part of the wartime experience.

Several key instances of this more carefully calibrated approach to musical performance can be seen in Keaton *Doughboys*. Among Keaton scholars and aficionados, *Doughboys* is not held in high esteem. As one of the MGM films made during Keaton's precipitous decline from the heights of his well-regarded silent work, this film, like his other early talkies (despite their financial success), is considered emblematic of the comedian's collapse into alcoholism. That opinion, cemented by years of repetition, has obscured the more interesting aspects of the work as one of the first sound films dealing with the Great War.[31] In *The Talkies: American Cinema's Transition to Sound, 1926–1931*, Donald Crafton admits that the film "does exhibit . . . some changes in MGM's sound techniques," specifically citing outdoor shooting with live recording and the occasional use of a single camera (versus a two-camera setup). Though he does not elaborate on the implications for the film, he also mentions that "there are some obvious examples of acoustic foregrounding."[32] This, at least, is an improvement over Barrios, who mistakenly asserts that "this time Keaton served mainly as a comedian, leaving the infrequent musical sequences to others."[33] In fact, Keaton is directly involved in two musical numbers, both of which are integrated into the plot as evocations of nostalgic memory.

As was so often the case in early talkies, underscoring in *Doughboys* is essentially nonexistent. However, music is introduced diegetically in two important instances. As Buster and his fellow soldiers make their way to Europe by boat, he and Cliff "Ukulele Ike" Edwards team up belowdecks to play ukulele and scat sing a version of "You Never Did That Before." The nature of this particular moment in the narrative is noteworthy—not a full-fledged musical number but rather a quiet moment shared among doughboys trying to amuse themselves during the voyage to France. The setting and situation would have been familiar to any veteran of the Great War, so while the interlude functions as a dramatic pause, it fits neatly into the realistic needs of the story and doubles as a gentle reminder of wartime experience.

A similar purpose is served by *Doughboys*'s later musical interlude. Keaton has offended the girl he loves (played by Sally Eilers), and his only chance to see her before being shipped to the front is to take part in a musical revue organized by the soldiers for their own entertainment. The musical number is important not only within the narrative but for several other reasons. First, it allows the studio to leverage the singing credentials of Edwards and the dancing experience of Eilers by displaying those skills in a full musical performance. Second, it permits Keaton an extended period of wordless physical comedy as he tries to improvise his place in the number (while appearing in drag). Third, the film experiments with the introduction and use of this interlude, combining all of these elements into an integral moment in the narrative. This particular integration is successful enough to later become a standard wartime trope seen in such films as *South Pacific* and *The Bridge on the River Kwai*. Soldiers performing for their own entertainment and assuming the part of absent female companionship is a recognizable part of the wartime experience that this sequence evokes.

The sequence thus represented an advance in the integration of sound and story. Perhaps most important, however, the show is ended by a sudden aerial attack in exactly the same way that Bosko's piano performance is ended in the later *The Dumb Patrol*. The extremely thin line separating animated and live-action comedy is thus crossed by sequences following the same pattern. In this instance, the appropriate integration of music successfully enables live-action cinema to achieve a freedom from realist obligations equivalent to animated films. This freedom mitigates the violence of the frontline combat scenes that conclude the film and allows the audience to compartmentalize the full implications of a battlefield narrative.

A similar integration of music and narrative occurs in Charley Chase's *High C's*, released a few months after *Doughboys*. The comic three-reeler includes numerous musical numbers, with a particular focus on traditional favorites such as "My Pretty Quadroon" and "Down by the Old Mill Stream." Applying the same usage as Keaton, Chase integrates the music seamlessly into the (thin) plot, which mostly involves Charley's desire to keep singing no matter what. The impulse is so strong that when a member of the singing group is shot in the throat, Chase replaces him with a captured German soldier, who joins in a German-language rendition of "Where, Oh Where Has My Little Dog Gone?" As in the earlier Keaton film, *High C's* uses the music to evoke a nostalgic sense of the camaraderie of the combat experience but blurs the line between animated and live-action comedy. This is especially apparent in a scene where Chase's group happily sings a rendition of "When You Were Sweet Sixteen" during a German bombardment of their entrenched position. Here again, serious events in a comic live-action film (a gunshot wound, a bombardment) free themselves from Chion's realist obligations by integrating a musical interlude in a manner similar to that of a cartoon.

The success with which these two Great War comedies found new ways to manipulate the inclusion of music argues for the importance of comic filmmaking as a part of the mechanism by which the industry determined appropriate methods for integrating musical sounds. Those methods extended beyond the use of music, however, to the inclusion of a second new type of sound. The use of spoken dialogue presented problems throughout the industry, but those problems were more intractable when it came to depicting the language of soldiers on the battlefield and even more problematic in a film with comic intent.

The particular rough-hewn rhetoric of men in combat was hinted at as soon as the cycle of World War I films began in earnest in 1925. Vidor's *The Big Parade* features several instances of profanity in intertitles, and at one key moment, the protagonist actively declaims against the brutalities of combat. Similarly, Walsh's *What Price Glory?* continues to be remembered (even if apocryphally) as a film that offended those who could read the lips of Quirt and Flagg as they profanely argued their way across the battlefields of France. This rough rhetoric serves a function beyond being a mere expression of the actors' linguistic practices, and there are moments in the battlefield sequences in which harsher language is put to use as an element of critical comment on the experience of combat.

The introduction of sound gave added strength to the increasing tendency toward linguistic realism, including the realistic talk of soldiers on the battlefield. In comedies of the period, this had three important results. The first of these was to codify the nuances of something as seemingly insignificant as grumbling in the ranks. Comments that would previously not have warranted full intertitles were now made audible on the soundtrack, more realistically reproducing the wartime experience. Examples of this appear in *Doughboys*, where the receipt of marching orders leads to a bantering exchange among the enlistees. While Elmer (Keaton's character) is eager to get back into the good graces of his beloved by proving himself in battle, others are not so sure:

> SOLDIER #1: "It won't be long now."
> ELMER: "Can't come soon enough for me."
> SOLDIER #2: "I'm not so anxious."
> ELMER: "I am. I'll show her. Bring on your war. I'll make her sorry..."
> SOLDIER #2: "Quite a cheerful fellow he is this evening."

The banter essentially contributes nothing to the plot but pointedly reflects the attitudes of the men as they march to the front.

The second use of speech resulting from the introduction of sound is the use of language to delineate foreignness. Here again, silent films such as *The Big Parade* had minimally established the trope in scenes such as those involving Jim talking to Melisande (the love interest, played by Renée Adorée). Intertitles involving intercultural communication frequently settled into pidgin English for the benefit of the audience, which could interpret meaning via minimal text and the performance of the actors. The addition of sound, however, demanded a new approach, and comics turned it to their advantage, manipulating the exotic foreignness of other languages to humorous effect. In *Half Shot at Sunrise*, for example, Bert and Bob pick up a carload of French women, to one of whom Bob whispers an inappropriate suggestion. The comedy results in part from the woman's inability to articulate her anger at the affront in English, leading to the universally understood retort of a slap in the face. *The Dumb Patrol* features a similar moment in which the French girl Bosko encounters cannot understand his broken French, so they communicate through the universal language of music.

This same approach was used in lighter moments of more serious wartime films, such as the German soldiers' interlude with French peasant women in *All Quiet on the Western Front*. The language barrier does not prove a bar to their straightforward exchange of food for sexual favors. At the same time, language could be used to define the otherness of the enemy as well as friends. In *Doughboys*, German soldiers speak only German, requiring the presence of an on-screen interpreter. In this case, Elmer is reunited with his German chauffeur, and their mutual cordiality leads to Keaton's promise to try to procure supplies for loudly enthusiastic (and starving) German troops. That comic moment was later inverted in *Heroes for Sale*, in which the chaos of a German field hospital is made more menacing for the American protagonist (and American audience), by a cacophony of German voices shouting orders and diagnoses. From the perspective of comedy, these moments reflect the trend (borrowed from radio) toward ethnic humor that relied heavily on accents (such as that of comedians Van and Schenk) but simultaneously comment on the experience of enlisted troops in a foreign land.

Over and above the ability to demarcate the otherness of foreigners, the third and perhaps most important use of language in war comedies is the ability to now fully articulate the brutality of the chain of military command. Again, though the suggestion of a demanding noncommissioned officer is not new, it receives added weight when that officer's diatribes can be heard rather than imagined. When a drill sergeant (played by Ed Brophy) in *Doughboys* is training recruits in the proper use of a bayonet, the sergeant's monologue is notable for its harsh, brutal unpleasantness:

> Why you stupid lug, pick it up, pick it up, get it on. It's guys like you that make work for stretcher-bearers. This is bayonet work. Cold steel, bloody business. I want you to show the tiger that's in you. I want you to come in growling . . . Ferocious as the wild beasts of the jungle! Because when the enemy sees a charging bunch of fighting, snarling,

growling, fighting men coming in with cold steel, ready to rip and tear through flesh and bone, they don't like it! . . . Get this blade right up against the enemy's blade. Grip it short. Get it around under his chin, ready to give it to him in the gullet. Man to man! Body to body! Eye to eye! You can feel your hot breath flowing right through the enemy! . . . And if you use it like men you'll come out like soldiers, not like a lot of dead ones! . . . The enemy's advancing! . . . Whaddya' do? . . . you give it to him right through the gullet! . . . Work it, tear, rip! You can feel his hot blood!

Most remarkably, this extended diatribe is being used for entirely comic effect. By the end of the sequence, all of the trainees have fainted at the graphic verbal description of proper bayonet use. It is difficult to imagine the sequence working in a silent picture, since the use of intertitles would be too disruptive to the functioning of the gag, which relies on the appalling buildup of the instructor's gory enthusiasm. At the same time, the hyperbolic language being used for comic effect is too extreme for use in a drama, in which the sergeant's overenthusiastic detail would be out of place. In a comic film, however, the zealous description of one man gutting another becomes acceptable fodder for humorous effect.

This sequence provides further evidence of the ways in which comedy opened up new avenues for discussing the brutality and violence of combat on film, given that the entire scene was essentially reused for dramatic ends in a 1937 MGM film, *They Gave Him a Gun*. In that instance, a raw recruit played by actor Franchot Tone takes the place of the Keaton character, but the two sequences are otherwise effectively identical. A tough drill sergeant schools a naive rookie, who faints at the blunt language and inescapable implications of his training. The dramatic version is more subdued in both language and performance, but the similarities are striking. *Doughboys* preceded *They Gave Him a Gun* by seven years, but the comic film provided a precedent for the later drama.[34]

The introduction of sound to film was a wrenching technical change for much of the professional industry. Questions of what was appropriate prompted debates throughout the filmmaking community, and that community included the makers of both animated and live-action comic entertainment. Though comic filmmakers were shielded from some of the most troubling aspects of this change by the ability to approach subjects from a more lighthearted perspective, the creation of comic films dealing with the Great War brought to the fore thorny questions about the new technology. Like their more dramatic counterparts, comic filmmakers were forced to apply new rules to established situations and to modify and develop tropes that were not yet entirely fixed. Their methods for introducing music and manipulating language reveal their ingenuity at solving the problems posed by new technology and at doing so in a way that suited their subject matter.

Between the signing of the armistice and the mid-1930s, as the makers of dramatic features created new conventions for dealing with the portrayal of the First World War on-screen, their comic brethren were not idle. By working to the strengths and advantages of their genre, those filmmakers introduced their own new ideas for expanding the vocabulary of the wartime experience. Building on the established precepts of his comic persona, Charlie Chaplin expanded the acceptable approach to the character of an enlistee, upending the traditional approach to wartime narrative. Drawing on their experiences in France, animators such as Messmer and Disney expanded the vocabulary of acceptable on-screen violence. Veterans such as Keaton and nonveterans such as Harman and Chase found ways to combine the new realism of sound technology with the surrealism of comedy while dealing with a subject as serious as combat. By stretching the limits of established approaches and experimenting with new technology for comic ends, these filmmakers created new tools for exploring the meaning of the First World War as well as new ways of depicting any warfare on-screen. The experiences and opinions of these filmmakers thus became an important part of the larger process of reevaluating the ultimate purpose and meaning of the First World War.

Chapter Four

RACE FILM AND THE DEPICTION OF AFRICAN AMERICAN MILITARY SERVICE, 1918–1939

AS MAINSTREAM FILMMAKERS STRUGGLED WITH AND BEGAN TO MODIFY existing narrative structures in response to their Great War experiences, a more specialized group of artists and business leaders turned their attention to the same topic. This group consisted of filmmakers working within African American "race" cinema. Unlike their mainstream counterparts, these individuals responded to a filmmaking tradition that began with narrow, stereotyped depictions created by white filmmakers but fought to expand it and make their own. Their efforts focused on shattering the racial preconceptions of mainstream cinema and led them to generate specific meanings and narrative approaches that addressed issues of Black masculinity and the place of African Americans in relation to the majority community. As Gerald Butters put it, "Motion pictures were a tool that African-American men used for uplift, instruction, and moral indoctrination."[1] Going even further, Jane M. Gaines suggests in her *Fire and Desire: Mixed-Race Movies in the Silent Era* that "if any group actually reconstructed the 'face of the race' in the 1920's it was not the celebrated black writers but rather the race movie producers."[2] A significant part of that effort related to African American participation in both the Great War and the armed services generally. Though the producers of race films reflected their mainstream counterparts in portraying the war as a locus of community pride, they differed in understanding the conflict as a chance not for young men to achieve manhood but for neglected citizens to prove their mettle and competence. At the same time, these filmmakers struck a harsher note of discord by acknowledging the realities of racial prejudice and difference that were generally completely invisible in the majority culture.

The Civil War films of the 1910s had generated and standardized a conventional approach to war narratives in mainstream filmmaking but solidified an entirely different pattern for Black audiences. As Thomas Cripps points out, "For Afro-Americans nothing could have been worse than the reunions, intersectional lovers, grizzled veterans, intertwined flags, blue and gray bunting, and loyal darkies.... The rush of movies commemorating the Civil War destroyed the chance for a humane treatment of Negroes on the screen. Instead they restored Southern lore to the screen and taught a new urban generation a false nostalgia." He continues, "Black characters gave their lives and fortunes for the cause of scores of white Southerners." In Cripps's view, these films preached a "celebration of Southern virtue and Negro fealty to it."[3] As the ultimate expression of these attitudes, D. W. Griffith's *The Birth of a Nation* might have been perceived as an unqualified success in filmic mythmaking for contributors such as Thomas Dixon (author of the source material) and Griffith himself, but the result in the Black community was quite different. According to Cripps, "If Dixon's motive had been to develop the race consciousness of the white North, he failed miserably. Instead the two most enduring by-products of *The Birth of a Nation* would be, first, a stimulation to the cinema as an art form, and second, a heightening of black awareness and identity that far outstripped Dixon's wildest hopes for white people."[4]

The release of *The Birth of a Nation* was the first of two major events that prompted the beginnings of an alternate film industry focused on America's growing Black urban communities. Griffith's film famously prompted the National Association for the Advancement of Colored People (NAACP) to spearhead a nationwide campaign by African Americans appalled at the depiction of their race in the Civil War epic. In terms of filmmaking, that outrage manifested itself most effectively in George and Noble Johnson's creation of the wholly Black-owned and -operated Lincoln Motion Picture Company. Noble was already involved in the industry, having joined the Lubin motion picture company in the early 1910s as an actor specializing in "ethnic" roles.[5] His brother George had previously been employed as a mail carrier.[6] Despite being consistently undercapitalized, their first two efforts—*The Realization of a Negro's Ambition* (1916) and *The Trooper of Troop K* (1917)—became the first nationally distributed films successfully made by and for African Americans.

Neither of these films has survived, but plot summaries and stills indicate the filmmakers' attitudes toward their subject. The plot of the three-reel *The Trooper of Troop K* indicates the vast difference between these films and typical cinematic portrayals of African Americans. The story revolved around a lower-class but upright character, Shiftless Joe (portrayed by Noble Johnson) who is in love with the middle-class Clara (Beulah Hall). When Joe is fired from his job for tardiness caused by his "deep sympathy for animals," he resolves (at Clara's suggestion) to join the army. She believes that Joe will benefit from military discipline and be able to improve himself. Her prediction is correct, and Joe becomes a model soldier who saves his captain in action around Carrizal, Mexico. When he returns, Clara accepts him over his middle-class rival, James (Jimmy Smith), who has outwardly desirable wealth but lacks Joe's demonstrated strength of character.[7]

The film was both a critical and financial success, with the Johnsons' investment in authenticity paying off on-screen (advertisements particularly noted the battle scenes and the use of many former members of the 9th and 10th Cavalries as extras).[8] The proud mention of the involvement of ex-servicemen certainly speaks to the attitude of the community toward that service, but the other key point of interest is the portrayal of the main character himself. Joe is described in terms that emphasize his lower-class status, and his military service is viewed as an appropriate and useful means for ironing out his rough edges. In her work on silent-era melodramas, Gaines argues that Joe's willingness to be improved is a key point in the narrative, especially given that Clara rejects her successful middle-class suitor in favor of the more upright Joe.[9] While audiences may certainly have perceived Joe as better because of his efforts at self-improvement, the film is of more interest for its replication of the typical traditional narrative, here functioning as a story of racial uplift. Participation in military action makes a shiftless character a worthy man, but the fact that a Black man can achieve this status through participation as a regular member of the armed forces also suggests that he is a made a worthy citizen.

The Black press praised the Lincoln films not only for the conditions of their production but also because they presented images that stood in opposition to the typical portrayal of Black characters on-screen. In the mid- to late 1910s, even Black-owned companies trafficked in the stereotyped tradition of comedic characters who ate watermelon and were afraid of ghosts. One of the few survivors of this tradition is the Ebony Film Corporation's *Spying the Spy* (1918), which depicts a Black lead character, Sambo Sam, who acts as a private investigator attempting to capture German undercover agents. Though nominally involving espionage, the film is much more in the tradition of a Sherlock Holmes spoof, in some ways very similar in tone to the earlier Douglas Fairbanks comedy *The Mystery of the Leaping Fish* (1916). Sam is shown smoking a Holmesian churchwarden pipe while wearing a loudly checkered overcoat and deerstalker, and the very loosely constructed plot involves his infiltration of the initiation rites of a secret society. The hooded members wear outfits resembling those of the Ku Klux Klan, and much is made of Sam's fear of these "ghosts" and of a skeleton they keep in their hideout. Throughout, the depiction of the hero relies on the exaggerated expression, genial incompetence, and irrational fear that defined the stereotypical image of Black characters in mainstream filmmaking despite the fact that Ebony made films catering specifically to a Black clientele. In contrast, the films made by the Lincoln Company depicted narratives of personal fortitude and redemption, enacted by noncaricatured performers, thereby speaking to the aspirations of an expanding Black middle class. This more measured approach became increasingly important with the advent of the second great spur to the development of the Black film industry, American involvement in the First World War.

Though there are individual cases in earlier conflicts, the first major use of specifically Black units in the U.S. armed forces took place during the Civil War, when a sizable minority of Union troops was African American. The success of these units led to their continuation following the war in two regiments of infantry (the 24th and 25th) and two of cavalry (the 9th and 10th). These regular troops (almost always under the command of white officers) were used primarily in the Far West but acquitted themselves well in Indian wars, the Spanish-American War, and skirmishes in Mexico. Byron Farwell suggests that they experienced lower desertion rates and higher reenlistment rates than did comparable white units.[10] For African American soldiers, U.S. entry into the First World War was initially viewed as another opportunity for these regular units to see combat. In fact, however, the federal government did not view a large war as an opportunity to encourage racial acceptance. As Arthur E. Barbeau and Florette Henri recount, army authorities quickly detailed the regular Black units away from Europe, dispatching the 9th to the Philippines and the 10th and the 25th to patrol the Mexican border. Most problematically, elements of the 24th were sent to Houston, Texas, where they came into conflict with the local population, leading to a violent clash that resulted in court-martials for 156 members of the battalion and the hanging of 19 of them.[11]

Black leaders may have been disappointed that the established Black units were not deployed to Europe but nevertheless viewed the war as an opportunity for African Americans to demonstrate their patriotism. In his autobiography, *A Man Called White*, Walter Francis White, head of the NAACP from 1931 to 1955, recalled that in 1917, "a 'flying squadron' of intensely patriotic young Negroes came to Atlanta during the courses of a Southern tour to induce Negroes to volunteer for the Negro officers' training camp which the War Department under pressure was planning to open at Fort Des Moines, Iowa.... When an eloquent appeal for volunteers was made, I found myself springing to my feet as one of the first to volunteer."[12] The pages of the NAACP's official journal, *The Crisis*, were full of war news throughout the period of active U.S involvement in the conflict and for almost a year after the armistice. In May 1918, for example, the organization's George Bradford declared, "I believe that this is Our War and not President Wilson's War and that no matter how many blunders the administration makes, or how many obstacles it puts in our way we must work the harder to win the war." He continued, "When men fight together and work together and save together, this foolishness of race prejudice disappears."[13] The general staff of the army faced the problem of reconciling these Black aspirations with white (especially Southern) unwillingness to serve in fully integrated units. As Jennifer Keene attests in her *Doughboys, the Great War, and the Remaking of America*, the general staff made a conscious decision to limit Black troops to noncombatant roles and to maintain white majorities during training.[14] This solution may have been imperfect, but the officials of the War Plans Division understood the extent of the difficulties. They were "leery" of complaints from Black lobbying organizations as well as of disciplinary problems that might arise when attempting to balance the interests and concerns of Black and white soldiers and civilians. The eventual compromise was "to maintain disciplinary control by segregating white and black troops as systematically as possible."[15] Earlier versions of the same thinking occurred during Wilson's first term when he created controversy by allowing the active segregation of African American workers in various federal agencies.[16]

The awkwardness of segregation did more than hinder military efficiency and discipline, however; it presented the government with a consistent public relations headache. While Black men were being drafted into the armed services to make the world safe for democracy, the Committee on Public Information (CPI) realized that it would need to acknowledge the participation of Black conscripts, at least within African American communities. The Lincoln Motion Picture Company arrived at the same conclusion, quickly offering its services to the government to provide a middle ground between Black and white versions of the experiences of Black troops.

On July 12, 1918, George Johnson sent a letter to Emmett Scott in Washington, DC. Scott had spent nearly two decades as Booker T. Washington's confidential secretary, and on October 5, 1917, the CPI announced that he had been "assigned to duty in the War Department as confidential advisor in matters affecting the interests of the 10,000,000 Negroes of the United States, and the part they are to play in connection with the present war."[17] According to Johnson, "The effectiveness of the motion picture is a proven factor insofar as to its value among the opposite races. Its value to the Government in a similar capacity with the Negro race is yet to be proven. And it is of this available opportunity that now exists that I respectfully call your attention [to the possibility of] the use of the motion picture by all of the various government departments in the task that now confronts them, of educating, encouraging and sustaining the morale of the folks at home, educated, and uneducated; Black and white; poor and rich." The letter goes on to suggest a variety of possibilities, including the establishment of a "Government Releasing Organization" (essentially an exchange network for Lincoln's films made for the government), the awarding of a contract to Lincoln to create "special" films for publicity purposes, particular film projects, and the establishment of a "Race pictorial news feature" to be released monthly.[18]

Three days later, Johnson sent similar letters to both George Creel, head of the CPI, and Charles Hart, the CPI's director of films. Johnson expanded on his arguments regarding the importance of film as a means of reaching a broad audience and the need to address a specifically Black constituency and offered more details regarding the messages to be sent via those films. Johnson proposed that Lincoln's employees be classified as members of a "war essential" industry, since "with all due respect to the Government order and with no intention of any of the members endeavoring to evade the draft laws; we firmly believe that each member of value into the Lincoln Firm can be of far more value and service to the Government and the people by remaining in their chosen profession and in conjunction with your committee, continue to produce and release the only photo-plays of their kind produced as a means of entertainment to the millions of Negro people." Most significantly, however, he stressed the moral and instructional qualities of films produced by Lincoln, declaring it "the only firm in the world producing high class, moral, instructive and entertaining photo-plays of, by and for the 12,000,000 Negro people, . . . the only company that has endeavored and succeeded in filming a photoplay other than comedies, containing a moral, and educational and instructive value, and one that appeases and upholds the ideals of the Negro Race without insult or offense of the white race, whether of the north or the south, [and] the only organization that has attempted and succeeded to cater to the desire of the 12,000,000 Negro people for wholesome attractive amusement in the form of photo-plays."[19] Johnson thus signals his willingness to use his films to create narratives conveying a particular "moral" and "wholesome" image of African American soldiers that would counter the standard stereotypes and instill pride among the entire Black community yet would avoid insulting white sensibilities.

In September 1918, Johnson was still trying to persuade government officials, sending Hart a memo that went into even further detail regarding the mechanics of his scheme and outlining possible subjects and projects.

The proposed productions included several fiction features with titles such as *The Black Devils* (intended as a seven-reel film) and *Why Uncle Sam Is Proud of His Negro Soldiers* (five or seven reels) as well as propaganda to "mould loyalty to the government" and short subjects addressing the Negro's relationship to various government agencies, departments, and religious denominations. In addition, there were to be films covering such subjects as education, social hygiene, and economic advancement.[20] Regardless of the breathtaking ambition and detailed business planning, indicated by this correspondence, none of these plans came to fruition. Instead, as Cripps notes, "Lincoln remained largely frozen out of the seats of power . . . unable to crack the white monopoly. . . . Instead of a Negro bureau, a lucrative contract, and good documentary film for ghetto audiences Lincoln lost out and was forced to buy stock footage from the French Government."[21]

Johnson's failure does not mean that the CPI completely ignored the African American film audience. In fact, Johnson himself must have been deeply disappointed to find that the CPI chose to address his concerns for the neglected Black community by signing a contract with the less ambitious Downing Film Corporation of New York. The company was a short-lived business venture of African American playwright, author, diplomat and businessman Henry Francis Downing. Downing's years in the U.S. Navy and in New York state politics as well as his many political connections may have given him an advantage in winning the government contract.[22] He was certainly more familiar with the nuances of government bureaucracy than an actor (Noble Johnson) and a postal clerk (George Johnson). Regardless of how Downing won the right to produce and distribute the two-reel documentary film *Our Colored Fighters*, he did bring the film to market, but as with most of the other films dealing with African American involvement in the war, it was not screened publicly until well after the armistice.[23] Though no print survives, Henry T. Sampson reports that *Our Colored Fighters* premiered in Manhattan on December 6, 1919 (though George Johnson saw the picture in late October), and Pearl Bowser and Louise Spence suggest that the film showed "the important place the American negro fighters are taking in the world war . . . the enlistment and the training of the colored soldiers in the cantonments and . . . their work overseas."[24]

Along with *Our Colored Fighters*, several other African American war films were released in the wake of the armistice, including *Our Hell Fighter's Return* (1919) and *Heroic Negro Soldiers of the World War* (1919). The most important of these was probably *From Harlem to the Rhine*, a five-reel opus that also incorporated a variety of slides and was apparently created by the War Department and released in May 1920. The film focused on the 15th

Regiment (known as the Harlem Hellfighters) and traced the unit from its inception to its return from France and victorious parade up New York's Fifth Avenue. Sampson includes a review of the film's midnight premiere at a Harlem theater, a standing-room-only affair featuring music performed by the 15th Regimental Band. According to reviewer Lester Walton, "The Negro can point with unbridled pride to one screen production featuring (without attempt to disparage) the colored soldier in the World War."[25] Despite the inadequacies of these films and the tardiness of their arrival on-screen, such comments justify Bowser and Spence's claim that "after the war, in the face of violent labor confrontations and escalating racial segregation and harassment, the Black soldier was still an important role model for many, a source of patriotic identity and a political tool, providing leverage in the fight for the rights of full citizenship."[26]

Though the government may have put forward the Black soldier as an ideal for African Americans, the actual meaning of Black servicemen as "a source of patriotic identity" or as a "political tool" remained an open question. Black and white audiences had very different conceptions of the meaning of minority military service, but since none of these films has survived it is difficult to assess their approach or attitude other than to posit that Black-dominated production companies might take a tack different from that of their white counterparts. George Johnson's ideas regarding middle-class uplift, for example, strongly suggest that his approach would differ from that of the white-owned Ebony Company or from those of other filmmakers authorized by the CPI to create and distribute documentary material. This notion receives support from the only surviving African American–themed war film with which the CPI was involved, *Training of Colored Troops* (1918).[27]

Unlike most of the other released films, *Training of Colored Troops* incorporates a fictional framework to dramatize parts of the Black serviceman's experience. The film begins with two crudely shot scenes that are essentially tableaux. The first depicts a young man speaking to two young boys, a woman, and an older man (presumably his father) while holding a document; on the wall behind the group are pictures of Booker T. Washington and Abraham Lincoln. Four more women, presumably neighbors and extended relations, enter the room and surround the young man, and an insert lets the audience read the induction notice for Edward Johnson of Louisville, Kentucky. One of the children puts his hand to his ear, thereby providing a bridge to the next tableau, in which the extended group has been joined by even more people as well as a deacon (the man does not wear a clerical collar) who prays over the kneeling inductee. These two shots are followed by the main body of the film, which consists of documentary footage of an

Training of Colored Troops makes a point of showing black soldiers in stereotyped situations, such as these recruits eating watermelon.

unnamed military base. Thomas Winter suggests that the film was made more to reassure white audiences than for the sake of Black filmgoers, and the scenes demonstrate a mixed sense of purpose. The first documentary shot shows Black men arriving on a train, but the train consists of only an engine, a boxcar, and two passenger cars. It thus neatly skirts the issue of segregated train travel by avoiding any intimation that white recruits would travel in separate accommodations. The pattern continues throughout the film, as the focus is on African American soldiers, but nearly every scene does double duty, striving to instill a sense of inclusive pride for a Black audience as well as reinforcing the racial views and attitudes of non-Black Americans. Though the enlisted men may be Black, they are supervised by white men at every turn—while being processed, engaged in close order drill, and standing in a mess line. In addition, the film features frequent sequences that include familiar stereotypes of African Americans. The enlisted men are shown jovially eating watermelon, performing the menial domestic labor of washing their mess kits, and singing and dancing with the "Receiving Station Jazz Band." One shot includes two soldiers, one abnormally tall and thin, the other extremely short. The only purpose of the shot seems to be the injection of humor by juxtaposing the two while perhaps implying that they are an odd fit for military service.

In this middle section, the troops appear increasingly professional thanks to the positive effects of military discipline and instruction, and their combat readiness is implied. They are pointedly never shown firing weapons,

Black trainees with bayonets practice under the supervision of a white instructor in *Training of Colored Troops*.

however, or in combat, though they are shown advancing in formation with charged bayonets and engaged in a friendly boxing match. The latter moment in particular seems to bear out Butters's argument regarding the importance of physicality as a defining characteristic of Black masculinity. He specifically relates the quality to fighter Jack Johnson, who remained one of the most well-known African Americans of the time and whose reputation is implicitly evoked by almost any scene featuring a Black boxer.[28]

Though Winter argues that "once removed from the direct surveillance of their Caucasian superiors, the film suggests African Americans will backslide into predictable behavior patterns," it is possible to read the final two scenes of this section as tracing an arc that affirms the salutary result of military training.[29] The first of the two scenes appears to show Black troops under the supervision of Black officers while a bureaucratic task is performed; the second is a simple shot of Black soldiers standing together in a group in full dress (and without the supervision of white officers), apparently ready to ship out.

The closing sequence returns to the fictional Johnson family as they receive a form postcard from Edward (who does not appear in any of the documentary sequences). The card is a note on Red Cross "soldier" stationery (perhaps asserting the nondiscriminatory nature of that organization) indicating the soldier's arrival overseas. Edward's parents and grandmother pointedly stand in front of a service star hanging in their window as they read it. The next scene shows the extended family gathered around Edward's

Black recruits shown under the supervision of black officers in *Training of Colored Troops*. The soldier sitting on the left appears to wear the insignia of a first lieutenant, while the man sitting on the right is presumably a quartermaster. The image therefore may show the disbursement of pay.

mother as she reads a letter he has sent from France. This letter, written on YMCA stationery "Somewhere in France," reads, "Dear Ma and folks, I am building the biggest dock in the world. Pushing a wheelbarrow is in the same language as ours, but I cannot understand the French talk. Tell grandma to send me a black berry pie. Hotziggity!!! The dinner bell has just blowed, so goodbye." Here again, the film's multiple goals include instilling pride in a serviceman and emphasizing the sameness of the military experience for African Americans yet also noting the ingrained differences of that experience. The Red Cross and YMCA stationery as well as the experience of an alien tongue would have been the same for most white soldiers, but Edward's building of "the biggest dock in the world" not only provides a source of pride but also clearly indicates that his duties involve not combat but manual labor. The final scene of the film involves Edward's father, inspired by the letter, digging out a Civil War–era sword and sharpening it on a whetstone. Once again, the multiple meanings of the sequence tread the line between white and Black audiences as the film invokes wartime service in previous conflicts for both white and Black veterans.

As the lone example of its kind, *Training of Colored Troops* delineates the difficulties faced by the government in trying to tread the ridge between Black and white audiences while still recognizing the presence of African

The framing story in *Training of Colored Troops* makes a point of showing the proud soldier's family, with a service star displayed prominently in the background.

American troops as part of the Allied Expeditionary Force. While Winter reads the film as an attempt by the government to create a sense of national unity (subtitling his article "A Cinematic Effort to Promote National Cohesion"), that argument appears generous given the tone of the film itself and the difficulties faced by anyone attempting to distribute and exhibit such material. It seems more plausible to read the film as a standard narrative of wartime service that awkwardly tries to graft those standards onto a community that the anonymous filmmakers approached from the perspective of outsiders. The result is a document that has something to both appeal to and offend either audience. It portrays African American service through a lens of white stereotype and condescension but does so in a way that tries to encourage the patriotism (and cooperation of) Black audiences.

Such films would not in any way fulfill the promise of George Johnson's hopeful correspondence with the CPI, and in fact the Johnsons' inability to crack the nut of government cooperation was the first step in the Lincoln Company's decline. Frustrated at the constant business struggles, Noble (the company's biggest star) resigned from the board and chose to focus on his career at Universal. (He is perhaps now best remembered as the native chieftain on Skull Island in RKO's 1933 version of *King Kong*.)[30] George eventually established a film-booking organization, shooting and distributing footage of the 10th Cavalry as well as distributing footage of Black troops in action in France acquired from another source. But his grand hopes of using film to convey a message that promoted and upheld the views and perspective of America's Black citizens remained an unrealized dream. After releasing two more short fiction films, the company dissolved in 1923.[31] It would become the task of other Black filmmakers to find new, more meaningful ways of expressing the image and importance of Black overseas service in later films of the 1920s.

The mixed messages contained in *Training of Colored Troops* were not clarified when those troops returned home. African Americans were understandably conflicted regarding their participation in the Great War. Despite assurances to Black leaders that at least 35 percent of Black recruits would be fighting men, the only units that saw regular combat were regiments of the 92nd and 93rd Divisions that were attached to the French army for the duration of the war, and only 20 percent of African American troops saw actual combat.[32] These Americans were under French control and issued French weaponry, and white American officers generally disowned them.[33] Most Black troops under U.S. control received little training and less equipment and were assigned to perform transport and supply duties overseas.

The combat regiments nevertheless acquired a solid record under fire, and when these men returned at the end of the war, they had every right to expect some recognition of their service. Instead, in the words of one writer, "For valor displayed in the recent war, it seems that the Negro's particular decoration is to be the 'double-cross.'"[34] Returning servicemen encountered a heightened degree of racial hostility, aggravated by concerns that well-traveled Black men would have their worst instincts affirmed by time spent in a more racially permissive French society. At the same time, hostilities increased since those "worst instincts" included a demand for increased respect from white society. Not surprisingly, W. E. B. Du Bois read Black wartime service through the lens of his notion of "double consciousness," writing in 1919 that "anti-Negro prejudice was rampant in the American army and the officers particularly were subjected to all sorts of discrimination" but also arguing that the internationalizing experience of serving in France presented African American soldiers with a more positive model of racial acceptance.[35] Through their interaction with unbiased French soldiers and citizenry, veterans would understand their dual natures as both Americans and as Black men while also being inspired to refuse to submit to America's established racial attitudes. Du Bois succinctly summarized this argument in a 1919 *Crisis* editorial: Black veterans "return at once bitter and exalted! They will not submit to American caste and they will ever love France."[36]

Within the mainstream Hollywood industry, the return of veterans did not initially alter the prevailing narrative methods of dealing with combat.

The traditional narrative remained the dominant discourse until it began to be transformed by filmmakers who had served overseas or by the more extended influence of returned veterans active in literature and the theater. The smaller size of the race film industry slowed this process of reconsideration even further for Black audiences, and the eventual result of that process differs notably.

At least two mainstream films of the early 1920s feature Black soldiers. Whether a response to the fact of African American wartime service or to the concurrent reality of the Great Migration of African Americans to northern urban centers occasioned by the conflict, these films apparently featured African American soldiers as equals of white troops, indicating at least the possibility (no matter how slim) of constructively addressing a divisive racial reality.

D. W. Griffith's *The Greatest Thing in Life* (1918) has been lost, but the plot involves a superior Southern aristocrat (played by Bobby Harron) who enlists in the U.S. Army and is sent to fight in the trenches. In combat, the racist Southerner is rescued by a Black soldier who at one point offers "his last drop of water so that his white buddy may live."[37] In what became the best remembered and most discussed scene of the film, Harron repays the favor by kissing the mortally wounded Black man as he calls for his "mammy."[38] Aside from adding further levels to the already Byzantine discussion of Griffith's racial attitudes, the film is noteworthy for portraying white and Black soldiers as equals on the battlefield. Richard Schickel reports that Lillian Gish felt "that if modern audiences could see the picture it would do much to correct what she insists is the false impression of Griffith as a racist."[39] Contemporary reactions, however, counter Gish's perspective. Writing for *Motion Picture Classic*, Frederick James Smith suggested that the scene was being touted as a moment of "extreme daring" that might be perceived as "atoning" for the racial sins of *The Birth of a Nation*, but he still found the film "conventional" and a "disappointment."[40] The reviewer for the *New York Times* made no mention of the scene, only characterizing the production as a whole as "not up to the Griffith standard."[41] The Black press seems to have taken no notice of the film whatsoever. As a contemporary effort to redress the balance of the negligence with which Black soldiers were treated, therefore, it seems to have made no real impression of any kind in either the Black or white communities.

The second film of the non-Black establishment to possibly include Black soldiers was Burton King's *The Lost Battalion* (1919). The film tells the story of the famous 77th Division advance, encirclement, and eventual relief as part of the Argonne offensive in October 1918. Led by Major Charles White

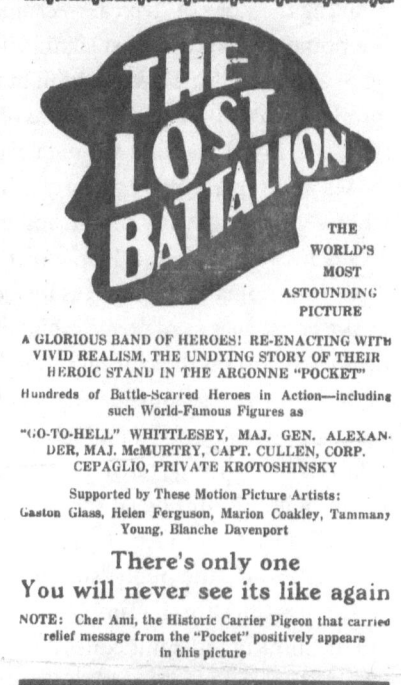
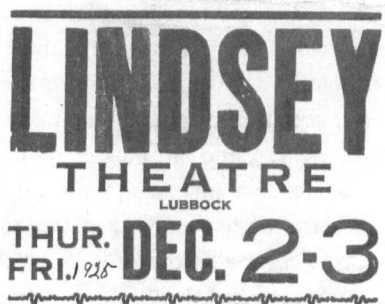

An original herald advertising *The Lost Battalion*. The "battle-scarred heroes" comprise a careful ethnic mix that may originally have included African American soldiers, but they are no longer in evidence in surviving materials.

Whittlesey, the roughly 550 men involved breached the German line of battle but did so without the support of the units on their flanks, which were turned back by enemy resistance. Surrounded and isolated, the Americans held out for five days before being rescued. King's film version of the event was made the following year and featured as many of the original participants as possible—including footage of the fabled carrier pigeon Cher Ami. Despite the frequent claims of authenticity, however, the film takes a great deal of dramatic license in detailing the story of "typical" recruits and their families and love interests back home. One of the most significant examples of this license is the detailing of a mixed ethnic composition that makes the unit a model of the type of propaganda seen so clearly in films of the Second World War such as *Bataan* (1943). As in the later film, the men of the unit come from all socioeconomic classes and represent a variety of ethnicities, including Germans, Jews, and Chinese. Conspicuously absent, however, are any African American soldiers. In his *Reel America and World War I*, Craig Campbell asserts that the battalion was originally "pictured as including blacks among its members" but that as a consequence of postwar bigotry, "the blacks seen in *The Lost Battalion* were . . . lost on the cutting room floor soon after the initial release."[42] Campbell provides no outside support for this claim, and the existing print of the film does not contain a single Black character or extra. Given that the film is using its narrative (as *Bataan* would later do) to posit an ideal moment of ethnic and racial solidarity, however, it would be significant if scenes including African Americans were initially included. As with *The Greatest Thing in Life*, the public showed little interest in the subject in the wake of the armistice (or, if Campbell is correct, just enough interest to be hostile to the film's broad-mindedness), so Black soldiers once again were denied even a brief nod of recognition on mainstream screens.

Much like the mainstream film industry, African American filmmakers needed several years before they began to address the legacy of the First World War within their community. There were, however, several key differences. White artists, writers, and filmmakers spent years struggling to overturn an established narrative model and replace it with something that more closely reflected their experiences. Black artists, however, immediately began to grapple with the contradictions of their involvement in military service less hindered by preconceived patterns. In large part, this attention was the result of the artistic and political movement that came to be known as the Harlem Renaissance.

In the years following the war, writers associated with the Harlem Renaissance developed two approaches for addressing African American participation in the military. The first treated servicemen in a more traditionally heroic mode and is exemplified by works such as Edward Christopher Williams's *When Washington Was in Vogue* and Henry Francis Downing's *An American Cavalryman: A Liberian Romance*. The second approach gave vent to the contradictions and bitterness felt by African Americans regarding their service and can be seen in such plays as Joseph Seamon Cotter Jr.'s *On the Fields of France* and Alice Dunbar-Nelson's *Mine Eyes Have Seen* and novels such as Claude McKay's *Home to Harlem* and T. S. Stribling's *Birthright*. Though film is generally excluded from discussions of the Harlem Renaissance, these two ways of addressing military participation emerged in the world of race filmmakers as well. Features such as *Injustice* and *The Flying Ace*, which were produced by segregated production companies and directed by white men, took the "traditional" path, often emulating the conventions of mainstream filmmaking and depicting their protagonists as exemplars of heroic values. However, the most important independent African American filmmaker, Oscar Micheaux, experimented with both approaches across a variety of films, trying to find a balance between the concurrent dual roles of Black soldiers as valorized heroes and reminders of racial intolerance.

As summarized by Henry Sampson, the plot of *Injustice* (1919) would make an appropriate pairing with Griffith's melodramatic *Hearts of the World*. The story involves a young woman, Irene Waterloo, being courted by a nobleman. When her competition for his affections discovers (and reveals) that Irene is actually Black (to Irene's own surprise), she runs away to France to join the Red Cross. When German soldiers attack her, she is rescued by her former butler, who is now serving with a Black infantry unit. After she nurses him back to health, they live happily ever after.[43] Though the star is a female, this is a thoroughly traditional story of redemption and follows the outlines of the traditional model. The main character begins as a spoiled child of privilege, finds redemption on the battlefield, and ends the story as a better person, rewarded with true love. As the African American *Chicago Defender* put it in a review, "The principals in the end, after many hardships and hair-raising adventures, sail into the peaceful valley of love and content, to the edification of their friends."[44]

Though the treatment appears to have been generally in line with the mainstream approach to similar material (with the exception of the subplot involving Irene passing as white), several points distinguish the film from the general run of such stories. First, as one newspaper put it, "Though it was produced with the idea of appealing exclusively to the Negro population, the picture has many good qualities which every fan will recognize."[45] In other words, though the story dealt with Black characters, its adherence to the prevailing norms of the white majority may have given it a broader appeal. At the same time, mention of those inequities that caused the Black community to be conflicted about the military experience drew divergent responses from white and Black reviewers. Though the writer for the *Defender* noted that the film showed "the petty prejudice as practiced against our people who were both in the uniform of the soldier and Red Cross" the reviewer for the white *Los Angeles Leader* was much less sympathetic to those issues, implying that their mere discussion was dangerous: "Los Angeles, fortunately, is in little

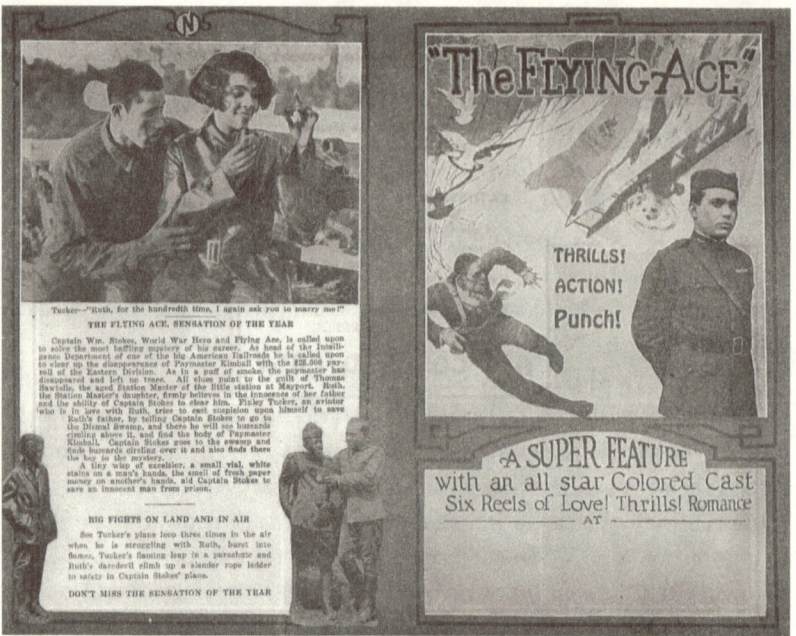

Images and advertising copy on this herald for *The Flying Ace* may suggest the roots of the story in a canceled serial but also emphasize the clean-cut, disciplined character of the military hero.

danger of ever being the scene of race riots.... But if such a danger existed, it certainly might be fanned into action by the picture play[, which] is a frank appeal to the emotions of colored folk to revolt against the social handicap that has been imposed upon them. Surely no good purpose can be served by such an appeal at the present time."[46] As a race film, therefore, *Injustice* apparently succeeded in bringing an African American view of military service to Black movie theaters, but that perspective remained problematic despite an acceptably conventional narrative framework.

Like *Injustice*, *The Flying Ace* (1926) was written and directed by a white filmmaker. Richard E. Norman owned and operated Norman Studios near Jacksonville, Florida. Perceiving a new market, he chose to focus on race films in the early 1920s, beginning with a Black-cast remake of his earlier all-white production *The Green-Eyed Monster* (1920). The films were free of negative racial stereotypes and were made specifically to appeal to a Black audience, so the racial attitudes portrayed in them are a useful reflection of the extent of progressive ideas concerning the Black community. *The Flying Ace* was Norman's last released film, and studio publicity made much of its expense and the technical know-how involved in the production: "When the picture was finally completed, it cost 75% more than the original estimate. This

Advertising for *The Flying Ace* makes a point of highlighting the airplane itself.

became necessary to make the picture mechanically perfect.... No company making colored pictures has attempted and successfully made a picture like *The Flying Ace*. It even has situations in it that haven't been shown in a white picture."⁴⁷ The publicity copy emphasizing the expense of the film and its creative use of aerial technology is enthusiastic, and the prominence of the airplane in advertising imagery cannot be denied. Phyllis Klotman over-reaches, however, when she writes that "the real star of the film is the plane. ... It is the symbol of Captain Stokes's heroism, his past triumphs, and his ability to use the new technology to good purpose."⁴⁸ In fact, the film is most fascinating for the way it which it combines the technology of the telegraph, the railroad, and the airplane as well as the hero's military service record into an otherwise fairly standard variant of the now-forgotten railroad genre. That genre was frequently the domain of serial heroines such as Pearl White and Helen Holmes, and the advertising copy for *The Flying Ace* drew intentional parallels between the narrative of the Norman production and the standard adventures of those established stars. Those similarities receive further significance from Barbara Lupack's extensive recounting of the film's gestation, which establishes that many story elements were adapted from various other aborted Norman projects, including *Zircon*, a multiepisode serial.⁴⁹

As it finally emerged, the plot of *The Flying Ace* revolves around the theft of a $25,000 payroll from a railroad paymaster and the hiring of a reliable railroad detective to solve the crime. That detective, Captain William Stokes, is indirectly introduced via a newspaper story:

> The many friends of Captain William Stokes, World War hero and Flying Ace, welcomed him back home by a banquet given last night at the Hotel Pennsylvania in his honor. Captain Stokes is credited with bringing down seven German planes during the "big push" and bears many scars of the encounter. Captain Stokes was a flyer of some ability before the War. Owning his own plane, he had learned to fly here on the local field and only a brief training was necessary before he was sent to France. Before his entrance in the war, he was a railroad detective for the M. N. & Q. Railroad and he was instrumental in clearing up mysterious freight thefts and bringing about the arrest of a clever gang of boxcar thieves operating on the railroad.

This story, which flashes by quickly enough on-screen that it would be difficult to read it all, immediately marks Stokes as a professionally and financially successful individual and insinuates that such success is transferable to his time in combat. The plane is not, as Klotman would have it, the symbol of Stokes's success, since Stokes is sufficient unto himself to perform that role. Breaking from the pattern of a traditional narrative, he is portrayed as a fully developed model individual. His wartime experience has not changed him but rather constitutes the fulfillment of his potential. Stokes is therefore less a reflection or comment on the effect of military experience than a model New Negro worthy of adulation.

Three other important pieces of evidence support Stokes's role as less a reflection of reality than an archetype. The first is his inordinate concern with his uniform, which he makes a point of straightening on several occasions, such as when he carefully puts on his cap after his initial on-screen appearance and when he neatens up his uniform following a brawl with the chief villain. The attention paid to how he looks emphasizes his role as an exemplar.

The second way in which Stokes is idealized is in the mutual devotion between the officer and his fellow veteran Peg. Peg is Stokes's mechanic and general right-hand man who lost his leg during the war. The two men travel together, displaying an easy camaraderie in their first appearance, smoking and talking after landing at the local airfield. Peg is tasked with the grittier jobs attendant to Stokes's investigation—that is, taking the train disguised as a hobo while Stokes flies or using a bicycle while Stokes rides in a car.

Their relationship is never spelled out beyond their mutual respect, but Peg is essential to Stokes's position as an idealized veteran. Stokes can fly because Peg takes care of the plane; Stokes can keep his uniform clean because Peg assumes a gritty disguise; Stokes can romance the love interest because Peg serenades them. They are not quite alter egos, but if any negative aspects of military service were displayed, they would be displaced to Peg, just as the one obvious potential drawback—physical injury—is made a defining characteristic of the less idealized sidekick.

Finally, Stokes embodies an idealized African American serviceman in that he is presented as a full member of the U.S. military, engaged in frontline combat with the enemy and enjoying a high degree of success. This is perhaps the most fantastical aspect of the film, given that no African Americans were permitted to fly missions for the United States during the First World War. The nearest models (as Klotman shows) were men who flew for the French or Canadians.[50]

Given the heroically idealized main character, the events and plot of the film are incidental. Standard crime fiction elements (a drug vial used to knock out a railroad employee, a mass escape by plotters who are conveniently assembled in one room while the hero explains their crimes) are interwoven with fairly typical plot points concerned with railroad activities (the stolen payroll, shots of telegraphers in action along the rail line, shots of rolling stock). The airplane footage is not uninteresting (especially when the villain attempts to rape the heroine midflight and she escapes by climbing from one flying airplane to another on a ladder lowered by the hero), but it adds little to the established impression of Stokes as a capable hero comfortable with technology or to his depiction as a stalwart model of the virtues of correct behavior and the benefits of military service.

As both *Injustice* and *The Flying Ace* demonstrate, race filmmakers were not entirely able to break free from the standard plot conventions of mainstream cinema when portraying Black military service, but that may have been especially true for white filmmakers catering to a specifically Black audience. The most significant Black filmmaker never addressed the topic directly, but he created a number of oblique portraits of military service that indicate a more complex understanding of the legacy of African Americans in the First World War.

Oscar Micheaux has become legendary as the first African American auteur, recognized as such more for his astonishing productivity and longevity than for the quality of his films. Ronald Green's strenuous arguments that Micheaux's aesthetic is an intentionally developed middle-class style, unhindered by the excesses (or standards) of mainstream Hollywood filmmaking, are not without interest but are never entirely convincing. Similarly, Jane M. Gaines's attempts to decenter the importance of Micheaux as auteur in favor of viewing the filmmaker as an entrepreneur and showman are an interesting corrective that is less useful in examining his attitudes toward military service. Though the theme of military service recurs periodically in his work, it is generally not central to the plot, and therefore does not register as an exemplar of showmanship.[51]

More compelling is the importance of literary influences on Micheaux's work, especially the frequent use of literature as source material for his films. As Lupack exhaustively argues, much of this source material is his own (he wrote seven novels and an unknown number of short stories), but he also drew plots from a number of successful if little-remembered authors such as Charles Chesnutt (three films), Henry Francis Downing (two films) and T. S. Stribling (two films).[52] Despite these literary attentions, Micheaux's middle-class tendencies, his forceful personality, and what Robert Jackson refers to as his "sometimes sketchy business practices" seem to have excluded him from serious artistic consideration by any of the leading lights of the Harlem Renaissance.[53] As Clyde Taylor puts it, "While the writers [of the Harlem Renaissance] identified with ordinary Black people and brought new vitality to Black writing through this identification, they apparently shied away from a personality from these ranks of the ordinary and from the poorly educated who tried to do what they did. They were, doubtless, ashamed of Micheaux because he menaced their need to gain the same respect given their White literary peers."[54] Micheaux's lifelong embrace of both pulp literature and popular filmmaking, entirely separate from any involvement with white guardians of cultural production, made him a threat to the greater acceptance of Black artists as a part of a larger cultural movement. Micheaux's independence made him untenable as a partner both for other Black filmmakers (after an early exchange of correspondence, George Johnson refused to deal with him, though Sampson asserts that Micheaux later offered Johnson a position in his company) and for leaders of the Black artistic community (including Chesnutt, who was wary of Michaux's adaptations).[55] That same individuality, however, makes him a useful bellwether for cultural attitudes toward military service outside of the usual narrative concerns of even those white filmmakers who attempted to address a Black audience.

Micheaux's attention to the question of military service manifests itself in two ways. Several films directly mention the issue of Black military participation in the First World War, including a brief documentary shown prior to the premiere of *The Homesteader* (which may or may not have been shot by Micheaux), a brief but significant mention in *Within Our Gates*, and both the silent and sound versions of Stribling's *Birthright*. In addition, Micheaux created characters who embody the virtues of military activity without specifically referring to the events of the Great War in *The Virgin of Seminole* and *A Daughter of the Congo*. This practice may indicate Micheaux's attempts to allude to the benefits of involvement in the armed forces without invoking the controversial realities of African American wartime participation.

Micheaux's first potential use of the war in his films is not directly incorporated into one of his narratives. In 1919, he released his debut film, a version of his autobiographical novel, *The Homesteader*. The film was preceded by a short documentary recording the homecoming of the Black Devils of the 370th Infantry of the 8th Regiment. Given Micheaux's proclivity for promoting himself and his work, the tendencies toward showmanship mentioned by Gaines came to the fore as he attempted to capitalize on the return of the African American military unit. It is not known whether Micheaux took the footage, but he clearly intended to make the most of the Black community's pride in its returning servicemen. His ideological beliefs regarding that pride are indicated by the concluding scenes of *Within Our Gates*, released the following year. As Dr. Vivian attempts to reassure the troubled main character, Sylvia, he tells her, "Be proud of our country, Sylvia. We should never forget what our people did in Cuba under Roosevelt's command. . . . And at Carrizal in Mexico. . . . And later in France, from Bruges to Chateau-Thierry, from Saint-Mihiel to the Alps!"[56] At this early point in the postwar period, Micheaux believed in the positive virtue of military service as a point of honor for Black veterans and expected that his audience would agree with his perspective.

The nature of participation in the Great War was less clear-cut in Micheaux's next approach to the subject. The silent version of his adaptation of *Birthright* apparently hewed fairly closely to its source. Stribling, who won the Pulitzer Prize for literature in 1933 and whose work inspired William Faulkner, created a novel that critiqued the ironies and inconsistencies of racial relations in the South. The hero, Peter Siner, is a Harvard-educated Black man who finds on returning to his Southern home that he can no longer comfortably fit in either Black or white society. On the train ride that begins both the novel and the film, he encounters an old neighbor, Tump Pack, returning from meritorious service in France. Though Stribling offers a nuanced depiction of the character, reviews of the film indicate that Micheaux was less temperate, with the *Chicago Defender* describing Tump as a "burley and loud spoken Negro" and the *New York Age* declaring him, "the colored bully of the town."[57] In this instance, Micheaux seems ambivalent regarding the returning veteran and is certainly far from applying a traditional approach to Tump's war record. Tump's buffoonish nature and his various run-ins with the law do not demonstrate that participation in the war has in any way improved his character. Though decorated, Tump was apparently portrayed as the villain of the film, a position that is a simplification of his role in the novel. In the book, Tump's befuddlement at so many of the events in the narrative indicates the inconsistency and contradictions of the racial attitudes that Stribling (and Micheaux) are criticizing. That the film was radically censored by New York, Maryland, Virginia, and Chicago before being approved for screening suggests that Micheaux initially succeeded at portraying at least some of this on-screen.[58] The film's overall approach seems to have radically differed from the prevailing mainstream discourse in presenting "an only too true story of conditions that have handicapped the harmony between the Races in a manner that emphasizes the lessons without reflecting discreditably upon the principal characters."[59] By delineating points of racial conflict—no matter how evenhandedly—Micheaux spoke to a narrative ignored by mainstream films that dealt with the Great War. The lessons that he emphasized must have had implications for the discussion of Black wartime service, though the absence of a surviving print makes it impossible to be sure how those lessons were expressed.

The films that embodied Micheaux's alternate approach to military service remain just as much of a mystery, given that no prints of any of them are extant. In both key examples, however, plot summaries indicate that the filmmaker took a route that may have constituted an attempt to capitalize on Black pride in military service while circumventing the censorship difficulties that plagued any frank assessment of the practical workings of such service. At the same time, this approach to some degree assumed a broader Black Atlantic perspective by expanding the geographic scope of the narratives to nations in which systemic racism would not interfere with professional progress. The plot of *The Virgin of Seminole* (1922) involves a man who travels to Canada and becomes (by virtue of the natural quality of his character) a member of the Mounties, eventually defeating the villain and winning the girl. The narrative itself is far from radical and seems to emulate typical mainstream fare. Available descriptions indicate, however, that the film reinforces the ideological message that military service (or in this case, pseudomilitary service) is a respectable avenue to success, which a Black character can achieve via an unbiased meritocratic system.

Though the first version of *Birthright* intervened, Micheaux made one other film utilizing this second approach. *A Daughter of the Congo* (1930) was a film version of Downing's 1917 novel, *An American Cavalryman: A Liberian Romance*. The story revolves around Captain Paul Dale, a Black serviceman detached to Liberia (along with Lieutenant Ronald Brown) to assist the constabulary force. En route, they rescue a jungle princess (Lupelta, actually a mulatto stolen at birth and raised by a jungle tribe) from Arab slave hunters. Lupelta and Dale are matched romantically, but it is unclear whether the film follows the book in its conclusion, which features the elimination of Lupelta as an acceptable mate when it is determined that she is actually white.[60] Micheaux again depicted a respectably noble soldier—in this case echoing the achievements of Black soldiers attached to French units during the Great War—who found success outside the boundaries of a racist and discriminatory American society.

Though neither *The Virgin of Seminole* nor *A Daughter of the Congo* directly depicted military action featuring Black American troops, Micheaux seems to have been experimenting with the correct way of portraying military service for the African American community. Especially by the late 1920s, the attempt to walk the line between a frank depiction of the subject and a representation that favored a more traditionally grounded approach made good business sense. By this time, Micheaux was receiving increasing criticism in the Black press for his willingness to portray an unflattering view of African American life. As Charlene Regester writes, "The central disagreement between Micheaux and the African-American press . . . was not his technique but his depiction of the unsettling behavior he observed and deplored in the black community."[61] At the same time, the problems he so frequently experienced with white censorship boards exerted insistent pressure to bring his filmmaking perspective and aesthetic in line with more mainstream productions. In this light, his decision to remake *Birthright* in 1939 can be read as a last, defiant effort to make an independent statement regarding aspects of Black life and culture, including his depiction of a Black World War I veteran.

Though it survives in only fragmentary form, Micheaux's 1939 talkie remake of *Birthright* takes on both the problematic character of Tump and the service of Black soldiers generally. As in the novel, Tump seems not to be depicted as a villain and is in fact wiser than Peter regarding the white townspeople's attempts to block the establishment of a school for Black children. Tump's antagonistic position in relation to the hero is a result of his jealousy over Cissie, the common love interest, and not a function of his bullying personality, as the silent version may have implied. As in the novel, Tump is no longer a threat when he discovers that Cissie is being arrested by the white sheriff, and he makes common cause with Peter to rescue her. As Green describes it, in a directorial touch that would have been impossible in the silent version, Tump assumes his former military demeanor, commanding himself to attention, shouting "right about face" and then "now, over the top." As Tump marches off to save Cissie, the non-diegetic sound overlay of bombs and gunfire reinforces the reference to the World War I combat experience as a toughening and validating influence on the domestic militancy of African-American veterans. Tump's determination to confront flagrant white racism . . . is tied to the experience of the militant protests of returning Black servicemen after having been given guns in World War I to fight for white American interests abroad; Tump is still wearing his World War I uniform throughout these scenes.[62]

This final statement of the theme, especially as part of a film version of a morally complex and successful novel, indicates that Micheaux has settled on a more nuanced version of the meaning of military service for the Black community. The character of Tump is a simple man who has not been made a better person in the manner of a traditional narrative but who is confused by the inconsistencies and paradoxes of his service. Combat has given him certain experiences that he may draw on for good or ill, but he (along with the entire community depicted in the film) remains deeply conflicted about the ultimate result of his time at war.

From the very beginning, the makers of race films faced enormous difficulties that relentlessly worked to confound them. The Lincoln Company lost its main star (Noble Johnson) because of pressure from competitor Universal. Richard Norman complained about the limited number of available venues for the screening of his films. Oscar Micheaux repeatedly clashed with hostile censorship boards. All of them experienced unending difficulties related to their undercapitalization and consistent lack of financing. In the face of these problems, they repeatedly sought acceptable ways to deal with ideas and social issues relevant to their audience. In the years of their greatest success, one of the most apparent of these issues was the response to Black service in the First World War. Filmmakers wrestled with the question of whether to valorize veterans and their time at war or to be blunt concerning the racial ambivalence and contradictions that greeted those men in the military and on their return. As Jacqueline Najuma Stewart puts it, "World War I crystallized the paradoxical relations between Black American identity and the cinema."[63] The insurmountable problems that afflicted their industry meant that race films never achieved a narrative consensus with regard to the issue and never resolved the paradox. Instead, support for such films began to decline as Hollywood began to pay more consistent, if circumscribed, attention to the Black audience in the late 1930s. Ironically, that attention not only subsumed the separate race film industry but also washed away the opportunity to create a coherent approach to the subject of African American wartime service on film.

Chapter Five

GIRLS IN HELL

The Changing Depiction of Women in the First World War

THOUGH IT IS NOW OFTEN FORGOTTEN, THE FIRST WORLD WAR PROVIDED the opportunity for the first officially sanctioned participation of women as members of the U.S. armed forces. Tens of thousands of American women served in the Great War in a variety of capacities, including as volunteers in various nonmilitary organizations and as regular enlistees in the navy and marines. As Lettie Gavin notes in *American Women in World War I: They Also Served*, more than eleven thousand women enlisted in the U.S. Navy by the time the armistice was signed, earning equal pay and full military benefits though they were not permitted in combat roles.[1] Kimberly Jensen points out in *Mobilizing Minerva: American Women in the First World War* that more than twenty-one thousand women served in the Army Nurse Corps during the conflict, and nearly eleven thousand of them served in France with the American Expeditionary Force. While army nurses were subject to military discipline, they were not treated as equals in any respect.[2] In addition, large numbers of female volunteers served in independent nursing units, as Red Cross and Salvation Army workers, and in various troupes of entertainers throughout Europe.[3] When they returned to the United States, many of them wrote memoirs of their experiences such as Ellen N. LaMotte's *The Backwash of War*, and Mary Borden's *The Forbidden Zone*. Like their literarily inclined male contemporaries, these women actively participated in the reformulation of literary conventions for dealing with armed conflicts.

On-screen, however, even as the depiction of the male wartime experience evolved through a decade of convolutions and adjustments, the depiction of the female experience remained largely standardized by a traditional romantic stereotype. However, the expected conventions did face some challenges. As with male-dominated stories of the Great War, those featuring female protagonists, though much fewer in number, underwent a decade-long evolution that addressed some of the same issues and concerns. But these films

A mother turns over her son to Uncle Sam for military service in this World War I recruiting poster.

labored under further handicaps that reflected an ambivalence concerning the place of women in the larger on-screen narrative of the conflict.

The late 1910s and early 1920s were a time of foment for women, in no small part as a consequence of the upheavals caused by the First World War. Images exhorting participation in the conflict on the home front included traditionally maternal, noble, and self-sacrificing women as well as those taking on more active roles as volunteers. Both became common in public discourse at the same time that women were assuming social and economic roles previously dominated by men. The onslaught of challenges to traditional conventions ultimately culminated in the passage of the Nineteenth Amendment, which granted women the right to vote, but the cultural currents leading to women's suffrage can also be seen in filmmakers' attempts to grapple with shifting social standards.

Women were called to actively meet wartime demands in any way they could.

In March 1919, D. W. Griffith released the last of his feature films to deal with the First World War. The title delineated a key aspect of the plot, but it also defined the most prominent initial methods of dealing with women in films set during time of war. *The Girl Who Stayed at Home* is by no means considered a major work in Griffith's oeuvre, but it reflects yet another way in which the narrative standards established prior to American involvement in the Great War persisted well into the early 1920s. For Griffith and many of his contemporaries, the subject of women's roles seemed incompatible with the discussion of a traditional narrative focused on the male experience and the growth of a young man into a fully enfranchised participant in the larger community. It is certainly true that the number of Great War narratives dealing with women in military situations beyond that of the helpless victim is limited. However, the evolution of women's roles between 1919 and the mid-1930s parallels the adjustments to both the depiction of male wartime service and the general attitude toward armed conflict.

Despite the mid-1910s prevalence of adventurous serial heroines such as Grace Cunard, Helen Holmes, and Pearl White, the on-screen portrayal of wartime female characters frequently resolved into two main types, both of which are on full display in *The Girl Who Stayed at Home*. Neither differed significantly from the Victorian-inflected versions of womanhood Griffith had displayed on movie screens since the beginning of his career. The plot of the film revolves around two sets of lovers swept up in the conflict. Ralph Grey (played by Richard Barthelmess) resolutely enlists when America enters the war, encouraged by the memory of a girl he fell in love with in France (Blossom, played by Carol Dempster). His dissolute brother Jim (Robert Harron) is shown to be a coward and a wastrel, an attitude their industrialist father encourages by declaring Jim essential to the family business. Jim is thus free to devote himself to the charms of a local showgirl, Cutie Beautiful (played by Clarine Seymour)—that is, until the local and district draft boards refuse to hear appeals from the senior Grey and Jim is drafted into the army. (The film was made in concert with the government to popularize the selective draft amendment.)[4]

Once both male characters are in the military, their stories unfold along predictable lines, with Ralph steadfastly masculine and Jim's character gradually molded into sober maturity by his time in combat, telling Cutie Beautiful, "If I get through alive and come back I'll be a different man." The two brothers meet serendipitously in the trenches, and the plot follows the lines of the story of *The Lost Battalion*, with Ralph fighting courageously with the surrounded unit and Jim wending his way through enemy lines to get help. His success allows the beleaguered men to hold out until a major American offensive can relieve them, with both brothers decorated for their valor.

As much as the stories of the male characters match narrative expectations, the female characters do precisely the same. In this film, as in most war films prior to the mid-1920s, women are portrayed in one of two ways, both dictated by their physical relationship to the field of combat. The titular "girl who stays at home" hearkens back to the Victorian ideals to which Griffith paid fealty. Confining women to the home front allowed them to be beacons of morality and stability in the face of wartime upheavals. They provided the solid foundation of home and hearth that gave male characters something to defend as well as something to return to. The maturity developed by virtue of military experience prepared men not only to take their rightful place as citizens but also to become heads of households.

Because Griffith uses his narrative to demonstrate models of correct behavior, *The Girl Who Stayed at Home* complicates the character of the American-based woman to depict the perils implicit in this role. The name

Cutie Beautiful signals that Seymour's character may approach life from a perspective that differs from what is traditionally considered proper. She is first seen dancing around her apartment, putting on makeup, and practicing the new song she will perform at a Broadway café ("Papa, There's Another Picture in Mamma's Frame"). Her willingness to step out with the louche Jim is also calculated to show her in a less-than-positive light. Before Jim is drafted, she allows "an old friend" (played by Tully Marshall) to make improper advances, accepting a necklace from him, though she balks at his attempts to extract sexual favors. She is thus primed to develop into the type of woman decidedly not worth fighting for.

When Jim returns from basic training on leave, his sincerity inspires Cutie Beautiful to confess her flirtations and assure him that henceforth she will "be so straight.... Just you forever." This is a key moment in the depiction of women on the home front. The fidelity of the women left behind is a constant concern for those engaged in military conflicts, but Griffith reinforces an idealized depiction of womanhood by arguing in extremis that even a woman of questionable character can be relied on to remain faithful (though the fidelity of the male characters is neither expected nor directly addressed). More important, through the use of intercutting, he parallels Jim's growing courage and virility on the battlefield with the Cutie Beautiful's struggles to remain true. Her eventual triumph over the advances of Marshall's character are directly matched with Jim's trek across no-man's-land to seek relief for the beleaguered soldiers of his unit. Her domestic victory is therefore the direct equivalent of his military success, and both characters have clearly fulfilled the duties expected of them. The final flurry of kisses when he returns home assures the audience that both characters' affections have been properly placed and that their wartime experiences have left them personally improved and ready for the future.

The second prominent role of women in immediate postwar films also centers on the domestic sphere. The difference is that for these women, the home front is placed in close proximity to the battlefield—not on the front lines but rather in a locale that allows female characters to maintain their domesticity behind the scenes of combat. At the same time, they are close enough to shifting battle lines to be imperiled by enemy advances at some point in the narrative.

Griffith ably illustrates this trope in *The Girl Who Stayed at Home* through the character of Blossom. Blossom is the daughter of an American expatriate, an unreconstructed adherent to the Confederacy who moved to France rather than surrender after the Civil War. She thus is suitably American enough to pair with Ralph yet also projects enough of a cosmopolitan air to fit comfortably into the French setting. Her engagement to a French aristocrat allows for a sacrificial death scene (he dies in her father's chateau, which has been converted into a field hospital), and her unavailability keeps her chastely distanced from Ralph. She inspires him to fight in a purely romantic way that also maintains her steadfast virtue. At the same time, her untiring devotion to the wounded and her vaguely defined service (she is shown working a treadle sewing machine and handling a bloody uniform) demonstrate her domestic skills and her dedication to the cause. Her purity is even more important as a contrast to Hunnish barbarity when the lines shift and Blossom and her father are caught up in the German advance. Predictably, she becomes the target of the ire of a German officer; he attempts to rape her, but she is saved by a wounded enemy soldier to whom she had earlier shown pity (played by David Butler, whose acting career was followed by years as a studio director). Blossom thus illustrates the second of the two options available for the depiction of women—as victims of circumstantial peril when they are trapped in a situation where they do not properly belong.

These variant treatments of female characters are seen both during the war and in the immediate postwar period. The women in such films as *The Little American* (1917), *Johanna Enlists* (1918), and *Hearts of the World* (1918) all conform to one of these two tropes, as do the female characters in *The Cradle of Courage* (1920) and *His Master's Voice* (1925). The larger message of these narrative devices is that women's wartime roles demand that they remain faithful, maintain their inspirational virtue, and understand the ways in which they would be compromised on the battlefield, where they would invariably be the object of barbaric and lustful attacks by an unscrupulous enemy. Generally speaking, no allowances were made for the depiction of women participating in the workforce or the military in any way that could compromise the contemporary requirements of femininity. Over time, however, and reflecting the new responsibilities women had assumed during the conflict, the portrayal of female characters and their place in war narratives underwent an adjustment equivalent to the evolution of the standard male role initiated by *The Big Parade* (1925).

Though war continued to be depicted from a primarily male perspective, a number of significant examples provide evidence that audiences were sympathetic to the difficulties faced by women who participated in the conflict. These films placed their female characters on the front lines but also dramatically separated them from anything resembling the traditional domestic sphere. Almost always in uniform, they came to France as part of various irregular units enlisted to support the armed forces. Entertainers, nurses, and Red Cross workers all make appearances in these films, and all were subject to varying degrees of military organization and discipline. This group of films co-opted the changes made in other films of the era but approached their narratives from a perspective that attempted to bring traditional notions of femininity into alignment with new realities. Perhaps most important, these films, like those featuring male protagonists, not only navigated the tricky shoals between versions of women's roles in the wartime experience but also became more complex and disillusioned.

Released almost exactly one year after *The Big Parade*, Paul Sloane's *Corporal Kate* (1926) was produced by DeMille Pictures and declares its perspective from the first title card: "In bestowing due praise upon the women of the Allied Nations for their services in the Great Conflict, let us not forget those who, as canteen entertainers, helped their soldiers endure war's tragedy." The entertainers are delineated as helpers who relieve the burden of the true soldiers, but it is also clear that women's roles have shifted in a way that might require a new kind of recognition. The story revolves around two manicurists, Katie O'Reilly ("half Irish and all American") and Becky Ginsberg ("all Jewish and all excited"), who volunteer to travel overseas to entertain the troops with an improvised musical act. They are posted to "Vivières, an advanced post on the crossroads of the Allied Armies," where they arrive in full uniform and are immediately billeted to a filthy stable. In the first of many instances, the film borrows a plot element from *The Big Parade*, with an extended scene of mucking out the barn that directly correlates to the arrival of the company in Champillon in the earlier film. Both scenes feature much complaining and much flying straw and manure, though the female version includes a failed attempt to charm the billeting officer into better accommodations.

As in *The Big Parade*, the bulk of the first half of the film involves a romance. In this case Jack, a wealthy playboy turned army mule driver has eyes for Kate and insistently pursues her. Several wooing scenes are directly comparable to romantic interludes of the earlier film in terms of tone, though Kate is more resistant to Jack's charms than Melisande was to those of Jim. The arrival of an additional female character provides a modicum of dramatic tension, especially given that Evelyn, "who has sacrificed the luxuries of a wealthy home for the hardships of the Red Cross," was a former friend of Jack's.

Corporal Kate includes representatives of each of the main organizations that encouraged women to travel to the battlefront. Entertainers, Red Cross workers, and the Salvation Army (in the form of a matronly woman whom Kate and Becky assist in her hospitality duties) are all actively involved with the troops. Aside from the brief romantic tension (quickly resolved in favor

The romance between Kate and Jack dominates the first half of *Corporal Kate*.

of Kate), these uniformed women repeatedly cooperate with each other for the good of the cause, and the film initially suggests that the battlefront is a locus of lighthearted romance, female camaraderie, and healthy adventure.

Again following closely in the footsteps of its predecessor, the narrative (and tone) of *Corporal Kate* take an abrupt turn with a single intertitle. "It was War—the great, cruel hammers were striking—a new German offensive had begun!" In short order, Becky is killed and Jack is shipped to the front after extracting a promise from Kate to watch over Evelyn. In a harrowing sequence, Kate does just that, fleeing before an enemy bombardment that eventually destroys their ambulance, seeking refuge in a shell hole, and losing an arm to wounds received on the battlefield. Her injury, of course, does nothing to dispel Jack's ardor for her, and the film ends with them kissing in a convalescent ward (where she is still gamely performing) as the armistice is announced.

Critics were not at all fond of *Corporal Kate*. The *Herald-Tribune* derided it as "just another war picture with a happy ending," and while another reviewer opined that it had "a few good sequences but they are buried in the ruck." The *Daily Mirror* claimed that it was "a good idea gone astray," and the *Evening Journal* suggested that it was "a splendid idea but weakly handled," indicating that there was something distinctive about the film's perspective. More succinctly, one review simply declared it "ghastly."[5] The negative criticisms are especially interesting in light of the film's resemblance to the much-lauded *The Big Parade*. *Corporal Kate* attempts to depict the war from a new perspective while maintaining a connection to the narrative conventions so adroitly manipulated by King Vidor. Unlike its predecessor, *Corporal Kate* was criticized as a comedy that veers into melodrama, though *The Big Parade* can also be seen as a comic romance that veers into wartime dramatics. The leeway granted to Vidor's and Stallings's reconfiguration of narrative conventions was thus not granted to director Sloane, though his handling of the actual battle material is quite adroit.

On December 26, 1926, the editors of the *Film Daily* acknowledged that *Corporal Kate* revealed a "New Angle in That the Story Presents the Woman's Side of the War" but argued that this new angle in no way excused the film's shortcomings. Hewing to the line that the film was primarily a comedy (an expectation perhaps influenced by the fact that women played the lead roles), the writers suggested that the audience would "expect more laughs but perhaps the novelty idea of having two girls as the principals might help to keep them interested."[6] The key concept here is the notion that the emergence of women as the narrative focus was merely a "novelty" and not a significant change. However, the marketing of that "novelty" suggested something else. To publicize *Corporal Kate*, the *Film Daily* suggested that theater owners "play up the story as dealing with the woman's part in the war and tell [audiences] about the team of Kate and Becky who went overseas to amuse the boys." In addition, they suggested that, "Girls in Red Cross outfits distributing throwaways and soliciting contributions for the local Red Cross bureaus might prove effective exploitation."[7] Though the focus on female protagonists might not have been perceived as a genuine narrative innovation at the time of the film's release, marketing suggestions hinged on acknowledging the changing role of women on the battlefields of the First World War.

As the larger transformation of the traditional narrative approach to war subsequently gathered steam, films began to depict characters who broke with the previously accepted portrayals of female involvement in the conflict. In Victor Fleming's 1928 film version of the popular stage play *Abie's Irish Rose*, a Jewish soldier, Abie (played by Buddy Rogers), falls in love with Rosemary, an Irish entertainer (Nancy Carroll) working to alleviate the suffering of troops at the front. The first two reels of the film do not survive, though some of the earliest footage on the third reel shows Rogers bidding farewell to Carroll, who is in uniform and assisting at a Red Cross canteen. As in *Corporal Kate*, Rosemary's primary purpose is eventually supplanted by the exigencies of the battlefield. She is present, assisting as she can, and interacting with the troops in ways that had not been part of the traditional narrative. The rest of the film hinges on the unconventional connection she shares with Abie, since their love leads them to marry in defiance of both social convention and parental expectations.

A better-known example of the changing depiction of women on the battlefield is Mary Preston, Clara Bow's character in William Wellman's *Wings*. We initially see her as the tomboyish girl next door, but her devotion to Jack (played by Buddy Rogers) leads her to volunteer for the Motor Corps so that she can be near him in France. Although she was ubiquitous in publicity materials, Bow has surprisingly little screen time in the film. Nevertheless, she makes an outsize impression, especially in the scenes at the front. When the setting of the narrative shifts to France, Mary is explicitly paired with the two male leads as a military veteran. The first intertitle to refer to the men using that term is immediately followed by one applying the word to her. At the same time, she embodies a study in the contradictions confronting filmmakers as they depicted women on the battlefield. She wears a uniform and assumes a sprawled-out, masculine pose as she drives a truck carrying medical supplies, but she is decidedly feminine in her expressions of remorse after her truck bumps into an infantryman (who then plays dead in the hopes of scoring a kiss). Surrounded by men, she cheers avidly for the two fliers chasing an attacking Gotha bomber, but only after she has blithely put herself in harm's way, seeking refuge from bombardment under her truck. Finally, her romantic devotion and prim sobriety lead her to find Jack in Paris to tell him that he has been recalled to the front, but the only way she can convince him to heed the message is by getting out of uniform and using her sexuality as a lure. This last act guarantees her return home when military police assume that she has engaged in immorality. These clashing elements of Bow's performance are condensed into a few minutes of actual screen time, and they demonstrate the changing social roles of women in the 1920s.

These examples indicate the limitations and difficulties of depicting a new kind of military experience in the First World War. These difficulties persisted throughout this period, but as with other wartime narratives, the portrayal of the female experience changed drastically over time. Though *Corporal Kate*, *Wings*, and *Abie's Irish Rose* raise key issues related to the portrayal of female characters on the battlefield, only with the coming of sound were the standard narrative conventions for the filmic depiction of women in the

Great War actively challenged. These challenges revolve primarily around three main issues—rank, romance, and relationships.

The issue of military rank presented difficulties for the various branches of the service as soon as women were permitted to serve. If women were to be considered legitimate members of the military, the fraught question of how male service members might react to a female superior was an immediate problem. The issue was comparable to the question of African American officers interacting with white troops who might be disinclined to take orders from Black men. In practice, both Black soldiers and women operated in largely segregated units that allowed the military to minimize the issue as much as possible. In filmed war narratives, the same strategy obtained. As a rule, women were shown performing supportive functions ancillary to actual combat situations, generally working under the supervision of men who provided either fatherly advice or strict discipline as needed. These superiors also allowed filmmakers to regulate the second major concern in such narratives—the functioning of romance on the front lines. The traditional conception of a damsel in distress was less relevant when women were in uniform, so filmmakers confronted new romantic scenarios. Finally, circumstances that allowed the introduction of one woman in uniform almost inevitably suggested that multiple women might be present, thereby requiring new and arguably more complex ways of thinking about story, character, and dialogue.

The first major sound film to depict women in combat raises all three of these issues but circumvents them by essentially simply treating its female protagonist as a man. Like *Abie's Irish Rose*, Henry King's part-talkie *She Goes to War* (1929) survives only in an incomplete state deriving from a 1939 abridgement that is approximately half the length of the initial release. The reduction in running time is partly achieved by the excision of all intertitles, but large swaths of the original narrative also are removed. The Rupert Hughes story on which the film is based is available, but conclusions regarding the film are necessarily incomplete.

Hughes's 1925 novelette takes an unabashed feminist tone. The story follows socialite Joan Morgan as she progresses from petulant debutante to volunteer on the battlefields of France. The primary focus is on her love-hate relationship with Tom Pike, a young man who is her social inferior at home but whom she grows to love while overseas. However, a major secondary focus of the plot is Joan's desire to be involved in the whirlwind of activities surrounding the war—specifically, in combat. She is an admirer of the Russian Women's Battalion of Death, and when told that "A woman's place is in the home" she reflects via internal monologue, "Now was the time to answer them once and for all. In Europe the women had achieved miracles of bravery and had shrunk from no task in France or at home. They pushed up to the front to nurse the shattered men, they ploughed the fields, risked their lives in the munitions plants, buried themselves in the smut and grease of the repair-shop. They were everywhere where they could be of use. American women must do as much and more."[8] She has very specific ideas about the prevailing standards for female participation in wartime activities: "Joan would not knit.... She madly resolved to disguise herself in the uniform, enlist and go abroad in the ranks. She would stow away on a transport if necessary. She had heard and read of numberless women who palmed themselves off as men and deceived their own companions, their own lovers even."[9] Setting out for New York in hopes of getting to France, she finds that "the strangest things were the girls of all ages going overseas in such numbers and varieties of uniform that it looked as if this were to be a woman's war."[10] She asserts that "women were at large for the first time after untold centuries of seclusion and suppression. There were new things ahead of them, and experiences more wonderful than could ever fall to any man, for, after all, these soldiers were going to do what men had always done. These women were going to do what had never been dreamed before."[11]

Once she arrives in France, the reality of war does not provide her with immediate options for military participation, but when the chance does arrive, Hughes (who had field experience against Pancho Villa but who served as a stateside military intelligence analyst during the Great War) adopts the same tone as literary contemporaries such as Laurence Stallings in describing the rigors of the battlefield. Joan seizes an opportunity to deliver food to men on the front lines, and Hughes paints a gruesome picture of her trip to the trenches: "The Germans had been shelled out of here a week ago and even the hatred of war could not refuse a further pity to riddled gray overcoats flung here and there with corpses in them.... They came at last to empty trenches recently abandoned, collapsed dugouts and monstrous open sewers.... The thing that just rolled under heel, was it the limb of a tree or a man? The unspeakable mess that just crumbled when it was trodden, was it an old log or—"[12]

While Joan is distributing food, a German bombardment costs her a finger on her left hand, but she brandishes the injury before her companions, crying, "I've got a wound!... I'm a soldier!"[13] More important than the vivid gruesomeness of Hughes's descriptions of the battlefield or the fact that the heroine is physically maimed in the line of duty is the key conclusion of the narrative, which is declared in the final paragraphs: "The women had proved their mettle in the universal conflict and they would not be denied their place in the everlasting war that is flattered with the name of peace. No more would they be denied their place as equals in the everlasting duel known as wedlock."[14] Though marriage remains the ultimate female goal, Joan has gone to war and achieved maturity, and she will return to society an improved (and more equal) participant. Because she and Tom share the experience of war they will be better equipped to face whatever hurdles might confront them in the future. Hughes has thus adapted a traditional narrative from a feminist perspective, but because these women went to do "what had never been dreamed before," he has entered the larger conversation regarding the depiction of war at a later stage, and the narrative standards that he is adapting are in a state of flux. The film adaptation of his tale seems to have taken advantage of that fact in ways that earlier efforts could not.

The feminist implications of Hughes story are much reduced in the surviving print of *She Goes to War*, although the screen version pushes the boundaries of female participation on the battlefield even further than its predecessors. Though Leslie Midkiff-DeBauche dismisses the film as having "simply replaced the typical male soldier with a woman," that step is much less simple and more radical than she implies.[15] Treating the female protagonist as a replacement for the "typical male soldier" automatically confers an equivalence to her experience and to her narrative authority. Though she is not in command, the romantic entanglements are superficial, and the depiction of Joan's relationships with other soldiers is ill-defined (thanks to the excision of any dialogue), *She Goes to War* introduces a female-centered narrative of combat and continues to advance the development of a comprehensive depiction of the Great War on-screen.

The extant footage of *She Goes to War* begins with a military sendoff at a train station, though surviving stills indicate that the social event that opens the novelette was filmed. The available footage provides only the barest introduction to the male lead, Tom Pike, Joan (played by Eleanor Boardman), and Joan's beau, Reggie (a character created for the film). Joan's excitement at the leave-taking is visually contrasted with the fearfulness of Tom's anxious mother, but the tone is much more somber than the patriotic revels that convinced Jim Apperson to enlist in *The Big Parade*. Sadness and fear are foregrounded in a way that marks this film as having been made in the late 1920s, when the cinematic portrayal of war was taking a darker turn. That tone is further confirmed in the following sequence, when some of the same soldiers are wearily returning from the front across a muddy and devastated landscape through a driving rain. They enter a bombed-out canteen building where Rosie Cohen (played by Alma Rubens) serenades the troops with a version of "There Is a Happy Land." These scenes are visually dismal and depressed, and Henry King pulls no punches in portraying the

Joan, Tom, and Reggie at the dance that opened *She Goes to War*. The sequence no longer survives.

effects of long combat on frontline soldiers. The song is ironic in the face of visual evidence of exhaustion and shell shock, but the addition of this musical number reflects a nostalgic reference point for the audience. This use of sound is similar to that discussed earlier with regard to World War I comic subjects. In addition, the sequence establishes the importance of the women, who nurse the men and provide a brief respite from the miseries of battle on the front lines. Though some of their work might be considered domestic (serving food, cheerfully singing, and so forth) the depiction of their involvement is grittier than anything seen previously.

At this point, Joan arrives (impeccably dressed), but the film has done little to establish any of the character motivations discussed in the book. The reissue edit likely excised any such scenes, as is evidenced by Joan's first exposure to the other women in the town. Surviving production photographs indicate more extensive interaction with her fellow female volunteers, but in the available footage she merely stands back and observes as wounded men are brought in by ambulance and then as Rosie comforts a dying soldier who is crying for his mother (which occasions a reprise of "Happy Land"). He dies in her arms, and Joan, moved by what she has seen, purposefully strides through muddy streets to her quarters (in a tracking shot that is nearly forty seconds long), where she puts on an apron and begins to scrub the floor. Establishing material is missing, and her response makes much more sense

Tom bids farewell to his mother in *She Goes to War*.

when the viewer is cognizant of the written story—in which Joan balks at such a lowly task until she is threatened with being sent home.

The missing character development confuses any discussion of larger motivations or character growth within the film, but we can also hypothesize that to some degree it was encouraged by King's initial approach to the story. The strongest evidence of this is the maneuver of essentially splitting the hero, Tom Pike, into two distinct characters, both of whom barely appear in the surviving footage. The stalwartness, bravery, and masculinity of Tom himself are never in question, but the whiny, cowardly, and effete Reggie offers a counterpoint. This Manichaean approach to the chief male protagonist reduces him to a stereotype (or two stereotypes), encouraging the viewer to simply focus on the implicit horrors of the action. It also dilutes any traditional narrative expectations by increasing the relative importance of the female characters.

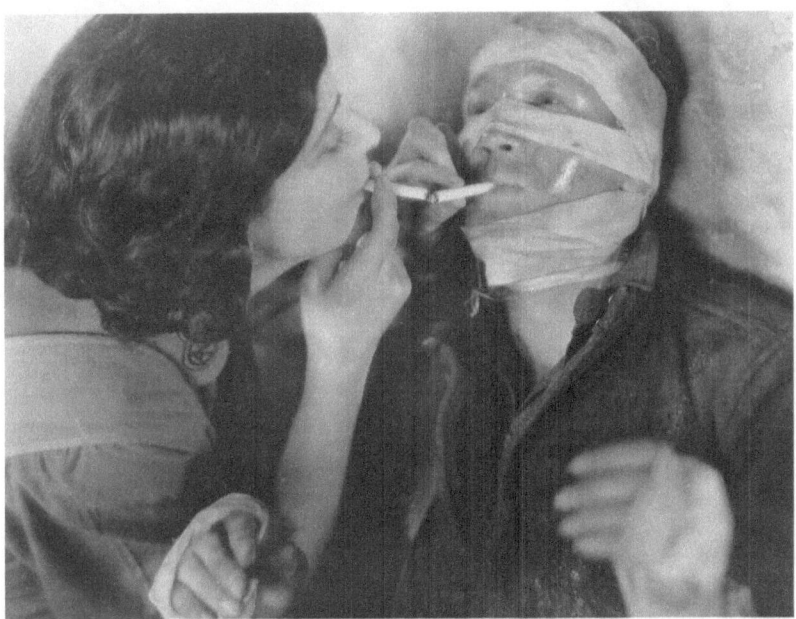

Rosie comforts a wounded soldier in *She Goes to War*.

Reggie comforts Joan before his act of cowardice leads her to take his place on the battlefield in *She Goes to War*.

Joan looks for the absent Reggie in *She Goes to War*.

When the bugles sound assembly for an Allied attack, the lack of fidelity to the characters depicted in the novel allows for a complete abandonment of the written source in favor of something much more brutal. As the men gather for the advance to the front, Joan (now in full military dress, though we have not seen her conversion to military discipline) finds Reggie in his quarters, drunk and wearing a silk robe next to a blazing hearth. Her attempts to sober him up fail miserably, but a fortuitously timed gas attack and the fact that she is already in uniform allow her to take his place among the lines of anonymous men whose faces are covered by protective masks. Though her ruse is soon discovered by nearby infantrymen, there is no way to return her to safety or treat her with any chivalric deference. Indeed, the only special treatment she receives consists of some unwanted attentions and crudities, which she mostly ignores. Instead, she takes her place in the attacking battle line and advances with the rest of the unit.

The matter-of-fact nature of these events speaks to the changes in the depiction of the Great War. As scenes of battle grew increasingly harsh in feature films, *She Goes to War* stands out, even in its eviscerated state, not only for the uncompromising brutality of the scenes of combat but also for the fact that it makes no allowances for the gender of its protagonist. Everyone is afraid, everyone is desperate, and everyone is equal. In the lines,

Joan is admonished for her fear and indecision in the face of the enemy in *She Goes to War*.

Joan's is just another body to be sent forward, and the egalitarianism of war subsumes all who encounter it.

For the remainder of the extant footage, Joan is under fire, and the action moves swiftly. The Germans roll barrel bombs down a hill toward the advancing Americans, decimating the lines and creating a hellish storm of flames. The arrival of several tanks provides a means through the fire, but the absolute terror of those inside the rapidly heating metal vehicles is palpable. Once through, the troops are pinned down by a machine-gun nest, but Joan (in part prompted by the continued harassment of her companions in a shell hole) eventually advances toward the German lines. She shoots the German machine gunner, then stands over him, pistol drawn, as he dies. Her scream of despair attracts Tom, who is taken aback when her helmet falls off, revealing her identity. As a long line of wounded troops return from the front lines through a devastated landscape, Tom brings up the rear, carrying Joan on his back.

Those responsible for the extant version of *She Goes to War* declare the intentions of their edit in a written prologue. They are presenting "for thoughtful consideration this vivid picture of the grimness and reality of the last war," and they are doing so to discourage participation in the looming Second World War. The focus on grim realities tilts the surviving material

The scenes of combat in *She Goes to War* are especially brutal.

away from "feminine" concerns (such as the love story or the development of Joan's character) and toward the rawest depiction of military engagement. Approximately half of the original film, much of which presumably did not include footage of combat, has been expunged in a deliberate attempt to color viewers' reading of what survives. However, the physical portrayal of the conflict in the surviving footage and the fact that the rigors of combat are seen through the eyes of a frontline female participant support the argument that the depiction of the Great War in the late 1920s and early 1930s had moved far beyond the narrative conventions seen over the preceding decade. The fact that the narrative of the film version moves so much further along those lines than the original story suggests that filmmakers were catching up to and surpassing their literary counterparts in their quest to reshape cultural perceptions of the conflict. Though the novel argues that Joan's experience at the front will provide her with equal standing when she returns home and marries Tom (which is only a slight twist on the traditional narrative form), the fact that the film depicts a female protagonist in uniform and in brutal combat acknowledges both the new realities created by the conflict and the necessity of finding new ways to portray them.

Despite the extreme nature of a narrative that placed its heroine in the midst of graphically portrayed scenes of combat, reviews for *She Goes to War* certainly did not dwell on the plot. *Photoplay* opined that "'*The Big Parade*'

Along with other infantry soldiers, Joan enters a tank in the hopes of breaching enemy lines in *She Goes to War*.

spoiled us for merely spectacular war pictures. This production falls short of greatness because it lacks heart interest." The anonymous reviewer praised both Boardman's performance and King's "superb" direction and "breathtaking" battlefield scenes yet maintained that the film as a whole "fails to grip you strongly."[16] The *National Board of Review Magazine* offered a more thorough analysis, but with regard to the central device of placing a woman in combat the reviewer merely commented that "she gets a taste of what war is really like and proves that she is made of heroic stuff." Of greater interest was the part-talkies use of sound effects: "The whistling and screaming of shells, the rattle of machine gun fire, the roar of the flames and the rumbling of the ponderous tanks add greatly to the realism of the action." What was perceived as most important was not the general approach to the role of women on the battlefield but the notion that the battle sequences "undoubtedly foreshadow a picture to come in which a battle scene on a large scale with full sound and voice effects will enable the screen to depict war in all its terror and emotional appeal."[17] Many such pictures were indeed on the way, and the first of them (John Cromwell's *The Mighty*) would be released in November 1929, less than six months later. The vast majority of these films predictably featured men as the protagonists, and while they would build on King's noteworthy use of sound, they ignored the implications of the unique female-centered narrative of *She Goes to War*.

The next major film to deal with the role of women in the First World War emerged from an unlikely and controversial source. Though her 1918 debut novel, *The Return of the Soldier*, is considered a touchstone of World War I literature, writer Rebecca West was involved in a second, less recognized, Great War project. References to the work and its authorship are muddled, but at some point in the late 1920s, West apparently made an agreement with *Cosmopolitan* magazine to write a serialized story for a fee of $10,000. Variously said to have been based on a diary, discarded notes for a different novel, or transcribed interviews with an anonymous source, *War Nurse: The True Story of a Woman Who Lived, Loved and Suffered on the Western Front* was published as a novel in 1930, but West, apparently unhappy with the results, disowned it and had her name removed from both the title page of the book and the film version.[18]

The novel relates the experiences of Corrine Andrews, a well-off society girl who volunteers to serve as a nurse in France. The primary concerns of the story involve the fluidity of morality in a wartime environment and the changing worldview that the war fosters in all who take part. Andrews herself lives comfortably in sin with a flier, Waldron, and there is much discussion of the ways in which sex becomes simply a release from the pressures and horrors of war. The war has in fact freed women from the conventions that prevailed in more settled times:

> For one thing, women in the past must have been enormously protected by the social assumption which used to exist that they did not have the same capacity for passion as men, and that if they should in rare cases develop it they became shameful and degraded. . . .
>
> But in my day that assumption no longer operated. It was beginning to leak out that women could find exactly the same pleasure in men that men find in women, and that it was fine that it should be so. . . .
>
> Also, in the course of my love-making I was doing something for Waldron which was so obviously a good thing to do that it seemed to have a moral sanction behind it. . . .
>
> It seemed hardly less important that our love-making was sanctioned by the god that ruled our lives those days—the war itself.[19]

As the end of the war approaches, Corrine returns to the United States for medical treatment necessitated by the physical stresses of her war work. The operation leaves her sterile, and while recuperating, she learns that her lover has married someone else. The book concludes with her reflections on the war and its effects:

The war had taken my youth and my health, it had thrust sex on me in its most cruel and barest form.... [I]t had taken my man from me, it had taken all prospect of children from me....

But I suddenly remembered how, quite early in my hospital career, I had looked down into a man's eyes and seen clear through into his throat; and hadn't dropped the tray of instruments I was carrying. I remembered how I had learned to carry on through every sort of discouragement and fatigue and disgust. I remembered how glorious it had been to find myself able to rise to every demand the war made of me, and what a sense of security, of assured and honorable occupation, it had given me to know that no day would pass when the war wouldn't make some such demand.[20]

The war has both freed and scarred the heroine, and the portrayal of the wartime milieu focuses on the moral implications in a way that prefigures the coming narratives of disillusionment.

MGM's 1930 film version of *War Nurse* demonstrates the difficulties faced by studios in transitioning to a new kind of war narrative. At the inflection point between the old and newly emergent ways of portraying the war on-screen, the filmmakers attempted to split the difference. They elected to soften the more radical feminist and moral issues raised by the novel as well as to include select elements of the unflinching depiction of a woman in combat seen in *She Goes to War*. *War Nurse* thus becomes emblematic of the problems of coming to terms with the new narrative paradigm, as director Edgar Selwyn and his team portray the experience of war from an uncommon perspective that featured some extreme narrative components but was infused with a fundamentally conventional romance.

As in the earlier film, the immediate problem of how to situate women institutionally on the battlefield is skirted thanks to the careful separation of the nurses from any larger organization (in this case, the group is not even related to the Red Cross). The women are volunteers acting under the command of the socialite who organized the unit. This fact reduces the role of men throughout the film and provides ample opportunities for the women to interact outside of the traditional confines of a war narrative. However, as in *She Goes to War*, *War Nurse* downplays the more nontraditional leanings of the written source material regarding gender roles in favor of a reversion to a more conventional romance. Though much of the film highlights women working together as an isolated group, the narrative framework relies on their interaction with standard, thinly drawn depictions of men at war. This leads to jarring disjunctions where conversations revolving around more conventional topics such as the number of unmarried soldiers or prospects for marriage are juxtaposed with discussions of the undesirability of marriage and children, medical inadequacies, rodents, and latrines. As with so many other films in this period, the transition from traditional standards to a new narrative approach is visible on-screen, but here the difficulties of that adjustment are made even more obvious by the focus on an underrepresented group of combatants.

The uncomfortable dichotomy between socially acceptable gender roles and the changing depiction of life on the battlefield is apparent within the first few minutes of the film. The moments following the opening credits begin with a brief, intense montage of combat scenes but quickly segue to a group of American socialites in Paris reading the latest headlines about the resumption of the Battle of Ypres and the "Frantic Need for Nurses." When one of them announces that she has "just signed up for the war" and will soon be arranging a unit of nurses, Babs (June Walker) sees it as an opportunity for romance: "With five million men up there, that's our place darling." There follows a montage of other women who will soon be recruits, including a schoolteacher in Kansas (played by Helen Jerome Eddy) and a class of graduates from a Catholic girls school (among whom is Joy, played by Anita Page). As in other films, this sequence provides thumbnail sketches of the various characters sufficient to emphasize the variety of backgrounds from which they are drawn. An intertitle allows a quick jump to the battlefield ("A hurried training in Paris—then on, toward the front, WAR NURSES!"), where the women quickly set to work preparing the hospital quarters.

Another intertitle ("Work! Work! Work! Nights of it! Days of it!") shifts the narrative from the establishing prelude to the more central concerns of the story. Primary among these is the appearance of Wally O'Brien (Robert Montgomery), Babs's love interest, but his bantering introduction is quickly countered by news of the death of the friend he has come to see. This is immediately followed by several brief anecdotes involving patients, one of whom has a piece of steel through both his eyeballs, one of whom dies quietly in his bed, and a third man suffering from shell shock. In a continuation of the pattern that persists throughout the film, Selwyn tries to balance the needs of a traditional love story with highly unconventional and shocking anecdotes drawn from the book. The novelist's rejection of acceptable sexual ethics is *too* unconventional, however, so the heroine's filmed manifestation is transformed into an upholder of more proper codes of sexual conduct. Explicit instances of the sexual adventurism of the novel are transferred to other female characters, while Babs remains resolute in drawing traditional boundaries between Wally and herself.

There are two major instances of this transference in the film, but only one has a parallel in the written story. At one point in the novel, Corrine discusses a woman from the Midwest who, swept up in the sexual maelstrom of the war, asks for advice regarding a rash on her chest. Corrine is horrified to recognize the symptoms of a syphilitic infection, partly because she understands how the war has transformed an otherwise "proper" woman into someone who will be unable to return to the society from which she came. In the film, the woman shows Babs her rash, but the audience has no way of diagnosing the problem. Given the film's earlier treatment of the afflicted character, it is inconceivable that the disease is sexual, so the viewer is only led to understand (from the look of horror on Babs's face) the extreme seriousness of the mystery ailment (which Babs reassuringly dismisses as nothing to worry about). The narrative then neatly disposes of the problem by having the woman die on the front lines as she tries to help a wounded soldier.

The second major comment on the sexual practices of the combat zone is embodied in the character of Joy. First seen as a virtuous Catholic schoolgirl, Joy is naive, though she quickly adapts to the rigors of the hospital. Almost immediately, however, she falls in love with a convalescing flier, Robin (Robert Ames), and offers herself to him in the belief that they are engaged. While he is away at the front, she discovers that he is already married, which leads her to further indiscretions. Threatened with being sent home for her conduct, she instead goes back to the hospital, knowing that the pregnancy that has resulted from her affair will preclude her readmittance into polite society. Robin eventually returns from battle mortally wounded and declares his love for Joy, but his death (combined with the stress of constant shelling) causes her to crack under pressure. She gives birth to her baby in the shattered ruins of the hospital, then promptly dies, leaving the boy orphaned. Here again, the film resolves the question of sexual mores on the front lines (the raison d'être of the novel) by reverting to traditional standards wherein transgressors are punished for their sins.

Babs's decision to remain chaste does not protect her from the unpleasant ramifications of combat. The hospital is gruesome, the battlefield is violent, and employment on the front lines results in numerous deaths among her friends in the unit of volunteers. These truths are manifested in ways that reflect the changing standards for the depiction of the conditions of combat. They also, however, allow Babs to fulfill the traditional qualifications for emerging from her experiences improved. In the final scene, she is reunited with Wally, to whom she introduces Joy's young son. He agrees that "nothing else but O'Brien would do" for the boy's last name, and the film ends with a shot of the newly constituted family that has emerged from the conflict.

Critics were not kind to *War Nurse*. *Screenland* dismissed it as "the horrors of war again, embroidered by a bevy of beauties.... Heavy drama occasionally enlivened by bright bits ... but mostly morbidly dull and dreary."[21] *Silver Screen* felt that "with a great story showing the woman's side of the war ... something glorious should have emerged from 'War Nurse.' Instead there is too much plot and too much movie suffering."[22] Mourdant Hall, writing for the *New York Times*, declared the film "a muddled, insincere piece of work which will hardly appeal to persons of finer sensibilities [and which] would have done better to emulate the early notes of 'The Big Parade.'"[23]

"Heaviness," "dreariness," and "suffering" were increasingly being incorporated into the narratives of the First World War, but in the case of *War Nurse*, as in other films of this period, the proportions of these elements were not settled in filmmakers' minds. Elements of a traditional narrative were combined with both increased amounts of violence and a pessimistic attitude toward the utility of previously accepted tropes. The application of these narrative standards to a story that focuses primarily on female protagonists further complicates matters, so that despite moments where a character may declare, "Remember we're soldiers just as the men are and our job requires just as much courage," the filmmakers are unsure of how to portray the full ramifications of that assertion. *War Nurse* is thus unable to provide a clear model for dealing with women in the context of new ideas about the experience of the Great War. Within a year, however, the problem would be resolved by the magnum opus of films addressing the issue of women in combat, *The Mad Parade*.

Like *War Nurse*, the original story on which *The Mad Parade* (1931) was based was written from a feminine perspective. The authors, Gertrude Orr and Dorothy Malloy, had served in France before moving to Hollywood to work in the film industry.[24] They were thus part of the wave of filmmakers with direct experience on the battlefields of Europe and were more than qualified to write a script reflecting on their time overseas. The story that they produced revolved around a group of Red Cross nurses serving on the front lines who become trapped in no-man's-land during a heavy bombardment. Most important, however, was the fact that no man appears directly on-screen. The minimal male presence is instead signified through the strategic use of shadow and off-screen voices. The major studios rejected this radical approach, but Herman Gumbin, treasurer of the independent Liberty Productions, felt that the script was worthwhile. The project, originally titled *Women Like Men*, was assigned to experienced director William Beaudine, who had signed a long-term contract with Liberty late in 1930.[25] Beaudine's career had begun at Biograph in 1911, and he was better known for the speed and efficiency of his direction than for any noteworthy dramatic or artistic skills, but the script apparently piqued his interest, and the results constitute one of the high points of his career.

The film opens with a montage of World War I violence similar to that which begins *The Last Flight* (released a month earlier) and *War Nurse*. The frenetic images of tanks, planes, and explosions eventually conclude with a long shot of a chateau that the camera approaches from above, settling on a sign identifying the building as a canteen: "This may not be a regular unit of this man's army—but if you think we don't make as good doughnuts as they do, come in and try 'em." The sign immediately establishes the complex task that the filmmakers have set for themselves, since it simultaneously asserts both the characters' equivalence and their inferiority (the women can perform a routine task as well as any man but cannot do so in the regular army). The sign dissolves to a shot of Mrs. Schuyler (Irene Rich) and Dorothy (Marceline Day) preparing doughnuts, which initiates a sequence introducing all of the women of the unit. From the outset, the traditional concerns of women are denigrated, especially through the person of Lil (Lilyan Tashman), who mocks one of the others (one of two twins played by Rosemary and Bluebell Jones) for excessive attention to her appearance. Their exchange demonstrates that Lil has no illusions regarding the ultimate desire of the male troops for sex and no patience for those who fail to understand that fact. As Lil walks to the wine cellar to refill her water bottle with contraband liquor, we hear a male voice discussing a report of misconduct with Mrs. Schuyler, and we see Lil putting a stop to the eavesdropping of Snoop (Fritzi Ridgeway). The misconduct report concerns Monica (Evelyn Brent) who has stayed at the local inn all night with a soldier who is engaged to one of the other women, Janice (June Clyde). The various tensions among the women add an additional layer of complexity to the depiction of conditions on the front lines and complicate any audience expectation of camaraderie among those who serve. Snoop is a particular irritant, constantly at odds with the rest of the unit.

Establishing a roll call of these characters is important because they are or will be disillusioned and damaged in the course of the narrative. Lil's alcohol-filled water bottle and brassy attitude easily set her apart as tainted goods, but even June, who appears to be less soiled by the war, speaks of green soldiers with the air of a seasoned veteran: upon returning from a supply run, she says, "After I loaded I gave a lift to a new bunch moving in. They hadn't been up before. Thought it would be a lark. Gee, their laughter hurt more than the screams of the wounded." The opening sequence ends with Dorothy sadly explaining that taps is being played for twenty-two gassed men brought to

Lil and Snoop confront Monica about her nihilistic behavior in *The Mad Parade*.

the hospital who had died during the night. The camera plays across the faces of each of the women, showing that they understand all too well the stresses and rigors of war; there is no question that as veterans, their understanding exceeds that of men with less experience.

The next sequence emphasizes that point further with the introduction of Monica, first shown only in silhouette putting on her stockings in a private room of the local inn as she talks to Tony. He is not seen, but the play of shadow on the wall shows that he is lying on the bed. His clothes are hanging on the bedstead and strewn about the room. As they talk, Monica distills the essence of the narrative of disillusionment into a few lines: "Funny what the war's done to people like us. It would've been different before. You can't go through three years of this . . . bandaging wounded, stopping their blood, watching 'em die." Then she justifies the importance of discussing the war from a female perspective by saying, "Y'know a woman is pretty much like a man, Tony. You can stand just so much." Here and later, she declares her love for him, but the film does nothing to affirm that their affair is anything more than a convenient way to relieve accumulated stress. The tone is similar to that of the "love" between the characters played by Richard Barthelmess and Helen Chandler in *The Last Flight* or Phillips Holmes and Nancy Carroll in *Broken Lullaby* (see chapter 6). These are convenient companionships but

In a scene missing from surviving prints of *The Mad Parade*, Monica sympathized with a prostitute.

not fully developed relationships. The war has drained all of these characters of the capacity to relate to others in that way.

In its original cut, the film included a scene immediately following Monica's departure from the inn that addressed one of the most common roles of women in a traditional war narrative—that of prostitute. Though the scene does not survive, a still photograph suggests the possibility that Monica may have been unconventionally sympathetic to the fallen woman she encounters, perhaps recognizing in her a kindred spirit similarly damaged by the detrimental effects of the conflict.

On Monica's return to the canteen, an air raid emphasizes the military dangers the women face, and a telegram informing Mrs. Schuyler of the death of Dorothy's beau reinforces the emotional stress of the war. Despite such pressures, however, Monica comprehends that she is no longer fit to return home. When Mrs. Schuyler declares that Monica's indiscretions may cause her to be sent away, she explodes: "I couldn't stand it. What would I do in the States? . . . I do my job, don't I? You bet I do—like a man. Does headquarters check up on every man in France who wants to live for a minute? No! It makes allowances for them. It knows it's war." When told that there is nothing new about war and that women have to carry on, she continues, "We're not women anymore. I'm not. You don't suppose I can go through it, living

Monica and Lil comfort Dorothy in *The Mad Parade*.

in mud, smelling the dead, and still come out of it like I was?" Finally, she concludes her tirade with an anecdote summarizing the way that women participate in this conflict and respond to it: "I kissed a man once. He was dying. He got in the way of a shell. I'll never forget the sight. Just a thing with two blind eyes. He was off his nut and thought I was his wife. I kissed him and heard the rattle. I went on my first bender after that. I got cock-eyed. It was the first time." Mrs. Schuyler assures Monica that the war is not going to last forever, but Monica responds, "Oh yes it is. For me. I couldn't stand peace now. That part of me's dead. That's why I can't go back to the States." In this brief exchange, *The Mad Parade* concisely crystallizes the argument of all of the forthcoming disillusionment films, neatly demonstrating that the war's effects are indiscriminate. The conflict scars everyone who is involved, no matter their background or their gender.

Given the truth of Monica's assessment of the war's effects, the remainder of the film lends further weight to her argument by reinforcing the implicit equality of the women's wartime experiences. The women are called forward to a field hospital even closer to the front lines, but the lead vehicles become lost and drive into the midst of a bombardment. One of the trucks is hit, and Dorothy is mortally wounded. Under fire, the women move to a shell hole, then to an abandoned American bunker. While there, Janice discovers

Trapped under fire in a frontline dugout, Janice confronts Monica about her affair with Tony (Janice's fiancée) in *The Mad Parade*.

the truth about Monica's indiscretion with Tony, and Snoop threatens to expose the affair to their superiors. In a fit of rage (and desperation), Monica throws a hand grenade at her tormenter, killing her instantly. On seeing the shattered body, one of the other nurses (Fanny, played by Louise Fazenda) runs screaming onto the battlefield in shock, but Monica defends her action with the last important monologue of the film. In a bold comment on both the priorities of war and her own shattered moral compass, Monica argues to Janice, "You think it's wrong to kill if you hate somebody. Well what about our boys killing men they've never seen? But that's right! It's right to kill if it's war, but if a dirty little sneak comes along and tries to knife you in the back it's wrong to defend yourself, to step on her like the rat she was."

By the time Mrs. Schuyler arrives in the trailing vehicle, the women have discovered that a devastating barrage is imminent, and they must decide who will traverse the battlefield to get help. Janice draws the short straw, but because she has refused to expose Monica and Tony's affair (which would ensure Monica's return to the States), Monica chooses to sacrifice herself. Crawling across no-man's-land, she is repeatedly wounded, but she reaches the American lines, forcing the cessation of the bombardment before she dies, surrounded by men who salute her courage. The last lines of the film are, "'Boy that dame had plenty of guts.' 'I'll say she did.'"

Monica's suicidal act of heroism both saves her comrades and ends her misery in *The Mad Parade*.

Reviewers were not kind to *The Mad Parade*, though the misapprehension of its virtues began with the publicity surrounding its production. There was constant pre-release mention of the novelty of an all-women cast, including a story written by Dorothy Woolridge that appeared in the May 1931 issue of *Picture Play* under the title "The Valiants Carry On" and that emphasizes that most of the actresses are "old-timers" who have achieved career success through their persistence. The article dwells primarily on their struggles as women in Hollywood, though it does briefly discuss the rough and dirty nature of the shoot for *The Mad Parade*.[26] This discussion of the role of women did not specifically relate to the plot of the film but was at least more open-minded than the actual reviews, many of which condemn the film for precisely those qualities that make it an important touchstone for the portrayal of the war on-screen. *The Film Daily*, in a review headlined "Weak Entertainment without a Man in the Cast," opined, "Apparently the idea back of this story was to do a female 'Journey's End.' Only one man figures in the yarn and he is never shown."[27] Both the *New York Times* and *Harrison's Reports* condemned the loose morals on display, with Mourdant Hall arguing that "one can scarcely imagine a like group of girls in uniform, for it should be borne in mind that those in charge of sending women abroad were extremely careful in their selection."[28] *Harrison's* faulted the executives at Paramount who bought the distribution rights from Liberty: "You would think that after producing pictures for twenty years, the Paramount executives would understand what are good and what are bad pictures when they see them.... 'The Mad Parade' is not entertainment.... In one of the scenes, the infuriated heroine is shown as hurling a hand grenade at another woman, who had been taunting her, and as killing her instantly, and afterwards as not feeling any remorse for what she had done. And yet the Paramount executives think, no doubt, that 'The Mad Parade' is a great picture."[29] Before the official premiere, the *Motion Picture Herald* (apparently having viewed a pre-release edit of the film) suggested that exhibitors show "light musicals or comedies" with the film "for best program balance."[30]

Despite these contemporary misapprehensions, *The Mad Parade* is an important film in the transformation of narrative standards for discussing the First World War. The incremental changes in the depiction of women's wartime service seen in films such as *Corporal Kate*, *She Goes to War*, and *War Nurse* are here carried to their fullest development, and that process entails a radical alteration in thinking about both women and the effects of combat. Though the films discussed previously in this chapter made concessions to contemporary gender expectations, this film essentially makes none. Despite the fact that the unit is not part of the regular army, it is playing an important role on the battlefield. There is no suggestion that these women are out of place, nor is their presence on the battlefield either frivolous or incidental. The reduction of men to an abstraction (in some cases literally) skirts the question of rank, but the chain of command and authority within the unit is clear. Moreover, men are entirely unnecessary. The women are capable of handling themselves, up to and including the fatal heroics of the conclusion. Like their male counterparts in other films, this self-reliance is hard-earned and encompasses bitter realizations about the nature of warfare that have changed these women forever. Any notions of romance or heroism are subsumed by the realities of the battlefield, and these women have no false notions about themselves or the men they encounter during their service. Though women in the military continued to fight for full equality for decades after the First World War and continue to do so today, this film was well ahead of its time in portraying the experience and effects of warfare on women as wholly equivalent to those of men. The enunciation of those effects, however, was very much of its time in relation to the larger changes taking place across the spectrum of films dealing with the Great War.

This small group of women-centered films becomes doubly important in light of the fact that the changing role of women in these narratives is a microcosm of larger trends. In increasingly stark, violent, and morally complex narratives filmed between 1919 and 1931, women progressed from characters whose primary wartime duties separated them from active involvement in the conflict to equals in the experience of the horrors of war. Though the reviewers of *The Mad Parade* may not have been ready to accept it, those experiences, filtered through the firsthand involvement of women who served, matched those of their male counterparts in many ways. The bravery exhibited by Monica on the battlefield was not only a result of the effort to save her companions. It was also a manifestation of her understanding that she would never be able to return to what had previously been considered a normal life. Because she had not stayed at home, her disillusionment matched that of her many male filmic companions, and her self-sacrifice was a way of achieving a peace that those who survived might never find. The elusiveness of that peace and the boldness of Monica's solution to the problem of achieving it are amply demonstrated by the full flowering of a new narrative of disillusionment in the final group of war films to be made before the introduction of the Production Code.

Chapter Six

FOR NO REASON AT ALL

Homecoming, Disillusionment, and the Failure of Tradition

AS THE 1920S GAVE WAY TO THE 1930S, THE AMERICAN FILM INDUSTRY FACED several major challenges. The Great Depression had arrived, with its attendant uncertainties. The question of how to portray new social and economic realities on-screen would roil popular filmmaking for the first half of the new decade. In addition, the process of adapting and integrating sound technologies into filmmaking technique continued. Though sound had been part of film exhibition from the very beginning, the industry-wide conversion to prerecorded dialogue, sound effects, and music beginning in the late 1920s gave centralized control of a powerful new tool directly to the filmmakers themselves and brought an additional level of verisimilitude to film production. Both of these factors would be crucial in the culmination of the development of the narrative of disillusionment that had begun in the mid-1920s. Ironically, however, both would also be crucial in the eventual demise of this narrative form, foreclosing further discussion of the First World War on American screens until the reemergence of the subject—in a much altered, more propagandistic mode—as the nation prepared for involvement in the second great global conflict of the twentieth century.

New ways of addressing the experience and meaning of the First World War occurred throughout the 1920s across a variety of film types (comedies, cartoons, race films, feature-length narratives). The final steps of this process occurred during the early part of the next decade as increasingly harsh depictions of the war and its effects portrayed an entirely useless conflict. While demonstrating the inhumanity of war as fought, these films also turned to the aftermath of the conflict and the ways in which veterans experienced and understood life after their time on the battlefield. By increasingly decoupling the veterans from any notion of a meaningful home front, these works marked the fullest progression of an approach that discounted the validity of any narrative that tried to draw positive messages from the wartime experience and created a new, modern narrative construct for the depiction of warfare and its results.

Howard Hawks's *The Dawn Patrol* (1930) features an early, though not fully developed, version of the percolating disillusionment narrative. Like William Wellman, Hawks acquired his lifelong love of flying in the military, but unlike Wellman, Hawks spent the war years as a flight instructor and never left the United States.[1] His service acted as a formative artistic experience, providing him with insights into the lives of World War I aviators. Hawks's experiences helped to generate the ideal Hawksian narrative situation—groups of men working together under great stress. Throughout his career, the director returned to this pattern in films as diverse as *Ceiling Zero, Only Angels Have Wings, Ball of Fire, Rio Bravo,* and *Hatari!,* but *The Dawn Patrol* is the earliest manifestation of this pattern. None of Hawks's prior films contain these elements, and his continued grappling with the subject indicates the importance of the pattern to his later development as a filmmaker.

Though the story and screenplay of *The Dawn Patrol* are credited to John Monk Saunders (author of the story of *Wings*), there is strong evidence that Hawks wrote the story himself, in part based on an earlier article by war correspondent Irvin Cobb. Hawks then paid Saunders $10,000 for the use of his name and claimed no credit when the story went on to win an Oscar.[2] The film portrays life in a squadron of English airmen, and the narrative demonstrates the stresses the fliers face and the mechanisms they use to cope with the effects of combat. The three main characters are the squadron commander, Major Brand (Neil Hamilton), his most reliable pilot, Dick Courtney (Richard Barthelmess), and Doug Scott, Courtney's affable, stalwart wingman (Douglas Fairbanks Jr.). The film implicitly comments on the war through its plot, which assembles generically typical events without significantly advancing to any sort of conclusion. The war is shown as a long, unending slog. Brand is burdened by the stresses of command and blamed by his men for the constant high casualties. When he is promoted away from the squadron, Courtney takes his place and in turn faces the accusations of butchery leveled against him by his men, including Scott. The pattern continues when Scott assumes the central role, and the film draws a clear equivalency between the three characters as they progress through the inexorable machinery of war. Hawks's concern with this process is the central narrative theme, made even clearer by the conscious elimination of any women from the script, thus focusing all attention on the soldiers, the workings of the squadron as a unit, and the characters' reactions to the stresses of combat.

The downbeat tone of the entire film and the narrative focus on the destructive stresses of war has frequently led to it being interpreted as an antiwar film, but a more detailed reading complicates that notion. The Hawksian focus on the men of the squadron as part of a professional group, working together to achieve a common goal, mitigates any criticism of the military at large or of the implicit rightness of winning the war. Both Michael Isenberg and Jeanine Basinger castigate the film for failing to promote enough of an antiwar agenda. Isenberg faults Hawks for portraying a "morally sound but rationally senseless devotion to duty which was given the gloss of high courage. Duty was treated as the highest virtue; there was never any talk about disobeying orders. The grim business of war was made tolerable by this strict perversion of morality and by sportsmanship." He suggests that the film fails to depict war in its full absurdity and asserts that "to depict war's viciousness and nothing more was simply to enhance the danger, emphasize the courage, and sanctify the sacrifice."[3] By doing so, Isenberg believed, the film sacrificed any credence with regard to an antiwar message.

Basinger is similarly dismissive of the film in her study of World War II combat films. While acknowledging its wide-ranging impact, she believes that *The Dawn Patrol* is part of an ambivalent group of films that "actually gloriously celebrate male bravery and heroism, and visually present exciting scenes of combat." For her, the film is "an adventure story about men and their comradeship, their grace under pressure, their nobility to their enemies, and their efforts to serve their countries in difficult situations."[4]

Both Isenberg and Basinger, however, begin with the assumption that the film must be part of a somewhat Manichaean universe that signals a pro- or antiwar perspective. Neither Isenberg nor Basinger seems to fully acknowledge or appreciate that *The Dawn Patrol* is part of the ongoing process of narrative change that had yet to see its fullest manifestation. The focus on personal valor, duty, and professionalism in Hawks's film is merely the last attempt to retain some part of the traditional narrative in the face of encroaching waves of disillusionment and suggests the progressive realization that those qualities do not adequately counter the overarching and inevitable rhythm of death so clearly put forward in the film. Courtney may tell a scared young flier, "If you should lose, be a good loser, just like you would in school," but that admonition in no way lessens the horror felt by the commander in sending the boy to his doom. Even the vaunted chivalry of the "knights of the air" does not negate (in this film) the sense of the grinding, purposeless machinery of military destruction. Courtney's final act of sacrifice (conducting a suicide raid over German territory) need not be read simply as an either/or act of heroism. It may be a self-sacrificing means of sparing the life of his best friend (and proof of his demonstrated manhood), but it is also a self-conscious act of suicide (and disillusionment) that enables him to escape both the horrors of the war and his role in it.

Dominick Pisano attempts to untangle these dichotomies by suggesting that *The Dawn Patrol* forms the basis of a developing air combat genre that reflects American notions of heroism. Like both Isenberg and Basinger, however, he gives short shrift to any reading of the film that might portray it as attempting to grapple with the horror and waste of the war, focusing instead on the display of actions he perceives as heroic. He tactically retreats from an initial claim that "*The Dawn Patrol* differs from its predecessors in that it begins to interpret the genre and stretches its boundaries by exploring the psychological pressures and stresses of wartime flying."[5] He is thus able to reconcile the more problematic aspects of the film's attitude toward the war with his contention that it is the progenitor of a heroic view of air combat that extends all the way to *Top Gun*.

In attempting to position the film within their own arguments, Isenberg, Basinger, and Pisano fail to take into account the larger pattern of narrative developments regarding filmmakers' approach toward the Great War. Given the steady progress away from the traditional narrative and toward a narrative of disillusionment, the attitudes expressed in the film are precisely what might be expected in a 1930 release. There is, for example, never any sense that the men are fighting for a particular cause. No awareness of a home front makes any appearance in the film, and the concept is not even considered in the abstract. At the same time, the main characters are depicted as fully mature and in no real need of proving their manhood, though they do demonstrate their bravery. The youngest of them are presented as little more than cannon fodder, and it is clear that they will have no time to mature on the battlefield. Those who survive quickly fall into the same pattern of drunken, brooding resignation that enables them to cope with their actions. Perhaps most important, the grinding inevitability of the plot itself points to the irredeemability not only of the war but also of the way in which war is fought. Men trudge perpetually toward death, and survival is frequently by mere luck. The continual churning of command demonstrates this repeatedly with three separate characters, as each replaces the next in the agonizing chain of responsibility. All of these elements position *The Dawn Patrol* as a not-yet-fully-formed example of the developing narrative of disillusionment, and the persistent ambivalence regarding this new approach continues to cause disparate and conflicted readings of the overall result. In the following three years, however, the uncertain and troubled attitudes expressed here would grow to full fruition.

The most important single element in the narrative of disillusionment is the gradual but insistent turn of war narratives away from combat itself and toward a hard-edged view of the aftereffects and unintended consequences of the war on those who fought it. Tales of returning soldiers are certainly not innovative in and of themselves, and most of the films discussed earlier in this book feature at least scenes of the protagonists' return to the safety and normalcy of their families. *The Cradle of Courage, His Master's Voice, Felix Turns the Tide*, and *The Big Parade* (to name only a few) feature homecoming sequences that demonstrate either that the soldier has come home a "better" man who will lead a reasonably productive life or that his service has saved him from the attentions of an unworthy woman.

In the late 1920s, the traditional pattern prevailed in the depiction of veteran homecomings, even as scenes of combat gradually modulated away from battlefield heroics toward a harsher approach to wartime service. Variant approaches to the depiction of the Great War and its aftermath could have become dominant but were supplanted by the more stridently negative narrative of disillusionment.

The plot of John Cromwell's unfairly neglected but surprisingly accomplished early talkie *The Mighty* (1929) revolves around gangster Blake Greeson (played by George Bancroft) and his conversion from criminal to responsible citizen. Drafted into the army, tough gunman Greeson ignores the summons until he is rounded up by a military police patrol. Once in France, however, he proves himself a soldier to be reckoned with, mostly because, as he says, "Gunmen are what they need over here!" Young lieutenant Jerry Patterson, under whom Greeson serves, finds this baffling, since Greeson is concerned only with killing and not with any of the ideals that the terrified officer holds dear. In a conversation following the ex-gangster's receipt of yet another medal for valor, Patterson angrily states, "I'd rather be dead than think the things you think, and I'd be willing to give up my life to do the things that you can do." Greeson's jaded response is to ask, "If those ideas you talk about were any good, wouldn't they make you do the things you want to do?" This exchange typifies the way in which the film treats the wartime experience, as Bancroft's character is correct about the violence of the war and the uselessness of platitudes regarding ideals that are nullified by combat. The battle scenes themselves are harsh and unforgiving, effectively using extended tracking shots (prior to *All Quiet on the Western Front*) to follow the American advance and making early use of a

Greeson is both heavy and hero in *The Mighty*, but the wartime experiences that utilized his toughness eventually lead him to make appropriately redemptive choices.

cacophonous soundtrack to create a verisimilar sense of the aural chaos of battle. When young Jerry is mortally wounded, Greeson promises to go talk to the dying man's family when he returns to the States, and here the film returns to a more traditional narrative format rather than pursuing the more radically critical ideas regarding wartime service that are suggested by the opening sequences.

From the moment he disembarks from the train in Jerry's hometown, Greeson is lauded as a hero, which eventually leads to both romance with the dead man's sister, Louise (played by Esther Ralston) and a commission to become the chief of police from the unnamed city's Committee on Public Safety with a grant of "full police power." Anticipating another later trend of depression-era film discourse, Greeson is told, "Ordinary police methods under ordinary police leadership have been proved unable to cope with" urban crime, so he will need to "make real war on the criminals."[6] Torn between loyalty to his old criminal comrades and his newfound love and

The moral support provided by Louise ensures that Greeson will make the right choices in *The Mighty*.

ideals, Bancroft's character must choose. In the end he intends to make a clean breast to the people of the city: "They can turn against me for what I used to be, but they'll never have that chance to hate me for what I am now." The final showdown with his old gang is brilliantly conveyed via sound effects in a mostly darkened warehouse room, and the film concludes with a slightly wounded Greeson being tended by his devoted sweetheart.

The narrative of this film most closely resembles the plot of the William S. Hart vehicle *The Cradle of Courage*. Like that film, the hero begins as a dysfunctional member of society whose military service gives him the tools to assume authority, contribute to civil life, and win the girl. The difference in this case is a question of tone. Though both stories are classifiable as traditional narratives, *The Mighty* suggests a way of modifying that narrative that allows the fundamental aspects of such stories to remain intact. The hero recognizes the validity of a home front and presumes that he will return after the war to make his way in society, and he is altered by his military service. Unlike Lambert Hillyer in the earlier film, however, Cromwell is entirely willing to convey a certain level of criticism of the war. Greeson is not incorrect when he characterizes combat as a place for thugs, and there is no effective retort to his condemnation of the empty ideals that Jerry holds so dear. When Greeson returns, he is ostensibly looking for the best angle to play, and only his love for the girl transforms him into a useful member of society. Because his relationship with her depends on the comradeship of arms, the war has served its purpose as a pathway to a better life, but the crucible of combat has not helped him to mature in and of itself.

Frank Borzage's *Lucky Star* (1929) took an entirely different tack in its approach to wartime service, but it too constitutes a road not taken in the treatment of the war. Charles Farrell plays a telephone lineman who enlists when war is declared. Injured in combat, he returns disabled and is eventually befriended by Janet Gaynor's character, Mary. The girl is portrayed as just past the cusp of adulthood, which allows the older Farrell to be simultaneously a paternal figure (thanks to his gender and age), a maternal figure (because of his demasculinized state), and a romantic interest. As Pat Kirkham points out in her article on Borzage's surviving late-1920s silent films, "The ideal man is one who is partly de-masculinised in order to be partly feminised; who is *deconstructed* to be *reconstructed*. . . . The de- and re-constructed man offered a fantasy hero capable of being reshaped according to women's wishes."[7] This interpretation posits a radical change in the late-1920s conception of virility, but Kirkham goes further in suggesting the positively transformative effects of the war: "Wounding makes men more accessible to women's imagination."[8] In this formulation, even a change in the definition of traditional standards of manhood fails to alter the parameters of the conventional pattern for portraying wartime service. Wounds sustained in combat provide an opportunity for the restructuring of masculinity, such that even additional femininity is a potential positive outcome of the traditional narrative.

By transforming the story of a maimed veteran into a lyrically charming romance, Borzage, like Cromwell, fails to fully develop the dark implications implicit throughout the story. Instead, Borzage is content to portray a similarly positive and virility-affirming outcome for the protagonist. Rather than act as a real handicap, Farrell's wounds provide a means for him to woo and win the girl, with almost no practical drawbacks (either in general or in terms of the courtship). He has no difficulty moving around his own home and is shown as entirely able to live independently. Mary accepts him for who he is, and he is arguably more helpful to her than she is to him. The two major exceptions to his social integration are her mother's objections to Mary's association with a "cripple" and his inability to attend the town dance with his sweetheart. Both difficulties are necessary to provide a level of tension in the plot, though both are also neatly disposed of in the final sequence of the film, in which Farrell rises from his wheelchair and struggles overland through the snow to prevent Mary's marriage to a cad. In effect, he is healed by their mutual love, and the narrative neatly encapsulates the view that neither military service nor grievous wounds sustained in battle are a bar to future personal success.

Borzage's penchant for romance is on full display here, but the film provides another alternative for looking at the war by tweaking the existing narrative pattern. Reducing the entire event and its aftermath to the level of a fable allows Borzage to express his true interest in the redemptive power of love rather than making any radical new comment on the reality of wartime service. As Herve Dumont states in his definitive biography of the director, *Lucky Star* "sums up with so much clarity and poetic imagination what amounts to the quintessence of [Borzage's] work. It contains a rare mixture of enchantment and cruelty that . . . emphasizes two solitary people. [These] two 'lost' individuals, victims of the evil that surrounds them, go beyond their selfishness . . . by rehabilitating themselves, by mutually stabilizing each other under the effect of their transcendent love."[9] This fabulist version of the aftermath of war had surfaced before, most notably in the 1924 version of *The Enchanted Cottage*, but in the final analysis it reflects a more fanciful version of the traditional narrative rather than any sort of new statement. Despite the hardships of physical scars, the war enables the protagonist's discovery of the benefits of a love that sustains him, justifies his service, rewards any sacrifice, and, by its own virtue, affirms Tim's manhood by making him whole.

Similar to Howard Hughes's *Hell's Angels* and Universal's *All Quiet on the Western Front*, *Lucky Star* faced the problematic introduction of sound partway through production. Like Hughes, William Fox decided to convert to the new technology midway through filming, but unlike the independent filmmaker, Fox tried to cover his investment by releasing both silent and sound versions of his film. For either Lewis Milestone or James Whale, the introduction of sound could only add an additional element to the already present verisimilitude of their depictions of combat. *All Quiet on the Western Front* was conceived as a sound film in the technologically hectic late silent period, but the lack of that sound in the more compactly edited "mute" version does not damage Milestone's overall depiction of warfare. It is nearly impossible, however, to imagine the effective addition of sound to a carefully controlled and deliberately nonrealist film such as *Lucky Star*. The approach to the material relies so heavily on a romanticized and fabulist tone that the increased reality touted as a benefit of the new technology would completely violate the mood that Borzage so carefully establishes.

Milestone's *All Quiet on the Western Front* (1930) is generally cited as the pivotal example of a radically new type of realistic war narrative that functions as the precise opposite of Borzage's film. Based on the successful novel by Erich Maria Remarque, the now familiar story of Paul Baumer's service in the German infantry (from schoolboy recruitment to his death on the front lines) demonstrates relevant changes in the portrayal of the war, but these changes are more incremental than they may appear at first glance.

In his *War on Film*, Isenberg declares that "critics have been unanimous in conceding that *All Quiet on the Western Front* was the finest picture made about World War I."[10] Isenberg then goes on to call this status into question. The focus on soldiers as low-ranking pawns, the caricatures of war supporters such as Himmelstoss and the village schoolteacher, and the insinuation that German soldiers held views about wartime service similar to their American counterparts make the narrative more palatable to an American audience. Rather than a radical break, in other words, a closer examination indicates that *All Quiet* was a shrewdly marketed and critically successful step in the continuing evolution of attitudes toward the war.

At its most basic level, the story is a version of the conventional journey to full manhood. The characters of *All Quiet* conform almost entirely to the standards of the traditional narrative. Baumer is a youthful protagonist led to enlist by patriotic zeal. His long-suffering mother is concerned but proud. The soldiers are a cross-section of standard combat types, from the comic relief of former comedian Slim Summerville to Louis Wolheim's older, gruffly wise sergeant. French farm girls are present for a sexual interlude, but they never approach the depth of character of Clara Bow in *Wings* or Renée Adorée in *The Big Parade*. These are all versions of previously seen types enacting familiar narrative arcs.

In *Fallen Soldiers*, his seminal work on the memory of World War I in popular culture, George Mosse specifically asserts that the novel "undoubtedly owed part of its enormous popularity to the fact that it could be read as a schoolboy's adventure story."[11] The film addresses this argument with an opening text that specifically denies that it is in any way an "adventure," but its key innovation for the standard narrative is that when Paul reaches that destination, he finds nothing worth having. With all of his friends departed, unable to reconnect to a home front that cannot conceive of the trials he has undergone, death is the only suitable conclusion for Paul's story. As expected, Paul has been changed by war, and he has matured, but he has also been broken by the experience. The film acknowledges this outcome in its opening text when it claims "simply to tell of a generation of men who, even though they may have escaped its shells, were destroyed by the war," but the final result is an advance toward disillusionment, not a complete transformation to a new narrative mode.

Moreover, grand claims for the film as condemnatory of war for all men and in all cases are to some degree undermined by the fact that the soldiers portrayed as putting forward these unconventional views are citizens of the defeated country. In fact, the critical reception in Germany was much less favorable; there, the film was perceived as an insult.[12] Thus, though the film successfully introduces ideas that were carried further in the years following its release, it fails to be as thorough a debunker of the previously established style as might initially appear to be the case.

Finally, as an early sound film, *All Quiet* is frequently lauded for its technical advances in the visual and aural depiction of combat. It takes nothing from the film's artistry, however, to point out that Milestone's visually sweeping shots of the trenches were accomplished in part by filming silent and then overdubbing the sounds of battle. In effect, Milestone and his photographer, Arthur Edeson, were simply restoring the mobility of the silent era by using exactly the same techniques and then grafting on a new element.[13] As Robert Sklar points out, "At its most basic level, sound was noise, and noise itself could be a source of thrills."[14] The creativity of this solution to the problem of merging sound and image pales even further in light of earlier work that applied versions of this same approach. Sound had previously been used to depict combat, both in the music and effects soundtracks of films such as the 1926 Movietone version of *What Price Glory?* and in lesser-known films such as *The Mighty*.[15] *All Quiet* was a success on many levels, but its Academy Award as Best Picture may elevate it in critical memory in a way that exaggerates its achievement. At heart it remains but another step toward the four films that encapsulate the final expression of the new narrative of disillusionment.

By 1931, the full application of sound technology combined with the continuing evolution of a dominant narrative of disillusionment to complete the transition to a new way of addressing the Great War on film. This new narrative displaced the standard conventions and assumptions of the traditional narrative by casting its protagonists adrift in a postwar world that held neither relief from the past nor promise for the future. The nature of friendships and romantic attachments were significantly altered in this new story. Even more changed was the fundamental conception of a home front that had welcomed returning veterans back with open arms, enabling them to assume their proper place as mature, productive members of society. The exemplars of this new narrative were William Dieterle's *The Last Flight* (1931), George Archainbaud's *The Lost Squadron* (1932), Ernest Lubitsch's *Broken Lullaby* (1932), and William Wellman's *Heroes for Sale* (1933).

The Last Flight (based on a story by John Monk Saunders that was first serialized in *Liberty* magazine as "Nikki and Her War Birds" and then issued as the novel *Single Lady*) marks one of the most advanced statements of the new attitudes toward the depiction of the war in film and establishes the fundamental conventions of the disillusionment narrative. The opening credits begin with the sounds of an artillery barrage, then segue into a loud, violent, half-minute-long montage of battlefield scenes, including firing artillery, rumbling tanks, and advancing infantry. All of these films feature a dramatic use of sound in brief establishing segments set during the war and showing the protagonists in combat. In *The Last Flight*, the opening montage transitions into a scene of air combat, as a pilot tries desperately to get his fiery plane under control, horribly burning his hands in the process. Both pilot and gunner survive the plane crash, and both are then seen in the hospital waiting as a clock ticks down to 11:00 a.m. on November 11, when hostilities will cease. Dieterle again provides an extremely effective use of aural and visual elements, as the face of the timepiece is overlaid with images of fighting and the soundtrack crackles with the noise of warfare. As the appointed time is reached, the sounds and images of combat fade away, replaced by the quietly ticking image of the clock.

The discharge of the wounded men displays a second characteristic of these films, as those in authority demonstrate complete ineffectiveness and ignorance regarding the reintegration of veterans into society. The doctor in charge sends off the two airmen with the suggestion that time will heal their wounds, advising them to return home as soon as possible. In conversation with a colleague, the head doctor encapsulates the argument of all of these films by delineating the ways in which the two men are emotionally and physically crippled by their participation in the conflict: "Their nervous systems are deranged, disorganized, brittle... spent bullets, that's it. They're like projectiles shaped for war and hurled at the enemy. They've described a beautiful, high-arching trajectory and now they've fallen back to earth. Spent. Cooled off. Useless. Even if they do take care of themselves, what good are they? What can you expect of them? I hate to think what may become of them."

From this bleak forecast, the locale shifts to Paris, so frequently a traditional scene of safety and escape. The armistice has been signed, and Cary (the pilot) has been joined by other former fliers mutually pledged to "Get tight" and "Stay tight." Unwilling to return to their homes in the United States, they constitute their own home front as they lead aimless lives of sleepless nights and heavy drinking. The notion of a meaningful return to society, in other words, has been completely upended. These men have nowhere to go and no one to go home to, so they cling to each other. Rather than the traditional buddy who is left behind at the end of hostilities in favor of a return to the place of origin, these men form a new family unit apart from everything they had known prior to their service. Their experiences on the battlefield have left them incapable of any connection to conventional social normalcy. The harsh realities of combat offer nothing redemptive and have left them socially and psychologically incompetent.

A similar pattern can be observed in the specific depictions of the central characters. Cary (played by Richard Barthelmess) is the ostensible leader of a group that includes Shep (David Manners), Bill (Johnny Mack Brown), and Francis (Elliott Nugent). Though nominally given a central place in the narrative (partly on the basis of his involvement with the only female in the story), Barthelmess is not truly a leader of this egalitarian assemblage. All of them have been made equal by their camaraderie fostered under the harsh conditions of combat. At the same time, there is no suggestion that these men can be led anywhere, let alone that they are moving toward either healing or maturity. The overarching sense of the characters is not of boys made men by combat but of men made weary by the conflict. In some cases (the character of Bill, in particular) the attempt to escape from the results of the war has made them arguably less mature and certainly less fit for participation in normal society. Bill, for example, tackles a horse on the streets of Paris on a whim and is endlessly fascinated by a pet turtle. This is a major change from the traditional pattern, where the position of the protagonist as soldier/veteran indicated the general direction of the narrative arc. Here, aimlessness is the central attribute of every character.

This aimlessness extends to the depiction of the main female character, Nikki (played by Helen Chandler). Nikki's simplicity and naivete appeal to the entire group, partly because these qualities make her as purposeless as any of them. Though she feels an attraction to Cary, the feeling can hardly be called romantic love. Her awkward comment on his burned hands arouses embarrassment, then sympathy, but to refer to her attitude as "love" would be unwarranted. The only "love scene" in the film is instigated when Nikki follows Cary to a cemetery where he hopes to be alone. His melancholy exposition of the tale of Heloise and Abelard causes only frustration when Nikki ignores the ramifications of the story and uses it merely as a source of names for her turtles.

Taken together, these characterizations redefine the conventions that existed in traditional cinematic depictions of war and its aftermath. There is no clear-cut protagonist, only an egalitarian group. The character of the woman is a cipher rather than a possible source of redemption. Figures of authority offer no useful advice or assistance, and the social normalcy of the home front offers only discomfort, not an opportunity for reintegration and advancement. Finally, it is always clear that the aftereffects of military service are not a pathway to maturity but instead are a gateway to extended psychological and social difficulties. Unlike the earlier approach, the central conception of combat has absolutely nothing to do with war as a site of personal growth, adventure, or romance. The dominant theme is a depiction of war as a complete destroyer of lives. The main characters are empty shells of men, masking their pain with alcohol and excess and finding solace nowhere except in themselves and in Nikki's reflection of them. Though we see only brief, concise scenes of battlefield action, further elaboration is unnecessary since the entire impact of the war can be traced through the problematic patterns of the survivors' lives. By the end of the film, two of them are dead, one is a refugee (and not expected to live long), and Cary and Nikki are left together to carry on with their lives. There is a fleeting suggestion that they may emerge from the problems that beset them, but the film evinces very little faith in this possibility and concludes very much in doubt.

Like *The Last Flight*, Archainbaud's *The Lost Squadron* begins with a scene of air combat over France. In this case, three pilots engage in dogfights with German competitors, with several of the pilots periodically checking their watches as they await the impending armistice. Promptly at 11:00 a.m., the enemies salute one another and return home to get drunk and congratulate themselves on surviving. The early return scene in the barracks establishes the three main characters Gibson (played by Richard Dix), Woody (Robert Armstrong), and Red (Joel McCrea), but it also strikes the one false note of the film, as drunken fellow pilots laud the ending of a "great war." Joined by their mechanic, Fritz, the three lead characters strike a more somber tone. They join in singing "Auld Lang Syne" and pledge to remain together when they return home, just as the characters in *The Last Flight* remain together in Paris. From the barracks, the scene cuts to footage of a victory parade down a major city street. The parade ends with an older politician haranguing surrounding veterans with a short speech: "These are our boys, our heroes who return to us. And their reward for all times will be the reward of heroes. And you boys, you who have returned to us, you will find everything—everything—exactly as you left it. And your services to your country will never be forgotten."

The scenes following the speech are a bitter rejoinder, as the film demolishes the politician's empty promises for each of the three main characters. Red declines to return to his former employment when he learns that it will force out an older man with a sick wife and many children. Woody discovers that his former business partner has betrayed him and left him destitute. Gibson learns that his girl back home did not remain faithful and is now the paramour of a producer who will benefit her acting career. Gathered together in a restaurant, the three pilots and their mechanic vow again to stay together, as their camaraderie is all that remains of their wartime experience. When Gibson offers a toast to the squadron, Woody amends it to include, "The birds that were lost," and Gibson agrees, toasting "the Lost Squadron." As in *The Last Flight*, what survives from the war is not maturity, social acceptance, or moral rectitude; it is only a shared affinity for those who endured.

In the remarkable sequence that follows, the lack of any profit from the experience of combat is driven home even more relentlessly. As the soundtrack plays a jaunty version of George M. Cohan's "Over There," a dissolving montage of newspaper headlines delineates the shift from positive to negative views of the returning veterans. "Nation Salutes Service Men! Country Greets Returning War Heroes Who Made the World Safe for Democracy" is followed by "Ex-Service Men Ask Help," "Congress Disputes Bonus," "Ex-Soldiers Clean City Streets!" and finally "Service Men in Bread Line." The final image dissolves into a shot of a boxcar on which a disheveled Gibson, Red, and Fritz the mechanic are bumming a ride to Hollywood, where they hope to meet up with Woody. The film has made its point regarding the results of the war for these characters, and it does so by offering a new form of verisimilitude. Made after the January 1932 march of Cox's Army on Washington, DC, the film used headlines ripped from current events to assert its own relevance and realism. As Paul Dickson and Thomas Allen demonstrate in *The Bonus Army: An American Epic*, the plight of unemployed veterans was a pressing public issue throughout the late 1920s and well into the 1930s. The depiction of beleaguered veterans would be familiar to American audiences primed to question the value of wartime service. The narrative presents protagonists who are adrift and unable to function, betrayed not only by the voluble politicians who welcomed them home but now also by society as a whole.

Once stated, the theme is reinforced by the balance of the film. The men find Woody, who is now flying dangerous stunts for a sadistic film director Arthur von Furst (played by the master of that trope, Erich von Stroheim). Though they make a steady living by risking their lives as stunt fliers, their employment indicates that they have not adjusted to a conventional life. Woody has become a drunk who lives only for the danger of flying (and who is killed in a plane crash engineered by von Furst). Gibson is tortured by the presence of his former flame (played by Mary Astor), who is now married to the director. Jealousy provides the motive for von Furst's engineering of the plane crash, and his accidental shooting in a scuffle with the three surviving members of the Lost Squadron is covered up by Gibson, who sacrifices his life to dispose of the body (suicide is another frequent trope of the disillusionment narrative). Red, the probable culprit in the shooting, is left alone to marry Woody's kid sister but must also deal with the guilt of knowing that his friend died to cover up his crime. The final sequence of the film indicates the depth of the displacement experienced by the members of the Lost Squadron as Red, Woody's sister, and Fritz stand before the tombstones of their departed friends, and the ghosts of Gibson and Woody, piloting their planes, salute each other as they soar into the clouds. Death has brought them peace from a postwar existence that caused them nothing but heartbreak and pain.

Released a few months before *The Lost Squadron*, Lubitsch's little-seen *Broken Lullaby* (also known as *The Man I Killed*), goes even further in fracturing the old conventions in favor of a more raw depiction of the results of warfare. The film is an uncomfortable fit with the general conception of Lubitsch's work as a source of comic entertainments like *Trouble in Paradise* (1932) or *Shop around the Corner* (1940) but demonstrates his mastery of the medium. Here, the director relates a deeply serious tale of postwar anguish, based on a play by Maurice Rostand (the son of Edmond Rostand, author of *Cyrano de Bergerac*). The story revolves around a young French soldier, Paul (played by Phillips Holmes), who is so crushed with guilt over the one man he killed during the war that he seeks out the man's family to beg their forgiveness. Misunderstanding, however, they take him for a prewar friend of their son, increasing his distress, which then grows even more when he falls in love with the dead soldier's fiancée. Once again, nearly every aspect of the film stands in opposition to the standards and tropes of the traditional narrative.

Lubitsch begins his story in Paris on the first anniversary of Armistice Day with a devastating opening montage. The director bluntly sets the tone with images and sounds of firing cannon, ringing church bells, and cheering crowds. Only after these brief establishing shots does he turn his camera on a military parade, with the shot framed by the crutches and remaining leg of an amputee as the viewer looks through the space left by the amputated limb. Unlike the shining safe haven so often depicted in more traditional war films, the City of Light no longer provides an exotic escape from the trials of war. Instead, the metropolis is a hypocritical place where crowds cheer and cannon boom in defiance of a "Silence: Hospital" sign (a hospital in which shell-shocked men scream, terrified at the disturbance). The same artillery salute that torments the hospitalized veterans segues into pealing bells, thereby facilitating a visual transition to the interior of a church full of soldiers in full regalia. The director skillfully cuts together shots of religious imagery (pews, hymnals, crosses) with the symbols of military pride (polished boots, swords, men in uniform). After the service, only Paul remains, desperately praying for forgiveness. Seeking out a priest, Paul begs for help, declaring that he has "murdered" a man and "can't get away from his eyes." When asked why he killed the man, Paul replies, "Why? Why? I don't know. For no reason. For no reason at all. And he didn't even raise a hand to defend himself. He just looked at me... looked at me." On the repeat of this phrase the camera moves in toward Paul's eyes, then dissolves to the eyes of a soldier in the trenches as the soundtrack erupts with the sounds of the battlefield. The trenches are shown as a muddy, disorienting hell in which the only living things are the two soldiers facing one another. The incessant pounding of shellfire increases the sense of chaos and isolation as we witness the aftermath of the death blow Paul has just administered. Shock and terror are written on the faces of both soldiers, and nothing remotely heroic or adventurous can be extracted from the scene. This same sense of despairing futility and horror is conveyed by the one other sequence set on the battlefront, a montage of chaos shown late in the film to reflect Paul's continuing anguish. In both cases, the portrayal of war is brief and effective, carefully calculated to achieve maximum effect. The battlefield is shown less as a setting for the narrative than as a specific source for the damaged psychology of the characters.

In keeping with the increased sense of the war as an experience shared by fighting men regardless of nationality, Paul and the dying German are seen to share the bond of music. Paul is a musician, and as the German dies, he reaches for a letter tucked into a biography of Beethoven. The viewer sees a close-up of the letter, which includes the lines, "Why? Whom am I going to kill and for what? For two years I lived in Paris and loved the French. And now I am told to kill them." These lines echo Paul's earlier declaration that he had killed "For no reason at all." Emerging from the flashback, Paul and the priest share an exchange in which the priest assures the troubled penitent that he has done only his duty and is free of all crime. Paul takes no consolation from the offered platitudes, however, crying out, "Duty to kill? Is this the only answer I can get in the house of God?... I came here to find peace and you haven't given it to me." Once again, the established authorities are completely incapable of assimilating the responses of returned veterans and are at a loss to help them deal with their wartime service.

Unable to accept absolution, Paul tries an alternate approach, and here Lubitsch applies another trope of the disillusionment narrative by completely realigning the definition of the home front. Paul's search for forgiveness leads him to the German hometown of the soldier he killed, which becomes his home (we never see him with his own relatives). Mistaken for a friend of their son when he is seen putting flowers on the dead man's grave, Paul is taken in by the family of the man he killed. Overwhelmed, he is unable to tell them the truth and increasingly takes the place of their lost child. His comfort in the country of his "enemies" is repeatedly reinforced by the events of the story. He is often invited to dinner, visits the cemetery, and courts the dead man's fiancée under the observation of the townspeople. In every way, in other words, Germany becomes his home. This is a complete inversion of the home front idea seen in traditional narratives dealing with the war. Paul is effectively cast out of his own society by the lack of understanding and sympathy for his experiences and finds release only among people who should hate him. The support and validation usually provided by a family and nation are here afforded by a source that is conventionally a diametric opposite.

This inversion extends to the roles of the central character types, with the loving parents and "girl at home" functioning as they would in a film dealing with any returning veteran but with the crucial difference that he "returns" to the home of his foe. The focus of the story remains so concentrated on Paul and the family that there is no room for any of the other stock character types we might expect to see in a film dealing with the war. The introduction of any fellow soldiers (other than the man Paul kills) would lessen the intense shock value of the scenes of combat by humanizing them. The only key character, then, is Paul himself. Here again, Lubitsch inverts the earlier patterns of defining the protagonist. Paul is an empty shell of a man, beyond the usual avenues of maturation or social redemption. This is made even more extreme by the lack of any comrades with whom he can bond (as in *The Last Flight* or *The Lost Squadron*) and by his sense of guilt. Holmes perhaps overplays the role, but Paul is utterly haunted by his actions, almost to the point of catatonia. He is without will or hope, and his acquiescence to the kindness of his German hosts is part desperation and part lack of will. Here again, heroism is completely abandoned as a character trait, and even the calculated emptiness of the men in *The Last Flight* is cast aside for the crushing weight of regret. Paul is crippled by his involvement in the conflict, and while he does make progress in his movement away from being an emotional and psychological invalid, it is hardly the advance to manhood seen in the traditional narrative. Assuming mature social responsibilities is of little importance when the main character is barely able to maintain his own sanity. Even the loving relationship of Paul and the girl (which would perhaps justify an argument that war leads to love in this instance) is of a highly dubious nature. It is not clear that love has been found as much as that Paul (along with the girl, who is solicitous of the dead man's parents) is desperate to maintain a fiction that will help them all to find some measure of psychological stability. Even aside from these concerns, the film disdains the notion that war can have any positive effect for anyone. Nothing emerges from the conflict except pain and anguish, and the attempt to repair those wounds has highly questionable results at best.

Beginning with the cannon, bells, and crowds of the opening sequence, Lubitsch repeatedly demonstrates a considered use of the soundtrack to support his arguments. In one especially effective instance, the director uses the sounds of cheers and marching in an empty street to indicate the irony of an army's "heroic" departure compared to the agony of their return. Holmes's pleas to the priest convey both the pain and the indignation of a man who has been deceived (and destroyed) by the standards of his society. Finally, the dialogue bristles with sentiments that could not have been expressed as clearly before the advent of sound film. In a central scene in a beer hall, Lubitsch slowly builds a conversation among German fathers who have lost their sons (and who resent the familiarities of the Frenchman in their midst), leading to an explosive outburst by Lionel Barrymore (as the dead soldier's father): "The fathers are responsible. I stood in front of this hotel when my son marched by. He was going to his death—and I cheered." The speech is punctuated by the approval of a wounded young veteran who stands to shake Barrymore's hand. The speech and the gesture could have been made in a silent film, as could the devastating opening Armistice Day montage, but both receive added weight through the use of sound effects and dialogue. Lubitsch manipulates every means at his disposal to convey a disillusioned sentiment that would not have been acceptable just a few years before, and the sum of those means allows him to express his ideas with a strength and conviction that would have been difficult (though perhaps not impossible) prior to the advent of sound.

Though Lubitsch comes very close to presenting the defining version of the new narrative form, he does cushion the effect of his story for American audiences. As Isenberg points out, the fundamental impact of *Broken Lullaby* is softened by the fact that the protagonist is a French lead character functioning in a German world: "American moviemakers were having their cake and eating it too." By peopling films of disillusionment with non-American characters, "they were able to condemn the war without involving either the war aims or the war conduct of the United States."[16] Because three of these four films present American characters, the criticism of *Broken Lullaby* does not ring entirely true, nor does Isenberg's rejection of Lubitsch's filmmaking skills as "slickness."[17] However, another skilled filmmaker most effectively summarizes the evolutionary changes in the depiction of the war from the mid-1920s to the mid-1930s. William Wellman's *Heroes for Sale* completes the move from a traditional narrative to a narrative of disillusionment in an entirely American setting and proves to be the culmination of Hollywood's decade-long assessment of the effects of the Great War.

Heroes for Sale is one of the most brutal films ever made about the American experience, painting an unstinting portrait of the fate of a typical American veteran of the First World War. There is no moral compass, no adventure, and no romance to participation in the conflict. Instead, the war experience sets the main character on a spiraling pattern of failure that destroys his life. As Thomas Doherty phrases it, the film "piles a Sophoclean weight of misfortunes upon its guiltless protagonist, a hero of the Great War discarded in its aftermath."[18]

The action of *Heroes for Sale* takes place almost entirely on the home front and in the aftermath of the war. As with the other three works discussed here, Wellman uses a vicious scene on the battlefield and a brief connecting scene in a hospital to set up the tone and arc of the narrative. The film opens with a tense meeting in a trench bunker between two officers. Roger Winston (played by Gordon Westcott) is receiving his orders to mount an intelligence mission to capture a German officer. The bunker is dark and dank, and the sound of explosions is omnipresent (as it is throughout the entire battlefront sequence). On asking how many men he should take, Roger's commanding officer tells him, "Nine or ten. That's all I can afford to lose." As in the other films, the notion of suicide is a precursor to action, though here the impulse occurs while the main character is under arms and in the service. In this instance, both men know that the mission is suicidal but undertake it because "suicide or not, it's orders." After a briefing with his men in another bunker, the scene cuts to the trenches, where Roger and Tom Holmes (played by Richard Barthelmess) prepare for the attack. Rain pours down, making the trench and battlefield a muddy mess and adding another sound to that of the explosions. As the order is given to advance, men fall to machine-gun fire and artillery, including one who falls facedown into a water-filled shell hole and another who falls on top of Tom. This battlefield is a chaotic, loud, messy place, and the men here are grim and afraid in ways not seen prior to the introduction of sound.

Tom is injured in combat and captured by the Germans. He is first taken to a field hospital, which offers few recuperative opportunities. The location is a bombed-out building, and beams and walls have fallen at strange angles, giving the scene an expressionistic feel. The use of sound adds to this feel, as the anguished groans of the injured combine with the foreign sounds of German dialogue. Here, unsubtitled, the German speech highlights the otherness of the doctors and nurses, isolating Tom even further in a roomful of enemies. The hospital locale remains central after a title card announces the signing of the armistice. The setting has switched away from the field hospital to the office of an army doctor in a more permanent facility. The doctor is releasing Tom, explaining that only morphine will ease the pain of his wounds. This sets up the first occurrence of a continuing pattern throughout the narrative: Tom's attempts to do right continually sow the seeds of further trouble.

The pattern is initiated when Tom arrives home after the war. Every site of his home life is converted into a scene of tragedy, pain, or suffering. His bedroom at the family home becomes a safe haven for the use of morphine (behind a locked door). His job at a bank interferes with (and exacerbates) his morphine addiction and tempts him to steal funds to buy drugs. Once again, characters who would traditionally wield social authority are entirely unhelpful to the veteran as he tries to deal with his problems. His doctor reports him as an addict, and the blustering bank president is enthusiastic about Tom's dismissal from a position as a teller. Ironically, his time in jail offers Tom the opportunity to get clean of his addiction and straighten out his life. Relocating to a city seems to offer hope of continuing revitalization but instead is only a source of further pain when Tom is involved in a riot. Repeatedly, then, the comfort and reassurance of the stable, even noble, nature of life at home seen in the 1910s and early 1920s is radically overturned or reversed in this film.

The same complete realignment and overturning of conventions is seen in the standard character types. There is no suggestion that Tom is a character in need of maturity or developing into manhood. The callow, naive youths of *The Big Parade* or *Wings* bear little relation to the soldier seen here. The initial scenes in the trenches depict him harboring a reasonable fear of the outcome of battle and weary of fighting. Despite the chaos of the battlefield, however, he acts responsibly, and none of the evils that befall him in combat, in the hospital, or in his later life are the result of any recklessness on his part.

Roger would play the buddy role in a traditional narrative. He grew up in the same town as Tom, and their families know one another, though Roger is wealthy and Tom is not. Instead of functioning as an anchor, companion, or guide, however, Roger consistently betrays Tom. Roger accepts praise (including medals, promotions, and a parade at home) that belongs to Tom (whom Roger believes has died on the battlefield). Even when Roger could make amends and confess his deception, he fails to do so, exhibiting none of the basic decency of a more traditional battlefield companion. His lack of resolve costs Tom a job at the bank (which Roger had procured for him out of guilt) and sends him to prison. The comrades of *The Last Flight* were bonded by their experiences, but these men are torn apart by their shared time in the trenches.

The last trope to be upended is the character of the girl, here played by Loretta Young. For a brief period, she seems to hold the promise of normalcy and redemption that Clara Bow represents in *Wings* or Renée Adorée symbolizes in *The Big Parade*. She and Tom marry and have a child, and a return to simple domesticity appears to be within their grasp. But their life together is shattered by a street riot of workers (whose jobs Tom has inadvertently helped to eliminate). In attempting to defend her husband, Tom's wife is killed in the melee. Rather than representing a hopeful future, the girl is only another element of a bitter and hopeless present.

In each of these cases, the traditional role of key character types is completely subverted by the narrative. Rather than assisting the development of the protagonist and enabling his assumption of a dominant social role, supporting characters tend to dismiss Tom, prevent his advancement, and hinder his recovery from his combat experience. *Heroes for Sale* thus offers a blunt reappraisal of the development and behavior of individuals in combat and in a postwar world.

Rather than trace the evolution to maturity of a main character, *Heroes for Sale* shows a man who has seen too much, as is apparent from his first appearance on-screen. Rather than depicting war as a site of adventure, the film sends Tom on a suicide mission, and in many ways, he never returns from it. Rather than finding romance and social acceptance as a reward for service, the "hero" glimpses happiness, only to have it ripped from his grasp. Rather than the development of group unity and cohesion, the film features a collection of desperate men who sabotage Tom at every step—either by design or as a consequence of their own weakness. As far as *Heroes for Sale* is concerned, every hope of betterment and improvement offered by the traditional narrative is a baseless lie.

These films have moved far beyond the parameters of the traditional wartime narrative originally utilized by D. W. Griffith and Thomas Ince. The fundamental values of verisimilitude, universal meaning, and maturation have been drastically transformed from their original applications. Though the verisimilitude of the presentation of combat was enhanced by the addition and skillful use of sound technology, the notion soon embraced the presentation of an accurate view of the veteran's later fate after his return home. The universal values so lauded in the traditional narrative—courage, bravery, devotion to duty—are not entirely cast aside but are downplayed in favor of a more unstinting look at the universal effects of war on those who experience it. This new view emphasizes previously unmentioned consequences—loyalty to friends over country, the inability to share the experience with anyone who did not also serve, discomfort at home, the probability of far-reaching psychological effects, and the acceptance of suicide, alcohol, and drugs as ways of dealing with these consequences. Finally, the notion of war as a mill that (to paraphrase an intertitle from *The Cradle of Courage*) grinds the stoop from the veteran's shoulders and the twists from his soul is completely absent in the fullest development of this new narrative. Instead, war has become a millstone that weighs down and crushes all who participate.

In his *No Man's Land: Combat and Identity in World War I*, historian Eric J. Leed writes, "The community of the front was formed by those uprooted from their social matrix to serve as instruments in the defense of the established order. In this defense many learned the indefensibility of this order. In the experience of war the 'home' became more alien than any enemy.... No 'rites of reaggregation' could efface the memory of utter defenselessness before authority and technology. No ceremonial conclusion to the war could restore the continuities it had ended, or recreate those 'fictions' that had been left behind in the labyrinth of trenches."[19] That harsh description of the aftermath of wartime service is precisely what is shown in the films that use the full-blown narrative of disillusionment. The characters of *The Last Flight*, *Broken Lullaby*, *The Lost Squadron*, and *Heroes for Sale* are all broken men, unable to readjust to conventional lives. Society has used them, betrayed them, and left them unable to reconnect. Though these films do not attempt to undermine the notion that veterans have done their duty and may have done so bravely, the presentation of the effects of their service and the ways in which it affects their lives have fundamentally changed. After ten years of negotiating a fundamental transformation of the dominant narrative, these films reflected the inadequacy of the traditional narrative of wartime service for discussing the rigors and hardships of the First World War.

Chapter Seven

MORALS AND MUCK

From Suicide to Superheroes

BY 1934, FILMMAKERS WORKING IN HOLLYWOOD DISPLAYED A CONSISTENT approach to portraying the First World War on-screen, and that portrayal was far from positive. Films that focused directly on the conflict depicted it as a waste beyond comprehension, damaging to the country and to anyone who served. The psychic aftereffects repeatedly either drove protagonists to the extreme of suicide or guaranteed them a life of perennial despair. Given the prevalence of this depiction, the logical next question is, What happened? If such an argument was developed in the late 1920s and early 1930s, where did it go? Like most such questions, the answers are not simple: a range of factors contributed to the suppression of the disillusionment narrative almost as soon as it was fully formed. Ironically, those factors included most of the subjects that the narrative directly criticized—the disjunction between public discourse and reality, the economic status of veterans, politics and war itself. Over nearly a full century, the disillusionment narrative has been continuously adapted, but it has never completely disappeared and indeed may be poised to reemerge in a new form. The passage of time never led to a complete effacement but rather led to a compartmentalization that allowed popular culture to acknowledge (grudgingly) the existence and horrors of the First World War while keeping it from "contaminating" the larger rhetorical framework for dealing with American war narratives.

The initial suppression of the disillusionment narrative can be attributed to a number of causes, the confluence of which made the subject of the First World War generally problematic. As capitalism seemed to teeter on the verge of collapse following the advent of the Great Depression, the popular mood initially encouraged films that questioned the government's efficacy and decision-making. The general sense of social pessimism is certainly reflected in the films dealing with the Great War, but it is also seen in a host of other projects that casually promoted radical political alternatives as solutions to the country's problems. Films such as *The President Vanishes* (1934), *Gabriel over the White House* (1933), and *This Day and Age* (1933) drew uncomfortably close to advocating either revolution or fascism as a means of enabling the nation's survival.[1] At the same time, gangster films such as *Little Caesar* (1930), *The Public Enemy* (1931), and *Scarface* (1932) depicted extreme violence as a natural aspect of the most raw, rapacious, and ruthless capitalistic endeavor—crime.[2]

As filmmakers freely ruminated on such subjects in their films, however, a variety of interest groups pressed for moral accountability in film culture. Especially enraged by the prominent use of sex and violence, those groups (the Catholic Legion of Decency is the most often cited) caused consternation in movie executives' offices by raising the specter of government involvement in the censorship of their product. The industry had previously dealt with such threats via half-hearted promises of reform, but by the early 1930s, such evasions were not enough to resolve the issue. Instead, the established Production Code was given teeth, and mechanisms were created to ensure that the industry regulated itself to avoid further criticism.[3] The specific practical effects of this self-censorship can be voluminously debated, but it is difficult to argue with Ruth Vasey's contention that "the general effect of industry regulation was to encourage the elision or effacement of sensitive subjects."[4] Foremost among such subjects was the depiction of America's involvement in the Great War.

Adding to the industry reticence to perpetuate a disillusionment narrative were two prominent political concerns, one international and one domestic. The European political situation threatened foreign film sales, as Vasey notes: "Between the World Wars, foreign revenues consistently accounted for about 35 percent of Hollywood's gross income," and Hollywood's "domination of the markets of the world depended, at least in part, upon its ability to convince foreign censors and trade representatives its output was culturally inoffensive and ideologically neutral."[5] In light of this consideration, most of the major studios found it strategically advantageous to assiduously avoid topics that might be perceived as politically sensitive. A review of Production Code administration files demonstrates these concerns even during the pre-Code period. Films such as *All Quiet on the Western Front* (1930), *Cock of the Air* (1932), and *A Farewell to Arms* (1932) raised major red flags among representatives of the industry as well as representatives of foreign governments.[6] By 1934 the safest option was to turn to other topics. It made little sense to allow the continuation of a narrative approach that questioned the value of military action in the face of a rapidly rearming Europe.

Domestic politics further complicated the problem. The depression left countless veterans unemployed and precipitated a political crisis.[7] In the summer of 1932, thousands of those men descended on Washington, DC, to demand government help. Calling themselves the Bonus Expeditionary Force or Bonus Army, they sought the early payment of funds authorized by Congress in 1924. Under the provisions of the World War Compensation Act veterans were to be paid monies based on their length of service. Depending on the circumstances, funds were not to be disbursed until 1945, though eligible veterans could borrow against the value of their claim. The Bonus Army sought the immediate payment of the promised money, but the Hoover administration did not find that demand fiscally tenable. Instead, concerned in part about the size of an encampment that might harbor antigovernment or communist sympathizers, the president authorized military action. In the melee that followed two Bonus Army veterans were killed by a military force led by Douglas MacArthur (and including George Patton and Dwight Eisenhower). The use of force against American veterans did not shower glory on any of those involved, with Hoover receiving the lion's share of the blame from a public already unhappy with his leadership. Though this particular incident may not have completely killed studio interest in stories featuring Great War veterans (*Gabriel over the White House*, *Heroes for Sale*, and the "Forgotten Man" musical number featured in *Gold Diggers of 1933* were all seen on America's movie screens in the following year), the topic was more politically fraught than it might have been otherwise.

The last major aspect of the move away from the Great War as an acceptable topic was the industry's willingness to position itself as a source of pure entertainment. Screwball comedies might address social issues such as divorce and remarriage, but they did not question the underpinnings of any nation's foreign policy. Musicals might also occasionally mention the economic plight of a nation but, unlike the veterans depicted in disillusionment narratives, Dick Powell, Ruby Keeler, and Shirley Temple never flirted with suicide as an acceptable escape from economic despair. It is possible, in other words, that the audience was no longer in the mood for films that told them that war was terrible when everyday life was already quite difficult enough. Given all of these considerations, the narrative of disillusionment lapsed into dormancy as Americans struggled with the effects of the Great Depression and Europe prepared for yet another military conflagration.

Despite this carefully maintained silence, Hollywood's reticence to discuss the gathering clouds of war was notably not shared by the scrappiest of the majors, Warner Bros. Though the true circumstances surrounding the studio's attitude toward Hitler and the Nazis are somewhat muddled by Jack Warner's propensity for self-mythologizing, the Warners came to believe in the perils of Nazism very early. Jack Warner claimed to have recognized the threat during a visit to Berlin in 1928, and Harry Warner made a firm anti-Nazi statement when he shut down the studio's German operations in July 1934.[8]

As early as 1935 the studio began to act on its anti-Nazi political convictions by producing a slate of films that directly engaged with the German threat. Short subjects, cartoons, and features promoted American ideals, countered negative feelings about the military, and directly mocked and/or villainized the Nazis. Perhaps the best remembered of these films, *Sergeant York* (Howard Hawks, 1941), moved beyond those sentiments to argue for the necessity of U.S. involvement in the Second World War by resurrecting and adapting elements of the dormant disillusionment narrative and turning it on its head.

As the most decorated American doughboy, Alvin C. York had enviable name recognition, but he also personally embodied the arguments of the disillusionment narrative.[9] In 1917, York's strong religious beliefs had led him to claim conscientious objector status, but when his request was denied, he reported for induction and eventually achieved unwanted fame through his battlefield conduct. Like the protagonists of *The Dawn Patrol* and *Journey's End* (both 1930), York believed that he was doing his duty, but he persisted in believing that war was a morally dubious endeavor that solved nothing. On his return to the States, he was acclaimed as a returning hero, but he never believed that his acts were heroic, frequently asserting that his role in the actions that led to his public recognition had been inflated by the press and public. When York attempted to use his popularity to achieve educational reform in his native Tennessee, he was consistently opposed by the political and social establishment. Much like the protagonist of *Heroes for Sale*, York met with repeated setbacks in his efforts to reintegrate into American society despite the potential advantage of his fame, and his attitude regarding war itself was not altered by his experiences. Throughout the 1930s, he continued to believe that it was a moral wrong from which nothing good emerged, and he spoke out publicly in favor of pacifism and nonintervention.[10]

Fervently wooed by producer Jesse Lasky (and in financial difficulties), York eventually agreed to cooperate on the production of a biopic, but he hoped that it would focus not on the war but instead on his life since returning from overseas. Such a focus might logically have led to a simple rebirth of the disillusionment narrative, detailing York's conviction that war remained a dubious and unprofitable activity and that pacifism remained the most desirable option. Though the parties involved initially agreed to such an approach, several elements mitigated against it. First, events in Europe increasingly warranted that the most interventionist of studios should use the film to promote America's involvement in the coming conflict, and York himself grew increasingly interventionist as the war in Europe expanded. Second, it made little dramatic sense for the film to minimize the events that made the protagonist most familiar to the audience. As the focus on wartime heroics increased, however, the studio was careful to tread a fine line between isolationism and interventionism. In doing so, they adjusted the disillusionment template in a significant way.

Rather than depict war as an entirely negative event that destroys the lives of those involved, *Sergeant York* presents it as a potentially negative event that sometimes must be tolerated. The most significant feature of this presentation is that York's pacifist views (and those of the disillusionment narrative) are not specifically denied. Avoiding conflict and its negative consequences remains the most important goal. This attitude is immediately in evidence with the dedication at the end of the opening credits, which posits a faith that "a day will come when man will live in peace on earth." As the film progresses, nothing undermines the premises that were so stridently presented in disillusionment narratives. For example, when York leaves home after being drafted, his sister asks, "Ma, what are they afightin' fir?" and their mother responds, "I don't rightly know, child." This is not a film involving unquestioned patriotism and moral clarity, nor is it a narrative recounting the main character's growth to manhood. (York was thirty when he was drafted.) Instead, it focuses on the philosophic and theological ramifications of taking up arms while eliding any consideration of negative personal aftereffects.

In one of the film's key sequences, York's commanding officers argue with him regarding the conflict between military service and religious conviction, and none of the participants deny the difficulties of reconciling the desire for peace with military action; in fact, they specifically agree with his convictions while arguing for their own. When he is given the choice of remaining in the military or being discharged, York retreats to a mountaintop with his Bible, finally settling on the argument that he should render unto Caesar the things that are Caesar's. This is not a counterargument for any of his reservations regarding the usefulness of war, and he specifically expresses his continuing qualms to his commanding officer when he reports back to camp. Instead, he recognizes that he must balance those reservations against his duties as an American citizen.

The final development of this argument is apparent in the scene of York's questioning by officers investigating his battlefield actions. He consistently invokes divine favor as an explanation for his success and is visibly uncomfortable with the matter-of-fact question of how many Germans he killed during combat. More pointedly, when directly asked how he decided that it was acceptable to kill, York states, "I'm as much agin' killin' as ever," but he asserts that his actions were taken to "stop them guns" and to save lives. Though it is implied that he is stopping German guns, that fact is not explicitly stated. York's actions save lives in a general sense, without regard to the nationality of those saved. Here again, the heritage of the disillusionment narrative is apparent. York is anguished over his involvement in the war and participates without introducing moral or patriotic claims to justify his involvement as well as without achieving any sort of positive growth as a result. York states this point baldly toward the end of the film in a scene where he declines a bevy of financial offers: "I ain't proud of what happened over there. What we done in France was something we had to do. Some fellows done it ain't a-comin' back. So, the way I figure, things like that ain't for buying and selling."

Sergeant York may certainly be read as a call for all Americans to question their consciences as a second great conflict approached. Warner Bros. films had pushed for intervention throughout the 1930s, and this film was not out of keeping with that pattern. But it does not undermine the philosophic legacy of the disillusionment narrative. Though the film was accused of warmongering and is still held up as an example of jingoistic patriotism, it depicts the experience of war as extremely troubling and scarring to both the nations and individuals involved. It may be a necessity, but it is not a source of pride, and many participants never entirely settle the matter in their minds.

Despite the possibility for a nuanced interpretation of *Sergeant York*, the film became the key building block in a retrenchment of the on-screen discussion of the First World War. The attack on Pearl Harbor swept away any lingering notions of the evils of war, completely sweeping up all hands (and all major studios) in supporting the war effort. The films that emerged from Hollywood over the next four years never questioned the necessity of this new conflict and could not possibly have done so. The injection of a Manichaean moral argument ("Good" Allies versus the "Evil" Axis) completely undermined a true narrative of disillusionment. No longer did the question involve the morality of all war and a consideration of its effects; rather, it was a simpler argument regarding which side was right. Hollywood's eager cooperation with government war aims both marshaled American public resolve and generated massive profits. In a larger sense, however, it also led to the enshrinement of this new type of war narrative, effectively sweeping away the vestiges of arguments made following the First World War. The new conflict is depicted as a "good war" that demands active participation by all as a consequence of the moral clarity of the oppositions it presents. Democracy must triumph over fascism, freedom over slavery, internationalism over narrow national interests. It is a fight for all humanity that has been forced on peaceful nations, and concerns over the effects of the war are no longer an issue. The serviceman depicted in typical films of the Second World War need not struggle with his conscience beyond determining that he wishes to stand with those on the side of right. In later years, when asked what he fought for, he will be able to say that he fought for good over evil. Unlike the First World War, no room for doubt existed at the conclusion of the conflict. Victory overwhelmingly confirmed a narrative pattern for the depiction of warfare that remained largely unchallenged for over a decade. War was a matter of tenacity and moral clarity from which America emerged righteously triumphant.

The advent of this new narrative had one other important effect: the Second World War effectively swept the First World War from public consciousness. With a few minor exceptions, more than a decade passed before the Great War again appeared as a significant topic on American screens, and when it did so, it returned in two films that adopted very different narrative approaches—William Wellman's *Lafayette Escadrille* (1958) and Stanley Kubrick's *Paths of Glory* (1957).

William Wellman's credentials for addressing the First World War on film are unassailable. Following the conclusion of his unofficial war trilogy, however, he made only one other film set entirely during the conflict. In some ways, however, that last film may be his most significant statement on the subject—not for its success but as a result of its failure. Even accounting for the fact that Wellman's personality is frequently discernable in his work, *Lafayette Escadrille* is the most directly autobiographical film he ever made. Wellman's commitment to getting the story on-screen involved his assumption of both producing and directing duties as well as his agreement to direct a second film (*Darby's Rangers* [1958]) as a condition of Warner Bros. financial support.[11] That film was made within the parameters of the prevailing post–World War II narrative and in direct contrast to the intended tone of its predecessor. Given Wellman's unique position as a veteran World War I combat pilot, the personal nature of the story, and the years of effort involved in bringing it to the screen, *Lafayette* could easily have emerged as a summation of the narrative developed by Great War veterans more than two decades earlier. It is therefore unfortunate that the final result is generally considered one of the weakest films in his entire filmography. At least in part, however, that weakness can be seen as a result of the radical nature of the story the director was trying to tell, its incompatibility with the expectations of the studio system, and the dominance of the post–World War

II war narrative. Continuing the revisionist trajectory traced throughout the entire group of his Great War films and despite many difficulties, Wellman manages to arrive at a deeply unpleasant conclusion.

The original story of *Lafayette* is markedly bleaker than any of its Wellman-directed predecessors, featuring a problematic main character who personifies the exact opposite of the traditional wartime protagonist. The story is true, and the characters were comrades of the director during his military service.[12] Portrayed (against Wellman's wishes) by studio heartthrob Tab Hunter, Thad Walker is an almost entirely reprehensible character from beginning to end. He is a spoiled man-child, running from the consequences of his own foolishness, who manages to exile himself from the armed forces by a lack of discipline (he both goes absent without leave and strikes an officer). When his fellow airmen help him break out of prison, he deserts, hides out with a prostitute with whom he has fallen in love, and then becomes a pimp. In the original story, a fortuitous encounter with an American officer offers a chance at redemption, but he wanders across the lines while flying to his first combat posting and is shot down by the Germans. In her grief, the former prostitute (whom he has married) drowns herself in the Seine.

As Frank Thompson recounts, the tragic nature of the story did not test well with Hunter's loyal fan base of teenage girls, so the ending was reshot to enable the survival of the romantic leads.[13] That modification does little to mask the general unsavoriness of the main character, his behavior, or the general tone of the narrative. Nor did postproduction changes temper the wildly varied tonal shifts in a film that attempts to function as tragedy, service comedy, love story, and elegy. Within this unworkable mélange, and despite the modifications wrought by the studio, two important elements stand out. Wellman's story does not idealize his characters in any way. Contrary to the prevailing post–World War II narrative, Wellman has entirely dispensed with any of the "heroic" conventions of a war story, and Thad and the young prostitute he loves are not depicted as anything other than what they are. In addition, the film's most striking sequences are those narrated directly by Wellman as he reminisces about the training of the novice flyers and their frequently tragic fates. These segments present the voice of a veteran not only remembering his youth but also memorializing friends who did not survive. The many years it took for Wellman to bring this project to the screen, even in a compromised fashion, may have enabled him to present a war stripped of conventional tropes and attitudes and to convey a degree of what is in some ways a more honest recollection of the conflict. Studio meddling in every aspect of the production prevented the director from fully realizing the story he intended to tell. Instead of presenting a retrospective version of the disillusionment narrative, the film disillusioned the filmmaker: he threw up his hands at the entire experience and retired.[14]

The failure of *Lafayette Escadrille* is also the failure of the last significant attempt by a veteran of the war to grapple with the experience on-screen. The failure is especially ironic given that within a few months, a film was released that has become synonymous with the Great War despite lacking the experiential authority that Wellman tried to bring to bear on his project.

As the first feature film about the Great War to be made by an American company without substantial participation by a veteran of that war, it is ironic that *Paths of Glory* is so frequently invoked as a significant World War I film. With the exception of Adolphe Menjou (who had served in the ambulance corps in France during the last months of the war), the key members of the creative team were all too young to have firsthand knowledge of the conflict.[15] They could not, therefore, be disillusioned in quite the same manner as their predecessors, and the film they created reflects that fact. Based on a novel by Humphrey Cobb, the story revolves around the machinations of two general officers who order a hopeless attack on an unassailable position. Enraged by the entirely expected failure of their troops, they single out three random soldiers for execution to set an example. At its base, the story could easily have encompassed the concerns of the disillusionment narrative. Senseless, meaningless killing is ordered for no sound reason and is followed by even more senseless killing. Rather than displaying the confusion and despair of the fully developed disillusionment narrative of the 1930s, however, *Paths of Glory* instead creates a hybrid narrative that grafts elements of post–World War II thinking onto the earlier conflict. Though the setting of Kubrick's film is a French battlefield in 1916, there are significant differences between how he treats his subject and how it was approached by his filmmaking predecessors. At the most basic level, the film features all of the expected, stereotypical, generic markers: trenches, a crater-filled no-man's-land, a shell-shocked soldier, a futile attack on an unassailable objective. It is also, however, a self-conscious allegory for a badly fought war—which is not precisely the same thing.

In his work on Kubrick, Alexander Walker argues that, *Paths of Glory* "shows one group of men being exploited by another group. It explores the social stratification of war.... The actual division, the deeper conflict, is that between the leaders and the led.... Only by implication is *Paths of Glory* a protest against war as such; it is much more pertinently an illustration of war as a continuation of class struggle."[16] Kubrick utilized the First World War as the backdrop for his argument but did so without regard for the tonal or thematic concerns of the disillusionment narratives of the early 1930s. Three elements demonstrate the ways in which he transplants later notions to a generically standardized setting.

The first key element indicating Kubrick's approach is his delineation of the characters. As the credited producer and star of the film, Kirk Douglas had every interest in making sure that Colonel Dax was portrayed in a positive light, and he is the hero of the piece despite his preordained failure to prevent the execution of the three scapegoat soldiers. Not only does he look the hero (when first seen on-screen he is impressively shirtless and none the worse for his time in the trenches), but he also demonstrates his unquestioned bravery in leading the doomed attack. While not quite a jingoist, he resolutely proclaims to his superiors, "We'll take the Anthill. If any soldiers can, we can." He is also portrayed as a brilliant lawyer—just the man to function as Kubrick's mouthpiece for arguing against the injustice about to be visited on three innocents. Douglas possesses the screen charisma necessary to oppose the beguiling portrayals of corruption presented by George Macready (General Mireau) and Menjou (General Broulard).

Mireau and Broulard are the primary villains of the film, personifying the ambition and ruthlessness of the aristocratic classes in direct opposition to the stalwartness of Dax. Kubrick fawns over their verbal abilities and self-possession while emphasizing their self-involvement and their lack of compassion for the troops under their command. A third villain seems to undercut Walker's contention that the film revolves around class warfare since the nonaristocratic underling Lieutenant Roget is a clear example of the conniving leadership Kubrick is so avidly condemning. His cowardice is of a different type than that of the two general officers, but he is no less evil than either of them, killing one of his own soldiers and conspiring to hide his crime by perpetuating the injustice of the executions.

In using a hero and villains, Kubrick replicates a key element of the Second World War narrative structure and imposes it on a story that is ostensibly about the First World War. The innovation of the film is that the obvious division of good guys and bad guys is not attached to the opposed battlefield combatants but instead revolves around opposing ranks of the same army. As Walker puts it, "No man's land is not really the great dividing barrier between the two sides in *Paths of Glory*; the 'two sides' actually wear the same uniform, serve the same flag, and hold the same battle line."[17] The disillusionment narrative in its fullest flowering proposed that all of the combatants of the Great War were equivalent victims of the conflict, so the notion of heroes and villains became irrelevant. Neither existed because everyone touched by the war was reduced to the same level. Heroism and villainy are quite beside the point, so to suggest either is irrelevant. The story of *Paths of Glory* not only encourages these categories, it hinges on the existence of both.

The second element of Kubrick's film that markedly differs from the previous World War I narrative develops directly from the structural existence of good and bad within the story. The existence of a hero and a villain indicates a moral imperative that is entirely at odds with the conclusions of the disillusionment narratives. In those stories, the war caused a complete disruption of clear moral categories that could not be reliably repaired. That rupture is the express cause of the suicides seen in such films as *The Lost Squadron* and *The Last Flight* (1931). Since life has become unmoored by the events of the war, previously accepted verities have lost all meaning. *Paths of Glory* does not suggest a clear solution to the problems it presents, but it does present them within a clear moral framework with which the audience is expected to sympathize. The actions of the hero and the villains slip neatly into expected dichotomous categories and the film does not—cannot—move beyond them.

This abandonment of the nihilistic side of the disillusionment narratives is the final element that indicates the extremity of the changes wrought by the Second World War on narratives of the earlier conflict. Kubrick is not interested in the existential conclusion reached by Phillips Holmes in *Broken Lullaby* (1932) that he killed a man for "no reason at all." *Paths of Glory* certainly suggests that war leads to waste and encourages injustice and venality. There is still an explanation for the awfulness that is depicted on-screen: the callous ambition of the generals and the cowardice of lesser officers may be a poor reason for the suffering of the troops, but it *is* a reason.

The post–Second World War narrative of victory precludes the full implications of a war that appeared to have no victor. Because of this fact, Kubrick's film utilizes the generic trappings of the earlier conflict, while ignoring the concerns of the fullest development of the World War I narrative of disillusionment. That *Paths of Glory* remains an oft-cited example of the treatment of the Great War in film, however, indicates that Kubrick's approach was taking the story in a new direction. While he may have been the first filmmaker to utilize these methods, his film initiated a new pattern that would dominate the portrayal of the First World War for the next fifty years.

The passage of time and the dominance of World War II on America's screens pushed the First World War ever further from public favor as a narrative subject. Occasional efforts such as *The Blue Max* (1966), *Darling Lili* (1970), and *Von Richtofen and Brown* (1971) emerged to remind the American audience that World War II had a predecessor, but the narrative of disillusionment did not enjoy a renaissance. Instead, these films drew from the pattern established by Kubrick. The Great War was seen as a brutal conflict, but in

The excitement and heroic adventure indicated by this herald for *The Blue Max* echoes that suggested by the images from *Wings* (chapter 1) and *The Flying Ace* (chapter 4).

each case a hero (or antihero) strove for recognition amid the chaos against a recognizable foe. The pattern received further support from an emphasis on military theaters that offered opportunities for personal accomplishment in situations allowing some degree of adventurous excitement. The world of spies (as in *Darling Lili*) or (especially) tales of reputedly chivalric pilots (as in *The Blue Max* and *Von Richtofen and Brown*) allowed characters to display virtues or vices that emphasized their personal motivations—whether noble or ignoble (more frequently the latter). Their ambitions supplied a clear direction for the narrative, and the achievement of those ambitions provided a reason for the events on-screen.

By the end of the 1960s, the increasing involvement of U.S. troops in the morass of Vietnam theoretically offered ripe conditions for the reemergence of the Great War as a subject for the screen. The conclusions that those earlier films reached about the meaninglessness of military action paralleled the feelings of a large segment of the American public in the Vietnam era. With one exception, however, the opportunity to resurrect the dormant narrative did not come to fruition, but that exception further advanced the repurposing of the First World War on-screen.

Dalton Trumbo's *Johnny Got His Gun* was arguably his most successful literary endeavor. Published in 1939, the novel relates the story of a typical American enlistee, Joe Bonham, whose body is destroyed in the trenches. His limbs, face, and ears are blown off, making him a living piece of flesh without the ability to communicate with the outside world. He reminisces about his life in various flashbacks and then communicates with a sympathetic nurse by tapping out Morse code messages with what remains of his head. His eventual request, which is denied, is that he be allowed to die.

Like Kubrick, Trumbo was using the First World War as a canvas on which to paint his larger message, but unlike Kubrick, Trumbo was born in 1905 and was thus old enough to remember—though not to participate in—the Great War. In his view, the unforgivable sin of the conflict was that it was "the last of the romantic wars," and in his preface to the 1959 edition of his novel, he reminisces about how "World War I began like a summer festival—all billowing skirts and golden epaulets. Millions upon millions cheered from the sidewalks while plumed imperial highnesses, serenities, field marshals and other such fools paraded through the capital cities of Europe at the head of their shining legions."[18] In January 1940, he seemed to see the same popular mood expressing itself in the buildup to the Second World War, and he was unsparing in his condemnation. In an article for *Hollywood Now*, Trumbo rejected "the thesis that this is a war between black and white—between evil and righteousness. To me and to humanity the blood of a German soldier is just as precious as the blood of a Finn, a Russian, a Frenchman, an Englishman or a Pole."[19] This declaration indicates that he had absorbed the arguments put forward on-screen through the disillusionment narrative.

That position was modified as the likelihood of U.S. involvement in the conflict increased. Though he continued to believe that war was a terrible choice, he also acquiesced to his publishers' decision not to reprint his novel, which he feared might be misappropriated by pro-Nazi groups willing to negotiate peace at any cost.[20] As Trumbo later said, "After Pearl Harbor its subject matter seemed as inappropriate to the times as the shriek of bagpipes."[21]

Instead, he continued to work in the studio system as it created the morally unambiguous narrative of the Second World War.

Though Trumbo grudgingly modified his antiwar position in the face of events, the harshly antiwar *Johnny* remained his most important literary achievement. During his tumultuous postwar years on the Hollywood blacklist, he considered several offers for the film and theatrical rights, but his desire to retain creative control over the way his story was translated to the screen contributed to his hesitance in finalizing any deal. In 1963, he worked with Luis Buñuel on a version, but financing could not be arranged.[22] The script that they developed became a top priority for the author, who endured a tortuous series of false starts, fruitless negotiations, and problematic business deals before finally securing financing for his dream project. In July 1970, principal photography commenced, with Trumbo sitting in the director's chair. The resulting film was a financial disaster.[23]

Trumbo had certainly expressed sentiments that placed him squarely on the same page as the filmmakers who created the disillusionment narrative of the early 1930s, and the novel reflects those sentiments. However, rather than simply taking up the mantle of that narrative, the film version of *Johnny Got His Gun*, like *Paths of Glory*, manipulates it for specific ends.

Like Kubrick's film, *Johnny* is superficially set during the Great War. The credit sequence consists of archival images from the era showing military parades, troops moving, and European and American politicians (such as Teddy Roosevelt and Woodrow Wilson) exhorting crowds. Most of the film, however, takes place in hospital facilities, with only a brief flashback to the trenches to describe the circumstances under which Joe (Timothy Bottoms) is initially wounded. Other flashbacks detail Joe's prewar life, while dream sequences relate conversations Joe has with Christ (played by Donald Sutherland). Throughout, Trumbo is completely uninterested in the specifics of the war itself. Instead, he poses larger philosophical (rather than historical) questions about the nature of warfare. The character of Joe contains autobiographical elements but is also an intellectual exercise in the nature of life itself. Does this twisted remnant of a human being continue to have value? How can any society justify an activity that reduces a person to this state? What is he owed by the society that tolerates such activities? How could any individual deal with a reality so terrible? These questions directly echo the narrative of disillusionment, but Trumbo has gone even further than Kubrick by reducing the historical context to a near nullity.

This maneuver redefines the First World War in film yet again. Like the creators of the fully developed disillusionment narrative, Trumbo universalizes the experience of combat. Joe's situation could be the fate of any combatant in any war, and the relevant philosophical questions would be the same. The film functions as a lament for those who suffer and die as a result of armed conflict. At the same time, Trumbo offers a reason for the suffering that is the film's central theme. Building on Kubrick's approach, Trumbo lays clear blame for Joe's situation, accusing both the doctors who keep Joe alive (in the naive confidence that his brain is incapable of more than the barest function) and the generals who lead the military of which Joe is now a broken fragment. This is made explicit during the scene in which Joe finally breaks through to an inspection party of high-ranking military men. Their horror at the situation is quickly subsumed by military priorities—especially the need to keep Joe's existence a secret. The officer in command castigates the lead medical officer for his hubris but also orders everyone present to maintain absolute silence regarding what they have seen. When he asks a priest to offer some words of comfort to the wounded man, the priest responds, "I'll pray for him for the rest of my days, but I will not risk testing his faith against your stupidity.... He's the product of your profession, not mine." There *is* a reason for Joe's suffering, and he stands before the broken body. Trumbo goes even further in the next scene, when the general prevents the sympathetic nurse from ending Joe's misery by cutting off his breathing tube. Joe's needless suffering will continue for the same reason that it began—because of the willful stupidity of men.

The message that war is terrible is clear enough in both *Paths of Glory* and *Johnny Got His Gun*. The most important aspect of both films, however, is that neither Kubrick nor Trumbo argues their "universal" verities about the nature of war by setting their films in the Second World War. In both cases, to make those arguments would be problematic, given the reputation of the latter conflict as a righteously fought "good war." This constitutes the most important key to the later evolution of the view of the First World War onscreen. The problematic outcomes of the Great War made it weak competition for its victorious sequel in popular media but allowed the earlier conflict to become a focus for the displacement of negative attitudes about war in the face of American post–World War II triumphalism. Yes, these films seem to say, war can be terrible—especially the dubiously fought trench warfare of the late 1910s. Bad generals and ambitious men kept victory from being truly won until the next generation—the "greatest generation"—could bring its moral power to bear in making the world truly safe for an American-style world order.

As Trumbo commented in 1959, "*Johnny* held a different meaning for three different wars"—the two world wars and the Korean conflict.[24] The film version, released during the Vietnam era, added a fourth war, but films set during the First World War again fell out of favor. The conflict in Vietnam provided a new set of tropes and a new set of ideas about warfare as well as initiating a struggle between two types of narrative. In some cases (*Coming Home* [1979], *The Deer Hunter* [1978], *Apocalypse Now* [1979]), those ideas suggested a new version of the disillusionment narratives, but at other times (*First Blood* [1982], *Uncommon Valor* [1983], *Missing in Action* [1984]), trends seemed to favor stories that reflected post–World War II triumphalism. In either case, the bitter politics of the contemporary conflict made the older war seem that much more out of date, so only a scant few American films addressed the conflict over the following decades. And when they did so, it was for purposes quite outside the goal of understanding the nature of the conflict. Instead, the war became shorthand for a hopelessly tragic situation, a stage on which an individual character might redeem violence and stupidity by achieving some measure of personal fulfillment. The most prominent examples of this approach are Tony Bill's *Flyboys* (2006) and Steven Spielberg's *War Horse* (2011).

By the time of their production, almost ninety years after the events they depict, almost no Great War veterans survived to be troubled by the films' historical inaccuracies and problematic romanticizing of the conflict. In both cases, there are clear heroes and villains in the Kubrick vein, combined with a touch of the Trumbo pessimism about war in general. There is also a heroic/romantic view of the conflict that is at odds with the films made by World War I veterans reflecting on their wartime experiences.

Flyboys is the story of American volunteer pilots flying for France, but the plot includes an amalgamation of anecdotes from both the Lafayette Escadrille and the Lafayette Flying Corps (Wellman's unit). The main focus is on the fictional Blaine Rawlings (played by James Franco), whose heroism and daring are portrayed with a minimum of nuance. Though war may be terrible, Rawlings nevertheless engages in romance, and the deaths of his fellow pilots goad him into further heroics rather than introspection.

War Horse is similarly problematic, melodramatically showing the "horrors of war" through the eyes of a horse drafted into the service. Any depiction of the war as an event or any attendant consideration of its effect on the characters is deeply compromised by the director's conception of the story (previously a novel and stage play) cited in a 2011 article in *The Atlantic*. Spielberg is quoted as having said, "I didn't pay a lot of attention to the First World War. I didn't know very much about it. And I also don't consider *War Horse* to be a war movie. . . . This is much more of a real story between the connections that sometimes animals achieve, the way animals can actually connect people together."[25] Once again, the war itself receives short shrift and largely serves as a convenient backdrop for other purposes—in this case, shorthand for a tragic situation that sweeps up characters on both sides—including the titular equine—who then suffer and redeem themselves.

The passage of time surely oversimplifies any historical moment, but by 2011, films dealing with the Great War had moved far from their origins more than ninety years earlier. The arc from *The Cradle of Courage* to *War Horse* was long, and depictions of the conflict had moved from the nihilistic response of dispirited veterans to moral arguments about class and ambition and finally to a trope-filled backdrop for battlefield heroics. The most recent attempt to explain the inexplicable suffering and despair—to finally find a reason for it all—would probably befuddle those who had originally tried to make sense of the conflict. They could never suspect that the most successful filmic version of their war would feature a heroine from a hidden island facing off against the god of war himself.

Wonder Woman's journey to the screen was fraught with decades of hardships and false starts, but her successful 2017 filmic debut seems to have justified all of the trouble. As a superhero movie headlined by a female heroine and directed by a woman, the film has been hailed for breaking new ground on several fronts. One of its more interesting facets, however, has gone largely unmentioned. Though Wonder Woman the comic book character appeared during the Second World War, the story of Wonder Woman the film character is set during the First World War. This change is rooted in a variety of considerations but ultimately continued the evolutionary arc of the Great War on film.

On a practical level, the change resulted from the trends that finally brought Wonder Woman to the screen. The overwhelming box-office dominance of superhero blockbusters beginning with *Batman Begins* in 2005 and *Iron Man* in 2008 led multiple "universes" of comic book legends to make the jump to the big screen. Among the ranks of these characters, several predate World War II (Superman, Batman), and several date to the Second World War itself (Captain America, Wonder Woman). While all four of these characters fought both Nazi and Japanese adversaries during the early 1940s, the identities of Captain America and Wonder Woman are intimately connected to their roots in the conflict. The superhuman powers of Captain America result from an attempt to perfect a serum that will create an Allied army of supersoldiers, while Wonder Woman was sent to the United States as part of a divine commission from the goddesses Aphrodite and Athena to assist the Allied cause. Speaking to Wonder Woman's mother, Queen Hippolyte,

Aphrodite declares, "Danger again threatens the entire world," instructing that Steve Trevor, a wounded American spy who has crash-landed on Paradise Island, must be delivered "back to America—to help fight the forces of hate and oppression." Athena is even more strident: "American Liberty and Freedom must be preserved! You must send with him your strongest and wisest Amazon—the finest of your wonder women—for America, the last citadel of democracy, and of equal rights for women, needs your help!"[26] While this is straightforward enough as a superhero origin story, the filmmakers were presented with a practical problem: Captain America beat them to the punch. With the success of *Captain America: The First Avenger* (2011), the Second World War had become the province of a different red, white, and blue superhero fighting to defend American ideals. It made sense to alter the Wonder Woman origin story to further distinguish her from the competition. The mechanics of that change, however, set up an interesting narrative situation.

In an interview in *Entertainment Weekly*, director Patty Jenkins said that she initially questioned the change of setting "because it wasn't her actual origin story, but very quickly I saw the genius behind it." She continued, "World War I is the first time that civilization as we know it was finding its roots, but it's not something that we really know the history of. . . . Even the way that it was unclear who was in the right of WWI is a really interesting parallel to this time. Then you take a god with a moral compass and a moral belief system, and you drop them into this world, there are questions about women's rights, about a mechanized war where you don't see who you are killing. It's such a cool time."[27]

The notion that "it's not something that we really know the history of" provides latitude to the filmmakers, freeing them from a variety of factual constraints. Enough time has passed since the conflict that the insertion of an Amazonian superhero on the battlefield is not seen as a problematic violation of history. The passage of time (and concurrent increase of forgetful ignorance) decreases the odds that any offense will be taken by the grafting on of fictional elements.

This assurance, in turn, allows the filmmakers to take Kubrick's approach to new levels. The war can now be made a pure allegory for whatever arguments the screenwriters and director may care to impose, since the specifics of the war are no longer relevant. Jenkins presents two possible topics for further exploration when she states that "there are questions about women's rights, about a mechanized war where you don't see who you are killing." The film does not grapple with either of these issues in any meaningful way, but it is not interested in doing so. More important is the notion that the narrative could extend in many directions, not all of which would relate to the originally central question of understanding the core nature of the conflict.

Though Jenkins has set her film during the First World War, she is approaching the story from a post–World War II perspective. The film bears out the validity of Wonder Woman's moral beliefs while specifically indicating which side is right and which side is wrong. The German General Ludendorff is purely evil, while Steve Trevor introduces himself to Wonder Woman as "one of the good guys." It also posits a clear explanation for the carnage in the form of the scheming God of War, Ares. Once Wonder Woman accomplishes her overarching mission to defeat her fellow immortal, the madness of war will stop, since it is Ares who leads humanity into such chaos. Though Wonder Woman achieves a moral breakthrough during her final struggle ("I glimpsed the darkness that lives within their light and learned that inside every one of them there will always be both. A choice each must make for themselves. Something no hero will ever defeat. And now I know that only love can truly save the world"), the platitudes she expresses would be of little comfort to those who had experienced the war. Generally speaking, moral complexity is not the bailiwick of a superhero, and despite an occasional feint in that direction, Jenkins does not credibly complicate the film's outlook. Right and wrong are clear, and although choices must be made, good may still triumph in the end.

The paltriness of this conclusion is especially reinforced by Jenkins's characterization of the Great War as "cool." The casualness of the claim is not entirely the fault of the director of a superhero movie. The passage of time encourages the processing and reprocessing of history in various ways, and the inescapable truth is that events pass from living memory into the realm of storytelling. The workings of that process are critical, however.

The version of the Great War that exists in current films bears little relation to what appeared on America's screens in the late 1910s. Even less does it grapple with the heartbreaking search for meaning initiated by veterans who sought to explore their ambivalence about the war through their literary and filmic endeavors. The failure to secure a clear victory, the devastations of the Great Depression, and the all-consuming nature of the Second World War have mostly swept the earlier conflict from sight, and it has now passed from living memory to narrative resource. Positioned as a counterpoint to its morally clear successor, World War I now offers generic notions of chaos without meaning, lives disrupted, and overwhelming sadness. In that sense, perhaps the narratives of the Great War have simply settled into the memory of most other wars, which, in the eyes of generations to come, are fought for no reason at all.

CONCLUSION

IN A 1973 INTERVIEW WITH CRITIC GENE SISKEL, FRANÇOIS TRUFFAUT famously asserted that "some films claim to be antiwar, but I don't think I've really seen an antiwar film. Every film about war ends up being pro-war."[1] Though that notion certainly applies to the vast majority of war-related films made over the past century, the films discussed in this book offer a strong counterargument. Given the astuteness of his critical skills, it is tempting to wonder if Truffaut might have modified his sentiment if he had seen all of these films. Until very recently, most of this material was extremely difficult to access, and the silent films fell into obscurity with the dawn of sound technology. (More than one scholar has lamented years spent seeking out obscure titles only to have seen them suddenly become available at the click of a button.) In addition, the World War I films are made even more problematic by their historical position. Stories of the conflict were quickly pushed aside by the tumult of the 1930s, the patriotic requirements of the 1940s, and the victorious postwar narratives that continue to recur on a regular basis. Unlike D. W. Griffith listening to tales of Civil War heroics at his father's knee or countless baby boomers fascinated by their parents' experiences and exploits, the generation of soldiers' sons and daughters that was best positioned to perpetuate a historical narrative of the first conflict was understandably more preoccupied with its sequel.

In her *Remembering World War I in America*, Kimberly J. Lamay Licursi contends that "the war was lost to collective memory because the interwar generation never established a 'collected memory' of the war."[2] On film, it is more accurate to argue that the problem is not a failure to reach an agreed narrative regarding the memory of the war but rather the massive inconvenience of that narrative in historical context. The adoption of the Production Code just as a consensus regarding the depiction of the war was reached tempered depictions of violence and challenges to established authority that were key components of the new narrative. At the same time, Hollywood's concern with avoiding the antagonization of foreign markets and the stridently antiwar sentiments of that narrative made it problematic in a world grappling with the rise of militaristic powers. The easiest (and perhaps most prudent) path was to put the subject aside.

It is, however, not entirely accurate to say that the First World War completely disappeared from public discourse, though its rhetorical use was constrained in the post–World War II era. As a conflict emblematic of the horrors of war, the Great War became a useful—if occasional—counter to the mythos of American military success. Though the problematic military outcomes and broad social fracturing caused by the war in Vietnam could conceivably have led to a reemergence of the Great War as a subject, history again took a hand in preventing on-screen comparisons. The collapse of the studio system, combined with the politically fraught nature of the topic, kept filmmakers from drawing parallels between an active military conflict and a war that had become shorthand for pointless combat, as seen in the exception that proves the rule, *Johnny Got His Gun*.

With the more recent U.S. involvement in extended conflicts overseas, ideas first explored in the films of the Great War have once again become part of the general conversation. Post-traumatic stress, emotional displacement from home and loved ones, and difficulty readjusting to civilian life are concerns that are familiar to veterans of any war. The notion that military results may be of questionable value, however, resonates especially strongly with the American public after nearly two decades of conflict in Asia and the Middle East. It is in fact quite striking to see the parallels between the ideas and issues discussed in these pages and concerns that are otherwise considered quite contemporary.

The shadow of the Civil War shaped initial attitudes and perspectives regarding involvement in the "war to end all wars." Young men of the early twentieth century were nurtured on gallant stories of the Civil War told by their fathers and grandfathers, and that tradition resonated across the screen via a narrative promoted by filmmakers such as D. W. Griffith, a proud soldier's son. In the early twenty-first century, the recruits who set off for Afghanistan and Iraq after 9/11 were nurtured on similarly heroic stories of World War II told not just by their forebears but also through on-screen narratives. Films and television shows such as *Saving Private Ryan* (1998) and *Band of Brothers* (2001) may be more bluntly brutal about the violence of combat, but both portray war as a challenging but morally uplifting experience. Though not as consciously didactic as their century-old predecessor, nothing in them contradicts the lessons learned by William S. Hart in *Cradle of Courage* (1920).

While short theatrical subjects are no longer a proving ground for new narrative ideas, television has stepped in to take their place. Instead of short comedies and cartoons, hours of documentary content on the Military Channel, the History Channel, and many others of their ilk have increased the acceptance of combat images in spectators' living rooms while encouraging the pursuit of "realism" in competing fictional narratives. Thanks to digital technologies, audiences can experience the violence of war through video games and re-creations that would have astonished the technicians of a century ago. The addition of sound technology forever altered the portrayal of the battlefield on-screen, but filmmakers continue to strive for innovations that will pull us into a combat experience from the safety of our own homes.

In some ways, we have retreated from the complexities of the World War I narratives. Though African Americans no longer serve in segregated units, they are perhaps at a filmic disadvantage compared to their earlier counterparts. Constant concerns about minority representation in popular media are somewhat tempered by the inescapable reality of Black soldiers in modern battlefield depictions. Ironically, however, the on-screen acknowledgment of a desegregated military does not compensate for the lack of representation behind the camera. The existence, no matter how tenuous, of a separate race film industry in the 1910s, 1920s, and 1930s provided at least the hope of a narrative that addressed the concerns and experiences of Black servicemen from a racially conscious perspective. The modern lack of such an industry makes the portrayal of minority concerns that much more difficult.

Similarly, though the number of films portraying the First World War from the perspectives of female protagonists may be limited, it is difficult to argue that significant progress has been made in bringing that perspective to more recent screen narratives. Though women play a more active military role than ever before, films about the military experience continue to skew heavily male. Recent filmmaking has not produced a narrative experiment as radical as *The Mad Parade* in its depiction of women on the battlefield.

In a 2002 article in *Cineaste* magazine, historian Thomas Doherty, discussing how the film industry might deal with the events of September 11, 2001, suggested that "a moral clarity heretofore the exclusive province of World War II will likely guide the sensibility of the cycle of the future while the built-in elements of high drama will provide a plethora of pre-tested plotlines."[3] While films such as Oliver Stone's *World Trade Center* (2006) might seem to fulfill that prediction, films about the ensuing military actions complicate the suggestion that 9/11 will encourage a new moral clarity. In many respects, *Home of the Brave* (2006), *In the Valley of Elah* (2007), *The Hurt Locker* (2008), and *The Messenger* (2009) reflect attitudes that would be entirely familiar to veterans of the First World War. Servicemen (and -women) worn down by the endless grind of a brutal conflict, questioning the ultimate usefulness of their sacrifices, and having trouble readjusting to life upon their return—all of these have been seen before. The films that most bluntly wrestle with those experiences remain those created between 1918 and 1934. Though they are now mostly forgotten and the Great War itself is pushed to the far reaches of public awareness, it is important to consider the ways in which the generation who fought in that conflict reflected on their experiences. The narrative they subsequently developed has now been reduced to a trope, but the evolution of that narrative demonstrates the ways that popular culture continually shapes our versions of the past and may shape our history in the future.

NOTES

INTRODUCTION

1. Library of Congress, "Frank Woodruff Buckles."
2. Associated Press. "Last American WWI Vet"; "D.C. War Memorial Controversy."
3. The National WWI Memorial in Washington, D.C. was opened to the public on April 17, 2021. In what might be seen as a reflection of the Great War's perceived importance, the memorial is located in Pershing Square Park and is not directly situated on the National Mall.
4. Goldstein, "Frank Buckles."
5. Katz, "Here's How ABC, NBC and CBS Are Covering the 75th Anniversary."
6. Auster, "Saving Private Ryan," , 212.
7. Creel, *How We Advertised America*, 117.
8. Brookman, *Helios*, 47–49, 63–67.
9. Fussell, *Great War*, 4.
10. Mosse, *Fallen Soldiers*, 6.
11. Jay Winter, *Sites of Memory*, 5.
12. Fussell, *Great War*, 158.
13. Mosse, *Fallen Soldiers*, 147.
14. Jay Winter, *Sites of Memory*, 142–43.
15. Jay Winter, *Remembering War*, 183.
16. Tudor, "Genre," 3.

CHAPTER ONE: THE CRADLE OF COURAGE: WARFARE IN AMERICAN FILM IN THE 1910S AND 1920S

1. Albert Smith with Koury, *Two Reels and a Crank*, 53.
2. Albert Smith with Koury, *Two Reels and a Crank*, 55–56.
3. Slide with Gevinson, *Big V* 35–36, suggests grounds for doubt regarding Smith's veracity regarding these adventures, but, as Slide points out, there is some inconclusive evidence that does support his claims. W. K. L. Dickson's *The Biograph in Battle* recounts the Boer War adventures of another film pioneer.
4. Strebel, "Imperialist Iconography"; Clarke, "'Wheelbarrows' and 'Real Soldiers'"; Bottomore, "Filming, Faking and Propaganda."

5. See, for example, McPherson, "Long-Legged Yankee Lies."
6. Logue, *To Appomattox and Beyond*, 131–32.
7. McPherson, "Long-Legged Yankee Lies," 75.
8. Wilson, *Patriotic Gore*, ix.
9. Crane, *Red Badge of Courage*, 109.
10. Hayden White, *Content of the Form*, 20.
11. Hayden White, *Content of the Form*, 21.
12. Though the "moral" of Henry's maturation in the course of the novel is sometimes questioned, a reading of Crane's later short story "The Veteran" provides further support for this interpretation. In the story, Henry, now a grandfather, admits his fear to his grandson while relating tales of his youth. He also dies while performing an act of bravery to which he commits without hesitation. The tone and the narrative of the story suggest that Crane viewed the war as a growth experience for the character.
13. Griffith, *Man Who Invented Hollywood*, 26.
14. Schickel, *D. W. Griffith*, 17–23.
15. Griffith, *Man Who Invented Hollywood*, 27.
16. Griffith, *Man Who Invented Hollywood*, 23.
17. Griffith, *Man Who Invented Hollywood*, 26.
18. In 1910, Griffith essentially directed more films on the Civil War than any other individual or than were produced by any other company. The sole exception is Sidney Olcott and the Kalem Company, which produced the serial *The Adventures of Nan the Girl Spy*. Most of these films are lost, though the plot summaries suggest that the Civil War provided a convenient starting point for the adventures of the heroine without (as in many other contemporary serials) dwelling on particular intricacies of plot development.
19. Ehrlich, "Civil War in Early Film."
20. Simmon, *Films of D. W. Griffith*, 104–36.
21. Taves, *Thomas Ince*, 1–11.
22. Slide, *Early American Cinema*, 79, places Ince's refinements in appropriate perspective.
23. The most insightful assessment of Hart and his career remains Kozarski, *Complete Films*. Also see Hart's autobiography, *My Life East and West*.
24. Tuska, *Filming of the West*, 151.
25. Kennedy, *Over Here*, 158, points out that the military struggled with this idea in practice but that it was a primary argument of those in favor of universal military training, who "saw military service as a means, at last, to effect 'Americanization.'"
26. Gunning, "The House with Closed Shutters," 141, provides the production dates. Gunning is fulsome in his praise of the film, calling it Griffith's "most complex Biograph Civil War film" (143), deserving of "an acknowledged place in film history" (146).
27. Simmon, *Films of D. W. Griffith*, 120.
28. Gunning, *D. W. Griffith*.
29. This clear perspective is similar to John Huston's simplification of battlefield confusion in his *Battle of San Pietro*, in which shots were printed in such a way that troops always attacked in the same direction (from right to left). Such techniques clarify the confusions of the battlefield for the audience and (in the case of Griffith) provide a consistent visual approach to narrative concerns.

30. Abel, *Americanizing the Movies*, 146–47.
31. Abel, *Americanizing the Movies*, 146.
32. Abel, *Americanizing the Movies*, 147
33. Abel, *Americanizing the Movies*, 165
34. John Ford included a similar scene in *The Horse Soldiers*, though Ford plays the sequence of children at war more as comic relief than as any sort of comment on the maturing effects of wartime experience.
35. In 1913, Ince also made the now-lost five-reel *The Battle of Gettysburg*.
36. Benbow, "Birth of a Quotation."
37. In a November 17, 1999, post to the usenet forum alt.movies.silent (https://groups.google.com/forum/#!topic/alt.movies.silent/fMLAZSPOz8I), historian Robert Birchard addresses the condition of the surviving print of *Civilization*, which was reedited and retitled for a 1930 rerelease. As Birchard suggests, the exact relation of the surviving material to the original is an open question.
38. Johnson, "Shadow Stage," 137.
39. Frederick James Smith in Slide, *Selected Film Criticism, 1912–1920*, 113; *Life*, April 18, 1918, in Slide, *Selected Film Criticism, 1912–1920*, 115.
40. *Life*, April 18, 1918, in Slide, *Selected Film Criticism, 1912–1920*, 115.
41. Johnson, "Hearts of the World," 48.
42. "Army Can Hook in with Bill Hart" 340.
43. "Army Can Hook in with Bill Hart" 340.
44. Slater, "June Mathis's Valentino Scripts," 106.
45. Studlar, *This Mad Masquerade*, 166–67.
46. Studlar, *This Mad Masquerade*, 169.
47. While applauding Slater's insistence on the importance of examining the scripts for Valentino's films and his assertion that Mathis played a key role in defining the actor's public persona, I disagree with the suggestion that the Terry character's influence in *Four Horsemen* extends beyond providing an impetus for Julio to enlist. The real redemption of his character occurs in the trenches without her involvement.
48. The use of a dog as hero is perhaps less remarkable than it might appear given the notable popularity of the real life dog hero Sgt. Stubby, whose taxidermied remains are on display in the Smithsonian's Museum of American History and who was the main character in an animated film released in 2018.
49. Souvenir book, Paramount Lasky Corporation, 1927, 2, in possession of the author.

CHAPTER TWO: COMBAT, LITERATURE, AND FILM: COMBAT VETERANS AND THE PRODUCTION OF NARRATIVES OF WARTIME SERVICE, 1925–1930

1. Gandal, *Gun and the Pen*, 5.
2. Stallings befriended Hemingway in the early 1930s and mounted a stage production of *A Farewell to Arms* in 1930. Stallings also befriended Faulkner, and Brittain suggests in *Laurence Stallings*, 42–43, that Faulkner's *Sartoris* is directly modeled on *Plumes*.
3. Brittain, *Laurence Stallings*, 17–23.

4. Stallings, *Plumes*, 241–42.
5. Stallings, *Plumes*, 243–45.
6. Ludington, *John Dos Passos*, 114–64.
7. Vidor, *Tree Is a Tree*, 111.
8. Simmon and Durgnat, *King Vidor*, 62.
9. Vidor, *Tree Is a Tree*, 111–12.
10. Simmon and Durgnat, *King Vidor*, 63.
11. Vidor, *Tree Is a Tree*, 112.
12. Vidor, *Tree Is a Tree*, 111–14.
13. "The Shadow Stage: The Big Parade," 46.
14. Robert Sherwood in *Life*, December 10, 1925, 24–25, reprinted in Slide, *Selected Film Criticism, 1921–1930*, 38.
15. "Watch Details for Perfection," 2.
16. Souvenir book, Gordon Press, New York, 1925, 10, in possession of the author.
17. Souvenir book, Gordon Press, New York, 1925, 2.
18. Dowd and Shepard, *King Vidor*, 150, 58.
19. Souvenir program, *The Play—The Picture*, 1926, 4, in possession of the author.
20. Brittain, *Laurence Stallings*, 45.
21. Anderson and Stallings, "What Price Glory?" 27.
22. Brittain, *Laurence Stallings*, 45.
23. Fussell, *Great War*, 32.
24. Anderson and Stallings, "What Price Glory?" 42.
25. Anderson and Stallings, "What Price Glory?" 59–60.
26. Jacobs, *Decline of Sentiment*, 133.
27. Jacobs, *Decline of Sentiment*, 137.
28. Jacobs, *Decline of Sentiment*, 155.
29. Robert Sherwood in *Life*, December 10, 1925, 24–25, reprinted in Slide, *Selected Film Criticism, 1921–1930*, 38.
30. Jacobs, *Decline of Sentiment*, 131, 157.
31. Curtis, *James Whale*, 14–20.
32. Sherriff, "Journey's End," 667.
33. Curtis, *James Whale*, 53.
34. Curtis, *James Whale*, 54.
35. Curtis, *James Whale*, 59.
36. In his *The Girl Who Stayed at Home* (1919), D. W. Griffith directly addressed the "problem" of such women in the heyday of his employment of the traditional narrative. Unlike the unrepentant Harlow, his sexually imperiled female realizes the error of her ways in the nick of time, preserving her virtue for the sake of her enlisted beau. See chapter 5.
37. Sherriff, "Journey's End," 640.
38. James Shelley Hamilton in *Cinema* 1, no. 5 (June 1930): 38, in Slide, *Selected Film Criticism, 1921–1930*, 151.
39. Curtis, *James Whale*, 96, states that both of these devices were used in an initial version of the screenplay but were rejected wholesale by Whale.

40. This is especially apparent in act 1, scene 1, as Hardy hands over command of the dugout to Osborne. See especially Sherriff, "Journey's End," 595–97.

41. A good example is the elimination of the pre-trench-raid discussion between Raleigh and Osborne of the ruins of a Roman road in Sussex in act 3, scene 1 (Sherriff, "Journey's End," 648).

42. Thompson, *William Wellman*, 13.

43. Thompson, *William Wellman*, 15.

44. McCarthy, *Howard Hawks*, 359.

45. Thompson, *William Wellman*, 4.

46. Though Saunders enlisted during the war, he served as a flight instructor in Florida and was never posted overseas. After the war, he wrote scripts or stories for a large number of films dealing with the war, including *Wings*, *Legion of the Condemned*, *The Dawn Patrol*, and *The Last Flight*.

47. Thompson, *William Wellman*, 76.

48. Hall, "Warriors of the Clouds," 26.

49. Ball and Saunders, *Legion of the Condemned*, 32.

50. Ball and Saunders, *Legion of the Condemned*, 91.

51. Ball and Saunders, *Legion of the Condemned*, 94, 93.

52. Ball and Saunders, *Legion of the Condemned*, 120, 124.

53. Thompson, *William Wellman*, 75.

54. Hall, "Warriors of the Clouds," 26.

55. William Wellman, *Go Get 'Em!* 130.

56. William Wellman, *Go Get 'Em!* 187.

57. William Wellman, *Go Get 'Em!* 182.

58. Ball and Saunders, *Legion of the Condemned*, 153.

59. William Wellman Jr., *Man and His Wings*, 43–44.

60. Gerblinger, "James Whale's Frankensteins."

61. Kelly, "Greatness and Continuing Significance," 23.

CHAPTER THREE: COMEDIES, CARTOONS, AND CARNAGE: WORLD WAR I IN AMERICAN COMIC SHORT FILMS

1. Fussell, *Great War*, 8.

2. Fussell, *Great War*, 30.

3. In *Colonel Heeza Liar at the Front*, *Colonel Heeza Liar in the Trenches*, and *Colonel Heeza Liar and the Zeppelin*.

4. In *Mutt and Jeff in the Outposts*, *Mutt and Jeff in the Trenches*, *Mutt and Jeff in the Submarine*, *Bobby Bumps Volunteers*, *Bobby Bumps' Tank*, and *Bobby Bumps' Submarine Chaser*.

5. For brief summaries of these films, see Campbell, *Reel America and World War I*; Lloyd, *Harold Lloyd Encyclopedia*.

6. Robinson, *Chaplin*, 185–88.

7. The film *The Bond* was donated to the government as Chaplin's contribution to the series of Liberty Loan shorts.

8. Robinson, *Chaplin*, 244.

9. These sequences have survived and may be viewed on home video releases of *The Chaplin Revue*.

10. Canemaker, *Felix*, 48.

11. Crafton, *Before Mickey*, 346.

12. Gabler, *Walt Disney*, 35–42.

13. Merritt and Kaufman, *Walt in Wonderland*, 63.

14. Merritt and Kaufman, *Walt in Wonderland*, 14.

15. Merritt and Kaufman, *Walt in Wonderland*, 15.

16. Crafton, *Before Mickey*, 292.

17. Merritt and Kaufman, *Walt in Wonderland*, 22.

18. *Alice's Little Parade* includes a similar gag, though in that film the pieces of the shattered Julius are reassembled as if he is a jigsaw puzzle. In addition, the hospital contains an entire shelf of "spare parts" that are used to replace a few missing pieces of the reconstituted cat.

19. Langdon used an arguably even more graphic gag in his *Soldier Man* (1926), in which he believes that a cow has swallowed dynamite that then detonates, showering him with raw meat. (The meat is actually from a butcher's basket blown into the air by the errant explosive.) Langdon's reputation as an overgrown infant is quickly dispelled by a viewing of his films, but the violence of these gags make them a key exhibit in the argument that his humor should be reassessed.

20. Watz, *Wheeler and Woolsey*, 100.

21. Watz, *Wheeler and Woolsey*, 95–96.

22. Watz, *Wheeler and Woolsey*, 101.

23. Prince, *Classical Film Violence*, 251.

24. Both men left Disney when Oswald was taken away from his creator. For further details, see Gabler, *Walt Disney*, 100–109.

25. Chion, *Film*, 38.

26. Chion, *Film*, 40.

27. Chion, *Film*, 42.

28. Bottomore, "Story of Percy Peashaker," 140.

29. Chion, *Film*, 46.

30. Barrios, *Song in the Dark*, 4.

31. According the American Film Institute Catalog, *Doughboys* was released almost simultaneously with *All Quiet on the Western Front* (August 30, 1930, and August 24, 1930, respectively).

32. Crafton, *Talkies*, 322.

33. Barrios, *Song in the Dark*, 272.

34. *They Gave Him a Gun* provides yet another (perhaps less direct) example of such influence in its opening credits, which explode across the screen as an artillery piece turns to fire directly at the audience. The sequence is notably similar to the opening of *Bosko the Doughboy*.

CHAPTER FOUR: RACE FILM AND THE DEPICTION OF AFRICAN AMERICAN MILITARY SERVICE, 1918–1939

1. Butters, *Black Manhood*, xvii.
2. Gaines, *Fire and Desire*, 128.
3. Cripps, *Slow Fade to Black*, 30, 33.
4. Cripps, *Slow Fade to Black*, 52–53.
5. Sampson, *Blacks in Black and White*, 531.
6. Cripps, *Slow Fade to Black*, 75.
7. Butters, *Black Manhood*, 114–15.
8. Butters, *Black Manhood*, 114.
9. Gaines, *Fire and Desire*, 109.
10. Farwell, *Over There*, 148.
11. Barbeau and Henri, *Unknown Soldiers*, 27–32.
12. Walter Francis White, *Man Called White*, 36.
13. Bradford, "Save," 7.
14. Keene, *Doughboys*, 83.
15. Keene, *Doughboys*, 84.
16. Wolgemuth, "Woodrow Wilson and Federal Segregation."
17. Scott, *Scott's Official History*, 40.
18. Wood, *Film and Propaganda*, 202–3. Typographical errors in the document have been silently corrected.
19. Wood, *Film and Propaganda*, 205–6.
20. Wood, *Film and Propaganda*, 212.
21. Cripps, *Slow Fade to Black*, 82.
22. Logan and Winston, *Dictionary of American Negro Biography*, 188–89.
23. Butters attributes the delay to "the logistical problem of acquiring footage of black soldiers from overseas and the necessity of cooperation with the U.S. War Department," though both of those conditions would have obtained for white filmmakers as well (*Black Manhood*, 100).
24. Sampson, *Blacks in Black and White*, 190; Pearl Bowser and Spence, *Writing Himself into History*, 239. The authors cite three trade papers and suggest that the descriptions are identical in all sources, positing that the source is a company press release.
25. Lester Walton in *New York Age*, May 5, 1920, in Sampson, *Blacks in Black and White*, 251.
26. Pearl Bowser and Spence, *Writing Himself into History*, 112.
27. Thomas Winter, "Training of Colored Troops," suggests that *Our Colored Fighters* and *Training of Colored Troops* may, in fact, be the same film. In the absence of compelling evidence one way or the other, I have elected to treat them as separate works.
28. Butters, *Black Manhood*, 102–3.
29. Thomas Winter, "Training of Colored Troops," 20.
30. Sampson, *Blacks in Black and White*, 132–36, reprints the minutes of the board of directors meeting at which Noble resigned. The reasons for his resignation remain cloudy, but the theory regarding his work at Universal remains the leading contender as an explanation.
31. Sampson, *Blacks in Black and White*, 140–41.

32. Barbeau and Henri, *Unknown Soldiers*, 43–44.
33. Barbeau and Henri, *Unknown Soldiers*, 113.
34. Barbeau and Henri, *Unknown Soldiers*, 174.
35. Du Bois, "Black Man," 222.
36. Du Bois, "Black Man," 223.
37. Cripps, *Slow Fade to Black*, 137–38.
38. Wagenknecht and Slide, *Films of D. W. Griffith*, 109–10.
39. Schickel, *D. W. Griffith*, 384.
40. Frederick James Smith, "Celluloid Critic," 45.
41. "The Screen," 9.
42. Campbell, *Reel America and World War I*, 75, 129.
43. Sampson, *Blacks in Black and White*, 256.
44. "Loyal Hearts," 3.
45. Unidentified Los Angeles newspaper, August 5, 1919, quoted in Sampson, *Blacks in Black and White*, 256.
46. "Loyal Hearts," 3; *Los Angeles Leader*, August 5, 1919, quoted in Sampson, *Blacks in Black and White*, 256–57.
47. Sampson, *Blacks in Black and White*, 217.
48. Klotman, "Planes, Trains, and Automobiles," 161.
49. Lupack, *Richard E. Norman*, 166.
50. Klotman, "Planes, Trains, and Automobiles," 161–66.
51. Gaines, *Fire and Desire*, 122–23.
52. Lupack, *Literary Adaptations*, 67–160.
53. Jackson, "Secret Life of Oscar Micheaux," 219.
54. Taylor, "Oscar Micheaux," 134.
55. Sampson, *Blacks in Black and White*, 149–50, 157; Lupack, *Literary Adaptations*, 139.
56. This is a direct transcription from the Library of Congress restoration intertitles.
57. Thomas, "Motion Picture News," 6A; "At the Lafayette Theatre," 6.
58. Pearl Bowser, Gaines, and Musser, *Oscar Micheaux and His Circle*, 250.
59. J. A. Jackson in *Billboard*, January 26, 1924, in Sampson, *Blacks in Black and White*, 285.
60. In fact, Lupelta is the child of a Black man who is passing, but that information is known only to the reader, not to the relevant principals. Given Micheaux's general tendencies with regard to the topics of miscegenation and passing, we might assume that the couple end up together, but there is no clear evidence. A *Pittsburgh Courier* review ("Daughter of the Congo," A7) refers to Lupelta as a mulatto but otherwise does nothing to clarify the conclusion of the film. A successful union for the couple might be interpreted as an appropriate reward for Dale's dedicated service, so the lack of a print is doubly frustrating.
61. Regester, "African-American Press," 48.
62. Green, *Straight Lick*, 242.
63. Stewart, *Migrating to the Movies*, 216.

CHAPTER FIVE: GIRLS IN HELL: THE CHANGING DEPICTION OF WOMEN IN THE FIRST WORLD WAR

1. Gavin, *American Women*, 2.
2. Jensen, *Mobilizing Minerva*, 120.
3. The last surviving officially recognized veteran of the Great War was a British woman, Florence Green, who enlisted in the Women's Royal Air Force in September 1918 and died at the age of 110 on February 4, 2012. Fox, "Florence Green."
4. Eileen Bowser, "Girl Who Stayed at Home," 9.
5. "Newspaper Opinions," 10.
6. "Corporal Kate," 8.
7. "Corporal Kate," 8.
8. Hughes, *She Goes to War*, 27.
9. Hughes, *She Goes to War*, 39.
10. Hughes, *She Goes to War*, 44.
11. Hughes, *She Goes to War*, 53.
12. Hughes, *She Goes to War*, 160–62.
13. Hughes, *She Goes to War*, 169.
14. Hughes, *She Goes to War*, 178.
15. DeBauche, *Reel Patriotism*, 192.
16. "Shadow Stage,"56.
17. "She Goes to War," 7–8.
18. Rollyson, *Literary Legacy of Rebecca West*, 46–48; Deakin, *Rebecca West*, 146
19. [West], *War Nurse*, 106–7.
20. [West], *War Nurse*, 212–13.
21. "Critical Comment on Current Films,"88.
22. "Silver Screen's Reviewing Stand," 40.
23. Hall, "Grins and Sighs," X5.
24. "Now We'll Have a Manless Picture," 36.
25. Marshall, *William Beaudine*, 134.
26. Woolridge, "Valiants Carry On," 54–55, 111.
27. "Mad Parade," 10.
28. Hall, "Snarling Beauties," X5.
29. "'Mad Parade' of Paramount-Publix," 160.
30. "Passing in Review."

CHAPTER SIX: FOR NO REASON AT ALL: HOMECOMING, DISILLUSIONMENT, AND THE FAILURE OF TRADITION

1. McCarthy, *Howard Hawks*, 46–47, provides the best summary of what we know about Hawks's military service. Hawks's service records are lost, so reliable information is scant.
2. McCarthy, *Howard Hawks*, 102–5, provides a summary of the tangled history of the story. Later in life (and years after Saunders's suicide), Hawks grew bolder about claiming credit.

3. Isenberg, *War on Film*, 125.

4. Basinger, *World War II Combat Film*, 87–88.

5. Pisano, "Dawn Patrol," 62.

6. Bergman, *We're in the Money*, 110–22, discusses films that propose the use of extragovernmental means to combat the woes of the early 1930s.

7. Kirkham, "Loving Men,", 107.

8. Kirkham, "Loving Men," 107.

9. Dumont, *Frank Borzage*, 153–54.

10. Isenberg, *War on Film*, 132.

11. Mosse, *Fallen Soldiers*, 142.

12. Kelly, *Filming All Quiet on the Western Front*, 102–32, details the reception of the film around the world, with particular attention to Germany and Austria (119–28).

13. King Vidor had used precisely this technique in his *Hallelujah* a year earlier.

14. Sklar, *Movie-Made America*, 176.

15. Crafton, *Talkies*, 93–94, discusses the Movietone version of *What Price Glory?*

16. Isenberg, *War on Film*, 139.

17. Isenberg, *War on Film*, 139

18. Doherty, *Pre-Code Hollywood*, 85.

19. Leed, *No Man's Land*, 213.

CHAPTER SEVEN: MORALS AND MUCK: FROM SUICIDE TO SUPERHEROES

1. Bergman, *We're in the Money*, 110–22.

2. Bergman, *We're in the Money*, 3–13.

3. Doherty, *Pre-Code Hollywood* is the most thorough history of the period.

4. Vasey, "Beyond Sex and Violence," 124.

5. Vasey, "Beyond Sex and Violence," 112.

6. PCA files for all three of these films were reviewed, as were the records for various other titles such as *Hell's Angels* (1930) and *The Road Back* (1937). The major topics that concerned the PCA across all of the reviewed material were sexuality and exportability.

7. Paul Dickson and Allen, *Bonus Army* provides a thorough version of the details covered here.

8. Birdwell, *Celluloid Soldiers*, 11, 19.

9. Birdwell, *Celluloid Soldiers*, chapter 4, is the main source for the details on York's life and attitudes in this and the following paragraph.

10. Birdwell, *Celluloid Soldiers*, 89–101.

11. William Wellman Jr., *Wild Bill Wellman*, 480.

12. William Wellman, *Short Time for Insanity*, 29–36.

13. Thompson, *William Wellman*, 261–62.

14. William Wellman Jr., *Wild Bill Wellman*, 498–99.

15. Menjou and Musselman, *It Took Nine Tailors*, 67–70.

16. Walker, *Stanley Kubrick, Director*, 66, 69.

17. Walker, *Stanley Kubrick, Director*, 69.

18. Trumbo, *Johnny Got His Gun*, 2, 1.

19. Quoted in Ceplair and Trumbo, *Dalton Trumbo*, 94.

20. Ceplair and Trumbo, *Dalton Trumbo*, 96.

21. Trumbo, *Johnny Got His Gun*, 3.

22. Ceplair and Trumbo, *Dalton Trumbo*, 488–89.

23. Ceplair and Trumbo, *Dalton Trumbo*, 505–31, recounts the film's troubled production history, including the financial consequences for Trumbo.

24. Trumbo, *Johnny Got His Gun*, 6.

25. Heller, "*War Horse* Is a War Film."

26. *All-Star Comics*, no. 8, December 1941–January 1942, in Joy, *Wonder Woman Chronicles*, 11.

27. Sperling, "*Wonder Woman* Filmmakers."

CONCLUSION

1. Siskel, "Touch That Transcends Violence," 3.

2. Licursi, *Remembering World War I*, 192.

3. Doherty, "New War Movies," 221.

BIBLIOGRAPHY

Abel, Richard. *Americanizing the Movies and "Movie-Mad" Audiences, 1910–1914*. Berkeley: University of California Press, 2006.

Altman, Rick. "A Semantic/Syntactic Approach to Film Genre." In *Film Genre Reader II*, ed. Barry Keith Grant, 26–40. Austin: University of Texas Press, 1995.

Anderson, Maxwell, and Laurence Stallings. *Three American Plays*. New York: Harcourt, Brace, 1926.

Anderson, Maxwell, and Laurence Stallings. *What Price Glory?* In *Three American Plays*, 5–89. New York: Harcourt, Brace, 1926.

Anthony, Brian, and Andy Edmonds. *Smile When the Raindrops Fall: The Story of Charley Chase*. Lanham, MD: Scarecrow, 1998.

"Army Can Hook in with Bill Hart in 'The Cradle.'" *Moving Picture World* 47, no. 3 (November 20, 1920): 340.

Associated Press. "Last American WWI Vet Wants Memorial." December 3, 2009. http://www.nbcnews.com/id/34265163/ns/us_news-military/#.WzGGYRJKjOR.

"At the Lafayette Theatre." *New York Age*, January 19, 1924, 6.

Auster, Albert. "Saving Private Ryan and American Triumphalism." In *The War Film*, ed. Robert Eberwein, 205–13. New Brunswick, NJ: Rutgers University Press, 2005.

Ball, Eustice Hale, and John Monk Saunders. *Legion of the Condemned*. New York: Grosset and Dunlap, 1928.

Barbeau, Arthur E., and Florette Henri. *Unknown Soldiers: Black American Troops in World War I*. Philadelphia: Temple University Press, 1974.

Barrios, Richard. *A Song in the Dark: The Birth of the Musical Film*. New York: Oxford University Press, 1995.

Basinger, Jeanine. *The World War II Combat Film: Anatomy of a Genre*. 1986. Middletown, CT: Wesleyan University Press, 2003.

Benbow, Mark. "Birth of a Quotation: Woodrow Wilson and 'Like Writing History with Lightning.'" *Journal of the Gilded Age and Progressive Era* 9, no. 4 (October 2010): 509–33.

Bergman, Andrew. *We're in the Money: Depression America and Its Films*. New York: Harper and Row, 1971.

Birdwell, Michael. *Celluloid Soldiers: The Warner Bros. Campaign against Nazism*. New York: New York University Press, 1999.

Borden, Mary. *The Forbidden Zone*. London: Heinemann, 1929.

Bottomore, Stephen. "Filming, Faking and Propaganda: The Origins of the War Film, 1897–1902." PhD diss., Utrecht University, 2007.

Bottomore, Stephen. "The Story of Percy Peashaker: Debates about Sound Effects in the Early Cinema." In *The Sounds of Early Cinema*, ed. Richard Abel and Rick Altman, 129–42. Bloomington: Indiana University Press, 2001.

Bowser, Eileen. "The Girl Who Stayed at Home." In *The Griffith Project*, ed. Paolo Cherchi Usai, 10:8–11. London: British Film Institute, 2000.

Bowser, Pearl, Jane Gaines, and Charles Musser, eds. *Oscar Micheaux and His Circle: African-American Filmmaking and Race Cinema in the Silent Era*. Bloomington: Indiana University Press, 2001.

Bowser, Pearl, and Louise Spence. *Writing Himself into History: Oscar Micheaux, His Silent Films, and His Audiences*. New Brunswick, NJ: Rutgers University Press, 2000.

Bradford, George. "Save." *The Crisis*, May 1918, 7.

Brittain, Joan T. *Laurence Stallings*. Boston: Twayne, 1975.

Brookman, Philip. *Helios: Eadweard Muybridge in a Time of Change*. London: Steidl, 2010.

Brownlow, Kevin. *The War, the West and the Wilderness*. New York: Knopf, 1979.

Butters, Gerald R., Jr. *Black Manhood on the Silent Screen*. Lawrence: University Press of Kansas, 2002.

Campbell, Craig W. *Reel America and World War I: A Comprehensive Filmography and History of Motion Pictures in the United States, 1914–1920*. Jefferson, NC: McFarland, 1985.

Canemaker, John. *Felix: The Twisted Tale of the World's Most Famous Cat*. New York: Pantheon, 1991.

Ceplair, Larry, and Christopher Trumbo. *Dalton Trumbo: Blacklisted Hollywood Writer*. Lexington: University Press of Kentucky, 2015.

Chion, Michael. *Film, a Sound Art*. Trans. Claudia Gorbman. 2003. New York: Columbia University Press, 2009.

Clarke, Liz. "'Wheelbarrows' and 'Real Soldiers': Advertising, Audiences and War Films of All Varieties." In *Beyond the Screen: Institutions, Networks and Publics of Early Cinema*, ed. Marta Braun, Charlie Keil, Rob King, Paul Moore and Louise Pelletier, 71–77. New Barnet, UK: Libbey, 2012.

"Corporal Kate." *Film Daily* 38, no. 73 (December 26, 1926): 8.

Cotter, Joseph Seamon, Jr. *On the Fields of France*. In *Lost Plays of the Harlem Renaissance, 1920–1940*, ed. James V. Hatch and Leo Hamalian, 21–25. Detroit: Wayne State University Press, 1996.

Crafton, Donald. *Before Mickey: The Animated Film, 1898–1928*. 1982. Chicago: University of Chicago Press, 1993.

Crafton, Donald. *The Talkies: American Cinema's Transition to Sound, 1926–1931*. Berkeley: University of California Press, 1999.

Crane, Stephen. *The Red Badge of Courage*. Ed. Sculley Bradley, Richmond Croom Beatty, E. Hudson Long, and Donald Pizer. 1962. New York: Norton, 1976.

Crane, Stephen. "The Veteran." In *The Red Badge of Courage*, ed. Sculley Bradley, Richmond Croom Beatty, E. Hudson Long, and Donald Pizer, 229–33. 1962. New York: Norton, 1976.

Creel, George. *How We Advertised America*. New York: Harper, 1920.

Cripps, Thomas. *Slow Fade to Black: The Negro in American Film, 1900–1942*. New York: Oxford University Press, 1977.
"Critical Comment on Current Films." *Screenland* 22, no. 3 (January 1931): 88.
Curtis, James. *James Whale: A New World of Gods and Monsters*. Boston: Faber and Faber, 1998.
"Daughter of the Congo All-Colored Picture at the Lando Next Week." *Pittsburgh Courier*, August 30, 1930, A7.
"D.C. War Memorial Controversy." Association of Oldest Inhabitants of D.C. Accessed April 15, 2021. http://www.aoidc.org/the-dc-war-memorial-controversy--the-centennial-of-world-war-i.html.
Deakin, Motley F. *Rebecca West*. Boston: Hall, 1980.
DeBauche, Leslie Midkiff. *Reel Patriotism: The Movies and World War I*. Madison: University of Wisconsin Press, 1997.
Dickson, Paul, and Thomas B. Allen. *The Bonus Army: An American Epic*. New York: Walker, 2006.
Dickson, W. K. L. *The Biograph in Battle: Its Story in the South African War Related with Personal Experiences*. London: Unwin, 1901.
Doherty, Thomas. "The New War Movies as Moral Rearmament: *Black Hawk Down* and *We Were Soldiers*." In *The War Film*, ed. Robert Eberwein, 214–21. New Brunswick, NJ: Rutgers University Press, 2005.
Doherty, Thomas. *Pre-Code Hollywood: Sex, Immorality and Insurrection in American Cinema, 1930–1934*. New York: Columbia University Press, 1999.
Dowd, Nancy, and David Shepard. *King Vidor*. Metuchen, NJ: Scarecrow, 1988.
Downing, Hugh Henry. *An American Cavalryman: A Liberian Romance*. 1917. College Park, MD: McGrath, 1969.
Du Bois, W. E. B. "The Black Man in the Revolution of 1914–1918." *The Crisis*, March 1919, 218–23.
Dunbar-Nelson, Alice. *Mine Eyes Have Seen*. In *Black Theater U.S.A.; Plays by African Americans from 1847 to Today*, ed. James Vernon Hatch and Ted Shine, 173–77. New York: Free Press, 1974.
Dumont, Herve. *Frank Borzage: The Life and Films of a Hollywood Romantic*. Jefferson, NC: McFarland, 2006.
Ehrlich, Evelyn. "The Civil War in Early Film: Origin and Development of a Genre." *Southern Quarterly* 19, no. 3 (Spring 1981): 70–82.
Eisenstein, Sergei. "Dickens, Griffith and the Film Today." In *Film Form: Essays in Film Theory*, ed. and trans. Jay Leyda, 195–255. 1949. New York: Harcourt Brace Jovanovich, 1977.
Farwell, Byron. *Over There: The United States in the Great War, 1917–1918*. New York: Norton, 2000.
Fox, Margalit. "Florence Green, Last World War I Veteran, Dies at 110." *New York Times*, February 7, 2012.
Fussell, Paul. *The Great War and Modern Memory*. New York: Oxford University Press, 1975.
Gabler, Neal. *Walt Disney: The Triumph of the American Imagination*. New York: Knopf, 2006.
Gaines, Jane. *Fire and Desire: Mixed-Race Movies in the Silent Era*. Chicago: University of Chicago Press, 2001.

Gandal, Keith. *The Gun and the Pen: Hemingway, Fitzgerald, Faulkner, and the Fiction of Mobilization*. Oxford: Oxford University Press, 2010.

Gavin, Lettie. *American Women in World War I: They Also Served*. Niwot: University Press of Colorado, 1997.

Gerblinger, Christine. "James Whale's Frankensteins: Re-Animating the Great War." *CineAction*, nos. 82–83 (Winter 2011): 2–9.

Goldstein, Richard, "Frank Buckles, Last World War I Doughboy, Is Dead at 110." *New York Times*, February 28, 2011.

Green, J. Ronald. *Straight Lick: The Cinema of Oscar Micheaux*. Bloomington: Indiana University Press, 2000.

Griffith, D. W. *The Man Who Invented Hollywood: The Autobiography of D. W. Griffith*. Ed. James Hart. Louisville, KY: Touchstone, 1972.

Gunning, Tom. *D. W. Griffith and the Origins of American Narrative Film: The Early Years at Biograph*. Urbana: University of Illinois Press, 1994.

Gunning, Tom. "The House with Closed Shutters." In *The Griffith Project*, ed. Paolo Cherchi Usai, 4:141–46. London: British Film Institute, 2000.

Hall, Mourdant. "Grins and Sighs." *New York Times*, November 2, 1930, X5.

Hall, Mordaunt. "Snarling Beauties." *New York Times*, September 27, 1931, X5.

Hall, Mordaunt. "Warriors of the Clouds." *New York Times*, March 19, 1928, 26.

Hammond, Michael. *The Great War in Hollywood Memory, 1918–1939*. Albany: State University of New York Press, 2019.

Hart, William S. *My Life East and West*.1929. Chicago: Donnelley, 1994.

Heller, Chris. "*War Horse* Is a War Film Even If Spielberg Doesn't Want It to Be." *The Atlantic*, December 23, 2011. https://www.theatlantic.com/entertainment/archive/2011/12/war-horse-is-a-war-film-even-if-spielberg-doesnt-want-it-to-be/250448/.

Higonnett, Margaret R., ed. *Nurses at the Front: Writing the Wounds of the Great War*. Boston: Northeastern University Press, 2001.

Hughes, Rupert. *She Goes to War, and Other Stories*. New York: Grosset and Dunlap, 1929.

Isenberg, Michael. "The Great War Viewed from the Twenties: *The Big Parade*." In *Hollywood's World War I: Motion Picture Images*, ed. Peter Rollins and John E. O'Conner, 39–58. Bowling Green, OH: Bowling Green State University Popular Press, 1997.

Isenberg, Michael. *War on Film: The American Cinema and World War I, 1914–1938*. Rutherford, NJ: Fairleigh Dickinson University Press, 1981.

Jackson, Robert. "The Secret Life of Oscar Micheaux: Race Films, Contested Histories, and Modern American Culture." In *Beyond Blackface: African Americans and the Creation of American Popular Culture, 1890–1930*, ed. W. Fitzhugh Brundage, 215–38. Chapel Hill: University of North Carolina Press. 2011.

Jacobs, Lea. *The Decline of Sentiment: American Film in the 1920s*. Berkeley: University of California Press, 2008.

Jensen, Kimberly. *Mobilizing Minerva: American Women in the First World War*. Urbana: University of Illinois Press, 2008.

Johnson, Julian. "Hearts of the World: A Review of Mr. Griffith's New Photodrama." *Photoplay* 14, no. 1 (June 1918): 48.

Johnson, Julian. "The Shadow Stage." *Photoplay* 10, no. 3 (August 1916): 137.

Joy, Bob, ed. *The Wonder Woman Chronicles*. Vol. 1. New York: DC Comics, 2010.
Katz, A. J. "Here's How ABC, NBC and CBS Are Covering the 75th Anniversary of D-Day." TVNewser, June 3, 2019. https://www.adweek.com/tvnewser/heres-how-abc-nbc-and-cbs-are-covering-the-75th-anniversary-of-d-day/404465/.
Keene, Jennifer. *Doughboys, the Great War, and the Remaking of America*. Baltimore: Johns Hopkins University Press, 2001.
Kelly, Andrew. *Cinema and the Great War*. New York: Routledge, 1997.
Kelly, Andrew. *Filming All Quiet on the Western Front: "Brutal Cutting, Stupid Censors, Bigoted Politicos."* London: Tauris, 1998.
Kelly, Andrew. "The Greatness and Continuing Significance of *All Quiet on the Western Front*." In *The War Film*, ed. Robert Eberwein, 23–29. New Brunswick, NJ: Rutgers University Press, 2005.
Kennedy, David. *Over Here: The First World War and American Society*. New York: Oxford University Press, 1980.
Kirkham, Pat. "Loving Men: Frank Borzage, Charles Farrell and the Reconstruction of Masculinity in 1920's Hollywood Cinema." In *Me Jane: Masculinity, Movies and Women*, ed. Pat Kirkham and Janet Thumim, 94–112. London: Lawrence and Wishart, 1995.
Klotman, Phyllis R. "Planes, Trains, and Automobiles: *The Flying Ace*, the Norman Company, and the Micheaux Connection." In *Oscar Micheaux and His Circle: African-American Filmmaking and Race Cinema in the Silent Era*, ed. Pearl Bowser, Jane Gaines, and Charles Musser, 161–77. Bloomington: Indiana University Press, 2001.
Kozarski, Diane Kaiser. *The Complete Films of William S. Hart*. New York: Dover, 1980.
La Motte, Ellen N. *The Backwash of War: An Extraordinary American Nurse in World War I*. Ed. and intro. Cynthia Wachtell. 1916. Baltimore: Johns Hopkins University Press, 2019.
Leed, Eric J. *No Man's Land: Combat and Identity in World War I*. New York: Cambridge University Press, 1979.
Library of Congress. "Frank Woodruff Buckles." Experiencing War: Stories from the Veterans History Project. October 26, 2011. http://memory.loc.gov/diglib/vhp-stories/loc.natlib.afc2001001.01070/#vhp:clip.
Licursi, Kimberley J. Lamay. *Remembering World War I in America*. Lincoln: University of Nebraska Press, 2018.
Lloyd, Annette D'Agostino. *The Harold Lloyd Encyclopedia*. Jefferson, NC: McFarland, 2010.
Logan, Rayford Whittingham, and Michael R. Winston, eds. *Dictionary of American Negro Biography*. New York: Norton, 1982.
Logue, Larry M. *To Appomattox and Beyond: The Civil War Soldier in War and Peace*. Chicago: Dee, 1996.
"Loyal Hearts." *Chicago Defender*, May 1, 1920, 3.
Ludington, Townsend. *John Dos Passos: A Twentieth Century Odyssey*. New York: Dutton, 1980.
Lupack, Barbara. *Literary Adaptations in Black American Cinema: From Micheaux to Morrison*. Rochester: University of Rochester Press, 2002.
Lupack, Barbara. *Richard E. Norman and Race Filmmaking*. Bloomington: Indiana University Press, 2014.
"The Mad Parade." *Film Daily* 56, no. 69 (September 20, 1931): 10.
"'The Mad Parade' of Paramount-Publix." *Harrison's Reports* 13, no. 40 (October 3, 1931): 160.

Marshall, Wendy L. *William Beaudine: From Silents to Television*. Lanham, MD: Scarecrow, 2005.
Mayer, David. *Stagestruck Filmmaker: D. W. Griffith and the American Theatre*. Iowa City: University of Iowa Press, 2009.
McCarthy, Todd. *Howard Hawks: The Grey Fox of Hollywood*. New York: Grove, 2000.
McKay, Claude. *Home to Harlem*. New York: Harper and Brothers, 1928.
McPherson, James M. "Long-Legged Yankee Lies: The Southern Textbook Crusade." In *The Memory of the Civil War in American Culture*, ed. Alice Fahs and Joan Waugh, 64–78. Chapel Hill: University of North Carolina Press, 2004.
Menjou, Adolphe, and M. M. Musselman. *It Took Nine Tailors*. New York: McGraw-Hill, 1948.
Merritt, Russell, and J. B. Kaufman. *Walt in Wonderland: The Silent Films of Walt Disney*. Baltimore: Johns Hopkins University Press, 2000.
Micheaux, Oscar. *The Homesteader*. Sioux City, IA: Western Book Supply, 1917.
Mosse, George L. *Fallen Soldiers: Reshaping the Memory of the World Wars*. New York: Oxford University Press, 1990.
"Newspaper Opinions." *Film Daily* 38, no. 68 (December 20, 1926): 10.
The New York Times Film Reviews, 1913–1968. 6 vols. New York: *New York Times* and Arno, 1970.
"Now We'll Have a Manless Picture." *International Photographer* 3, no. 3 (April 1931): 36.
"Passing in Review: The Mad Parade." *Motion Picture Herald*, 103, no. 5 (May 2, 1931): 42.
Pearson, Roberta. *Eloquent Gestures: The Transformation of Performance Style in the Griffith Biograph Films*. Berkeley: University of California Press, 1992.
Pisano, Dominick. "The Dawn Patrol and the World War I Air Combat Film Genre: An Exploration of American Values." In *Hollywood's World War I: Motion Picture Images*, ed. Peter Rollins and John E. O'Conner, 59–78. Bowling Green, OH: Bowling Green State University Popular Press, 1997.
Prince, Stephen. *Classical Film Violence: Designing and Regulating Brutality in Hollywood Cinema, 1930–1968*. New Brunswick, NJ: Rutgers University Press, 2003.
Regester, Charlene. "The African-American Press and Race Movies, 1909–1929." In *Oscar Micheaux and His Circle: African-American Filmmaking and Race Cinema in the Silent Era*, ed. Pearl Bowser, Jane Gaines, and Charles Musser, 34–49. Bloomington: Indiana University Press, 2001.
Robinson, David. *Chaplin: His Life and Art*. New York: McGraw-Hill, 1985.
Rollins, Peter C., and John E. O'Conner, eds. *Hollywood's World War I: Motion Picture Images*. Bowling Green, OH: Bowling Green State University Popular Press, 1997.
Rollyson, Carl. *The Literary Legacy of Rebecca West*. San Francisco: International Scholars, 1998.
Sampson, Henry T. *Blacks in Black and White: A Sourcebook on Black Films*. 2nd ed. Metuchen, NJ: Scarecrow, 1995.
Schickel, Richard. *D. W. Griffith: An American Life*. New York: Simon and Schuster, 1984.
Scott, Emmett. *Scott's Official History of the American Negro in the World War*. 1919. New York: Arno, 1969.
"The Screen." *New York Times*, December 23, 1918, 9.
"The Shadow Stage." *Photoplay* 36, no. 1 (June 1929): 56.
"The Shadow Stage: The Big Parade." *Photoplay* 24, no. 2 (January 1926): 46.
"She Goes to War." *National Board of Review Magazine* 4, no. 6 (June 1929): 7–8.

Sherriff, R. C. "Journey's End." In *Sixteen Famous British Plays*, comp. Bennett A. Cerf and Van H. Cartmell, 591–668. New York: Modern Library, 1942.

"Silver Screen's Reviewing Stand." *Silver Screen*, 1, no. 3 (January 1931): 40.

Simmon, Scott. *The Films of D. W. Griffith*. New York: Cambridge University Press, 1993.

Simmon, Scott, and Raymond Durgnat. *King Vidor, American*. Berkeley: University of California Press, 1988.

Siskel, Gene. "The Touch That Transcends Violence and Death." *Chicago Tribune*, November 11, 1973, section 6, 3.

Sklar, Robert. *Movie-Made America: A Cultural History of American Movies*. New York: Random House, 1975.

Slater, Thomas, "June Mathis's Valentino Scripts: Images of Male 'Becoming' after the Great War." *Cinema Journal* 50, no. 1 (Fall 2010): 99–120.

Slide, Anthony. *Early American Cinema*. Metuchen, NJ: Scarecrow, 1994.

Slide, Anthony, ed. *Selected Film Criticism, 1912–1920*. Metuchen, NJ: Scarecrow, 1982.

Slide, Anthony, ed. *Selected Film Criticism, 1921–1930*. Metuchen, NJ: Scarecrow, 1982.

Slide, Anthony, with Alan Gevinson. *The Big V: A History of the Vitagraph Company*. Rev. ed. Metuchen, NJ: Scarecrow, 1987.

Smith, Albert, with Phil Koury. *Two Reels and a Crank: From Nickelodeon to Picture Palaces*. Garden City, NY: Doubleday, 1952.

Smith, Frederick James. "The Celluloid Critic." *Motion Picture Classic* 8, no. 1 (March 1919): 45.

Spehr, Paul. *The Civil War in Motion Pictures: A Bibliography of Films Produced in the United States since 1897*. Washington, DC: Library of Congress, 1961.

Sperling, Nicole. "*Wonder Woman* Filmmakers Explain Why They Changed Heroine's Origin Story." *Entertainment Weekly*, May 30, 2017. https://ew.com/movies/2017/05/30/wonder-woman-world-war-i-setting/.

Stallings, Laurence. *The Doughboys: The Story of the AEF, 1917–1918*. New York: Harper and Row, 1963.

Stallings, Laurence. "The Big Parade." *New Republic*, September 17, 1924, 66–69.

Stallings, Laurence, ed. *The First World War: A Photographic History*. New York: Simon and Schuster, 1933.

Stallings, Laurence. *Plumes*. New York: Harcourt, Brace, 1924.

Stewart, Jacqueline Najuma. *Migrating to the Movies: Cinema and Black Urban Modernity*. Berkeley: University of California Press, 2005.

Strebel, Elizabeth Grottle. "Imperialist Iconography of Anglo-Boer War Film Footage." In *Film before Griffith*, ed. John Fell, 264–71. Berkeley: University of California Press, 1983.

Stribling, T. S. *Birthright, a Novel*. New York: Century, 1922.

Studlar, Gaylyn. *This Mad Masquerade: Stardom and Masculinity in the Jazz Age*. New York: Columbia University Press, 1996.

Taves, Brian. *Thomas Ince: Hollywood's Independent Pioneer*. Lexington: University Press of Kentucky, 2012.

Taylor, Clyde. "Oscar Micheaux and the Harlem Renaissance." In *Temples for Tomorrow: Looking Back at the Harlem Renaissance*, ed. Genevieve Fabre and Michel Feith, 125–35. Bloomington: Indiana University Press, 2001.

Thomas, D. Ireland. "Motion Picture News," *Chicago Defender*, March 15, 1924, 6A.

Thompson, Frank. *William Wellman*. Metuchen, NJ: Scarecrow, 1983.
Trumbo, Dalton. *Johnny Got His Gun*. 1939. Secaucus, NJ: Citadel. 1970.
Tudor, Andrew. "Genre." In *Film Genre Reader II*, ed. Barry Keith Grant, 3–10. Austin: University of Texas Press, 1995.
Tuska, Jon. *The Filming of the West*. Garden City, NY: Doubleday, 1976.
Vasey, Ruth. "Beyond Sex and Violence: 'Industry Policy' and the Regulation of Hollywood Movies, 1922-1939." In *Controlling Hollywood: Censorship and Regulation in the Studio Era*, ed. Matthew Bernstein, 102–29. New Brunswick, NJ: Rutgers University Press, 1999.
Vidor, King. *A Tree Is a Tree: An Autobiography*. 1953. Hollywood, CA: French, 1981.
Wagenknecht, Edward, and Anthony Slide. *The Films of D. W. Griffith*. New York: Crown, 1975.
Walker, Alexander. *Stanley Kubrick, Director*. 1971. New York: Norton, 1999.
Ward, Larry. *The Motion Picture Goes to War: The U.S. Government Film Effort During World War I*. Ann Arbor, MI: UMI Research Press, 1985.
"Watch Details for Perfection." *New York Times*, July 5, 1925, sec. 7, p. 2.
Watz, Ed. *Wheeler and Woolsey: The Vaudeville Comic Duo and Their Films, 1929—1937*. Jefferson, NC: McFarland, 1994.
Wellman, William. *Go Get 'Em!* Boston: Page, 1918.
Wellman, William. *A Short Time for Insanity*. New York: Hawthorne, 1974.
Wellman, William, Jr. *The Man and His Wings*. Westport, CT: Praeger, 2006.
Wellman, William, Jr. *Wild Bill Wellman: Hollywood Rebel*. New York: Pantheon, 2015.
[West, Rebecca]. *War Nurse: The True Story of a Woman Who Lived, Loved and Suffered on the Western Front*. New York: Burt, 1930.
White, Hayden. *The Content of the Form: Narrative Discourse and Historical Representation*. Baltimore: Johns Hopkins University Press, 1987.
White, Walter Francis. *A Man Called White: The Autobiography of Walter White*. New York: Viking, 1948.
Wilson, Edmund. *Patriotic Gore: Studies in the Literature of the American Civil War*. New York: Oxford University Press, 1962.
Williams, Edward Christopher. *When Washington Was in Vogue: A Love Story*. New York: Amistad, 2003
Winter, Jay. *Remembering War: The Great War between Memory and History in the Twentieth Century*. New Haven: Yale University Press, 2006.
Winter, Jay. *Sites of Memory, Sites of Mourning: The Great War in European Cultural History*. New York: Cambridge University Press, 1995.
Winter, Thomas. "The Training of Colored Troops: A Cinematic Effort to Promote National Cohesion." In *Hollywood's World War I: Motion Picture Images*, ed. Peter Rollins and John E. O'Conner, 13–25. Bowling Green, OH: Bowling Green State University Popular Press, 1997.
Wolgemuth, Kathleen. "Woodrow Wilson and Federal Segregation." *Journal of Negro History* 44, no. 2 (April 1959): 158–73.
Wood, Richard, ed. *Film and Propaganda in America: A Documentary History*. Vol. 1, *World War I*. New York: Greenwood, 1990.
Woolridge, Dorothy. "The Valiants Carry On." *Picture Play* 34, no. 3 (May 1931): 54–55, 111.

FILMOGRAPHY

SHORTS

The Fugitive (Griffith, 1910)
The House with Closed Shutters (Griffith, 1910)
The Battle (Griffith, 1911)
Drummer of the 8th (Ince, 1913)
Granddad (Ince, 1913)
A Submarine Pirate (Syd Chaplin, 1915)
Luke Joins the Navy (Roach, 1916)
Luke's Preparedness Preparations (Roach, 1916)
The Realization of a Negro's Ambition (Gant, 1916)
A Trooper of Troop K (Gant, 1917)
The Bond (Charlie Chaplin, 1918)
Kicking the Germ Out of Germany (Goulding, 1918)
Our Colored Fighters (1918)
Shoulder Arms (Charlie Chaplin, 1918)
Spying the Spy (Phillips, 1918)
Training of Colored Troops (1918)
A Sammy in Siberia (Roach, 1919)
From Harlem to the Rhine (1920)
Felix Turns the Tide (Messmer, 1922)
All Night Long (Edwards, 1924)
Alice's Little Parade (Disney, 1926)
Soldier Man (Edwards, 1926)
Great Guns! (Disney, 1927)
High C's (Horne, 1930)
Bosko the Doughboy (Harman, 1931)
The Dumb Patrol (Harman and Ising, 1931)

FEATURES

The Birth of a Nation (1915)
Director: D. W. Griffith

Producer: D. W. Griffith
Screenplay: D. W. Griffith based on the novel *The Clansman: An Historical Romance of the Ku Klux Klan* by Thomas Dixon (New York, 1905)
Cast: Lillian Gish, Mae Marsh, Henry Walthall, Miriam Cooper, George Siegmann
Production Company: David W. Griffith Corporation
Distribution Company: Epoch Producing Corporation

The Coward (1915)
Director: Reginald Barker
Producer: Thomas Ince
Screenplay: Thomas Ince
Cast: Charles Ray, Frank Keenan, Gertrude Claire
Production Company: New York Motion Picture Corporation, Kay-Bee
Distribution Company: Triangle Film Corporation

Civilization (1916)
Director: Reginald Barker
Producer: Thomas Ince
Screenplay: C. Gardner Sullivan
Cast: Herschel Mayall, Lola May, Howard Hickman
Production Company: Thomas Ince

The Little American (1917)
Director: Cecil B. DeMille
Screenplay: Jeanie MacPherson
Cast: Mary Pickford, Jack Holt, Raymond Hatton, Hobart Bosworth
Production Company: Mary Pickford Film Corporation
Distribution Company: Artcraft Pictures Corporation

The Greatest Thing in Life (1918)
Director: D. W. Griffith
Producer: D. W. Griffith
Screenplay: S. E. V. Taylor credited as Captain Victor Marier
Cast: Lillian Gish, Robert Harron, Adolphe Lestina, David Butler
Production Company: D. W. Griffith
Distribution Company: Famous Players–Lasky Corporation

Hearts of the World (1918)
Director: D. W. Griffith
Producer: D. W. Griffith
Screenplay: M. Gaston de Tolignac, S. E. V. Taylor credited as Captain Victor Marier
Cast: Lillian Gish, Robert Harron, Dorothy Gish, Josephine Crowell
Production Company: D. W. Griffith

Johanna Enlists (1918)
Director: William Desmond Taylor
Screenplay: Frances Marion based on the short story "The Mobilization of Johanna" by Rupert Hughes, *Hearst's*, September–October 1917
Cast: Mary Pickford, Monte Blue, Douglas MacLean, Wallace Beery
Production Company: Pickford Film Company
Distribution Company: Famous Players–Lasky Corporation, Artcraft Pictures

The Girl Who Stayed at Home (1919)
Director: D. W. Griffith
Producer: D. W. Griffith
Screenplay: S. E. V. Taylor
Cast: Carol Dempster, Richard Barthelmess, Robert Harron, Clarine Seymour
Production Company: D. W. Griffith
Distribution Company: Famous Players–Lasky Corporation, Artcraft Pictures

Injustice (aka *Loyal Hearts*) (1919)
Director: Leslie Peacocke
Screenplay: Leslie Peacocke
Cast: Thais Nehli-Kalini, Maurice Stapler, Vera Lavassor
Production Company: Democracy Film Company, L-Ko Pictures Corporation
Distribution Company: Bookertee Film Exchange

The Lost Battalion (1919)
Director: Burton King
Producer: Edward A. MacManus
Screenplay: Charles Logue
Cast: Major-General Robert Alexander, Lieutenant Colonel Charles W. Whittlesay, Major George McMurtry
Production Company: MacManus Corporation
Distribution Company: W. H. Productions Company

The Cradle of Courage (1920)
Director: Lambert Hillyer
Screenplay: Lambert Hillyer
Cast: William S. Hart, Ann Little, Thomas Santschi, Barbara Bedford
Production Company: William S. Hart Company
Distribution Company: Famous Players–Lasky Corporation, Artcraft Pictures

Within Our Gates (1920)
Director: Oscar Micheaux
Producer: Oscar Micheaux
Screenplay: Oscar Micheaux
Cast: Evelyn Preer, Jack Chenault, Charles D. Lucas

Production Company: Micheaux Film Company
Distribution Company: Micheaux Film Company, Quality Amusement Corporation

The Four Horsemen of the Apocalypse (1921)
Director: Rex Ingram
Screenplay: June Mathis based on the novel by Vicente Blasco-Ibanez
Cast: Rudolph Valentino, Alice Terry, John Sainpolis, Alan Hale
Production Company: Metro Pictures Corporation
Distribution Company: Metro Pictures Corporation

A Sailor-Made Man (1921)
Director: Fred Newmeyer
Producer: Hal Roach
Screenplay: Hal Roach, Sam Taylor
Cast: Harold Lloyd, Mildred Davis, Noah Young
Production Company: Hal Roach Studios
Distribution Company: Associated Exhibitors

The Virgin of Seminole (1922)
Director: Oscar Micheaux
Producer: Oscar Micheaux
Screenplay: Oscar Micheaux
Cast: Shingzie Howard, William E. Fountaine
Production Company: Micheaux Film Company

Birthright (1924)
Director: Oscar Micheaux
Producer: Oscar Micheaux
Screenplay: Oscar Micheaux based on the novel by T. S. Stribling
Cast: J. Homer Tutt, Evelyn Preer, Salem Tutt Whitney
Production Company: Micheaux Film Company

The Enchanted Cottage (1924)
Director: Jack Robertson
Screenplay: Josephine Lovett, Gertrude Chase
Cast: Richard Barthelmess, May McAvoy
Production Company: Inspiration Pictures
Distribution Company: First National

The Big Parade (1925)
Director: King Vidor
Producer: King Vidor, Irving Thalberg
Screenplay: Laurence Stallings, Harry Behn
Cast: John Gilbert, Renée Adorée, Hobart Bosworth, Claire McDowell, Karl Dane, Tom O'Brien

Production Company: Metro-Goldwyn-Mayer Corporation
Distribution Company: Metro-Goldwyn-Mayer Distributing Corporation

His Master's Voice (1925)
Director: Renaud Hoffman
Producer: Samuel Sax
Screenplay: J. Henry McCarty, James Tynan, Frank Foster Davis
Cast: Thunder the Dog, George Hackathorne, Marjorie Daw
Production Company: Gotham Productions
Distribution Company: Lumas Film Corporation

Corporal Kate (1926)
Director: Paul Sloane
Producer: C. Gardner Sullivan
Screenplay: Albert Shelley La Vino, Zelda Sears, Marion Orth, John W. Krafft
Cast: Vera Reynolds, Julia Faye, Kenneth Thompson, Fred Allen
Production Company: DeMille Pictures Corporation
Distribution Company: Producers Distributing Corporation

The Flying Ace (1926)
Director: Richard E. Norman
Producer: Richard E. Norman
Screenplay: Richard E. Norman
Cast: J. Lawrence Crimer, Kathryn Boyd, Steve Reynolds
Production Company: Norman Film Manufacturing Company
Distribution Company: Norman Studios

What Price Glory? (1926)
Director: Raoul Walsh
Producer: William Fox
Screenplay: James T. O'Donohoe, Malcolm Stuart Boylan based on the play by Laurence Stallings and Maxwell Anderson
Cast: Victor McLaglen, Edmund Lowe, Dolores Del Rio
Production Company: Fox Film Corporation
Distribution Company: Fox Film Corporation

The Patent Leather Kid (1927)
Director: Alfred Santell
Producer: Alfred Santell, Richard Rowland
Screenplay: Winifred Dunn, Adela Rogers St. Johns, Gerald C. Duffy
Cast: Richard Barthelmess, Molly O'Day, Lawford Davidson
Production Company: First National Pictures
Distribution Company: First National Pictures

FILMOGRAPHY

Wings (1927)
Director: William Wellman
Producer: Adolph Zukor, Jesse L. Lasky, B. P. Schulberg
Screenplay: John Monk Saunders, Hope Loring, Louis D. Lighton, Byron Morgan, Julian Johnson
Cast: Charles "Buddy" Rogers, Richard Arlen, Clara Bow, Jobyna Ralston
Production Company: Paramount Famous Lasky Corporation
Distribution Company: Paramount Famous Lasky Corporation

Abie's Irish Rose (1928)
Director: Victor Fleming
Producer: B. P. Schulberg
Screenplay: Jules Furthman, Anne Nichols, Herman J. Mankiewicz, Julian Johnson based on the play by Anne Nichols
Cast: Charles "Buddy" Rogers, Nancy Carroll, Jean Hersholt, J. Farrell MacDonald
Production Company: Paramount Famous Lasky Corporation
Distribution Company: Paramount Famous Lasky Corporation

Legion of the Condemned (1928)
Director: William Wellman
Producer: Adolph Zukor, Jesse L. Lasky
Screenplay: John Monk Saunders, Jean De Limur, George Marion Jr.
Cast: Gary Cooper, Fay Wray, Barry Norton
Production Company: Paramount Famous Lasky Corporation
Distribution Company: Paramount Famous Lasky Corporation

Lucky Star (1929)
Director: Frank Borzage
Producer: William Fox
Screenplay: Sonya Levien, John Hunter Booth, Katherine Hilliker, H. H. Caldwell
Cast: Janet Gaynor, Charles Farrell, Guinn "Big Boy" Williams
Production Company: Fox Film Corporation
Distribution Company: Fox Film Corporation

The Mighty (1929)
Director: John Cromwell
Screenplay: William Slavens McNutt, Grover Jones, Robert N. Lee, Nellie Revell, Herman J. Mankiewicz
Cast: George Bancroft, Esther Ralston, Warner Oland, Raymond Hatton
Production Company: Paramount Famous Lasky Corporation
Distribution Company: Paramount Famous Lasky Corporation

She Goes to War (1929)
Director: Henry King

Producer: Victor Halperin, Edward Halperin
Screenplay: Howard Estabrook, Mme. Fred De Gresac, John Monk Saunders
Cast: Eleanor Boardman, John Holland, Edmund Burns, Alma Rubens, Al "Fuzzy" St. John
Production Company: Inspiration Pictures
Distribution Company: United Artists Corporation

All Quiet on the Western Front (1930)
Director: Lewis Milestone
Producer: Carl Laemmle, Carl Laemmle Jr.
Screenplay: Maxwell Anderson, George Abbott, Del Andrews. C. Gardner Sullivan
Cast: Lew Ayres, Louis Wolheim, Slim Summerville
Production Company: Universal Pictures Corporation
Distribution Company: Universal Pictures Corporation

A Daughter of the Congo (1930)
Director: Oscar Micheaux
Producer: Oscar Micheaux
Screenplay: Oscar Micheaux based on the novel *The American Cavalryman* by Henry Francis Downing
Cast: Kathleen Noisette, Loretta Tucker, Clarence Reed
Production Company: Micheaux Film Company

The Dawn Patrol (1930)
Director: Howard Hawks
Producer: Robert North
Screenplay: Richard Barthelmess, Douglas Fairbanks Jr., Neil Hamilton
Cast: John Monk Saunders, Dan Totheroh, Howard Hawks, Seton I. Miller
Production Company: First National Pictures
Distribution Company: First National Pictures

Doughboys (1930)
Director: Edward Sedgwick
Screenplay: Richard Schayer, Al Boasberg, Sidney Lazarus
Cast: Buster Keaton, Sally Eilers, Cliff Edwards, Edward Brophy
Production Company: Metro-Goldwyn-Mayer Corporation
Distribution Company: Metro-Goldwyn-Mayer Distributing Corporation

Half Shot at Sunrise (1930)
Director: Paul Sloane
Producer: William LeBaron, Henry Hobart
Screenplay: James Ashmore Creelman, Anne Caldwell, Ralph Spence, Edwin K. O'Brien, Rube Bernstein
Cast: Bert Wheeler, Robert Woolsey, Dorothy Lee, Edna Mae Oliver
Production Company: RKO Productions
Distribution Company: RKO Radio Pictures

Hell's Angels (1930)
Director: Howard Hughes, James Whale
Producer: Howard Hughes
Screenplay: Howard Estabrook, Harry Behn, Marshall Neilan, Joseph Moncure March
Cast: Ben Lyon, James Hall, Jean Harlow
Production Company: Caddo Company
Distribution Company: United Artists Corporation

Journey's End (1930)
Director: James Whale
Producers: George Pearson, Gerald L. G. Samson
Screenplay: Joseph Moncure March (based on the play *Journey's End* by R. C. Sherriff, [London, December 9, 1928])
Cast: Colin Clive, Ian MacLaren, David Manners
Production Companies: Tiffany Productions, Gainsborough Pictures 1928
Distribution Company: Tiffany Productions

War Nurse (1930)
Director: Edgar Selwyn
Screenplay: Becky Gardiner, Joseph White Farnham
Cast: Robert Montgomery, Anita Page, June Walker
Production Company: Metro-Goldwyn-Mayer Corporation
Distribution Company: Metro-Goldwyn-Mayer Distributing Corporation

Young Eagles (1930)
Director: William Wellman
Screenplay: Grover Jones, William Slavens McNutt based on the short story "The One Who Was Clever" by Elliot White Springs, *Red Book Magazine*, August 1929, and the short story "Sky-High" by Eliot White Springs, *Red Book Magazine*, July 1929)
Cast: Charles "Buddy" Rogers, Paul Lukas, Jean Arthur
Production Company: Paramount Famous Lasky Corporation
Distribution Company: Paramount Famous Lasky Corporation

Frankenstein (1931)
Director: James Whale
Producer: Carl Laemmle Jr.
Screenplay: Garrett Fort, Francis Edwards Faragoh, Richard Schayer (based on the novel *Frankenstein* by Mary Shelley [London, 1818] and the composition of John L. Balderston from the play *Frankenstein* by Peggy Webling [1927])
Cast: Colin Clive, Mae Clarke, Boris Karloff
Production Company: Universal Pictures Corporation
Distribution Company: Universal Pictures Corporation

The Last Flight (1931)
Director: William Dieterle
Screenplay: John Monk Saunders (based on the novel *Single Lady* by John Monk Saunders [New York, 1931])
Cast: Richard Barthelmess, David Manners, Helen Chandler, Johnny Mack Brown
Production Company: First National Pictures
Distribution Company: First National Pictures

The Mad Parade (1931)
Director: William Beaudine
Producer: Herman M. Gumbin, M. H. Hoffman
Screenplay: Henry McCarthy, Frank R. Conklin, Gertrude Orr, Doris Malloy
Cast: Evelyn Brent, Irene Rich, Louise Fazenda
Production Company: Liberty Productions Company
Distribution Company: Paramount Publix Corporation

Broken Lullaby (1932)
Director: Ernst Lubitsch
Producer: Ernst Lubitsch
Screenplay: Samson Raphaelson, Ernest Vajda (based on the play *L'homme que j'ai tué* by Maurice Rostand [Paris, January 15, 1930] and the English-language adaptation, *The Man I Killed*, by Reginald Berkeley [London, 1931])
Cast: Lionel Barrymore, Nancy Carroll, Phillips Holmes
Production Company: Paramount Publix Corporation
Distribution Company: Paramount Publix Corporation

The Lost Squadron (1932)
Director: George Archainbaud
Producer: David O. Selznick
Screenplay: Wallace Smith, Humphrey Pearson, Herman J. Mankiewitz, Robert Presnell (based on the novel *The Lost Squadron* by Dick Grace [New York, 1932])
Cast: Richard Dix, Mary Astor, Robert Armstrong
Production Company: RKO Radio Pictures
Distribution Company: RKO Radio Pictures

Pack Up Your Troubles (1932)
Director: George Marshall
Producer: Hal Roach
Screenplay: H. M. Walker
Cast: Stan Laurel, Oliver Hardy, Donald Dillaway
Production Companies: Hal Roach Studios, Metro-Goldwyn-Mayer Corporation
Distribution Company: Metro-Goldwyn-Mayer Distributing Corporation

Heroes for Sale (1933)
Director: William Wellman
Producer: Hal B. Wallis
Screenplay: Robert Lord, Wilson Mizner
Cast: Richard Barthelmess, Aline MacMahon, Loretta Young
Production Company: First National Pictures
Distribution Companies: First National Pictures, Vitaphone Corporation

The Road Back (1937)
Director: James Whale
Producer: Charles R. Rogers
Screenplay: R. C. Sherriff, Charles Kenyon based on the novel *The Road Back* by Erich Maria Remarque, translated by A. W. Wheen [Boston, 1931])
Cast: John King, Richard Cromwell, Slim Summerville, Andy Devine, Noah Beery Jr.
Production Company: Universal Pictures
Distribution Company: Universal Pictures

They Gave Him a Gun (1937)
Director: W. S. Van Dyke
Producer: Harry Rapf (based on the novel *They Gave Him a Gun* by William Joyce Cowen [New York, 1936])
Screenplay: Cyril Hume, Richard Maibaum, Maurice Rapf
Cast: Franchot Tone, Spencer Tracy, Gladys George
Production Company: Metro-Goldwyn-Mayer Corporation
Distribution Company: Metro-Goldwyn-Mayer Distributing Corporation

Block-Heads (1938)
Director: John Blystone
Producer: Hal Roach
Screenplay: Charles Rogers, Felix Adler, James Parrott, Harry Langdon, Arnold Belgard
Cast: Stan Laurel, Oliver Hardy, Patricia Ellis
Production Companies: Hal Roach Studios, Metro-Goldwyn-Mayer Corporation
Distribution Company: Metro-Goldwyn-Mayer Distributing Corporation

Men with Wings (1938)
Director: William Wellman
Producer: William Wellman, William LeBaron
Screenplay: Robert Carson
Cast: Fred MacMurray, Ray Milland, Louise Campbell, Andy Devine
Production Company: Paramount Pictures
Distribution Company: Paramount Pictures

Birthright (1939)
Director: Oscar Micheaux

Producer: Oscar Micheaux
Screenplay: Oscar Micheaux (based on the novel *Birthright* by T. S. Stribling [New York, 1922])
Cast: Carman Newsome, S. O. Moses, Alec Lovejoy
Production Company: Micheaux Pictures Corporation
Distribution Company: Micheaux Pictures Corporation

Sergeant York (1941)
Director: Howard Hawks
Producers: Jesse L. Lasky, Hal B. Wallis
Screenplay: Abel Finkel, Harry Chandlee, Howard W. Koch, John Huston (based on the book *Sergeant York: His Own Life Story and War Diary* by Alvin C. York, as edited by Tom Skeyhill [New York, 1928])
Cast: Gary Cooper, Walter Brennan, Joan Leslie
Production Company: Warner Bros. Pictures
Distribution Company: Warner Bros. Pictures

Paths of Glory (1957)
Director: Stanley Kubrick
Producer: James B. Harris
Screenplay: Stanley Kubrick, Calder Willingham, Slim Thompson (based on the novel *Paths of Glory* by Humphrey Cobb [New York, 1935])
Cast: Kirk Douglas, Adolphe Menjou, George Macready
Production Company: Bryna Productions
Distribution Company: United Artists Corporation

Lafayette Escadrille (1958)
Director: William A. Wellman
Producer: William A. Wellman
Screenplay: A. S. Fleischman, William A. Wellman
Cast: Tab Hunter, Etchika Choureau, Marcel Dalio
Production Company: Warner Bros. Pictures
Distribution Company: Warner Bros. Pictures

Johnny Got His Gun (1971)
Director: Dalton Trumbo
Producer: Bruce Campbell
Screenplay: Dalton Trumbo (based on the novel *Johnny Got His Gun* by Dalton Trumbo [Philadelphia, 1939])
Cast: Timothy Bottoms, Donald Sutherland, Charles McGraw
Production Company: Robert Rich Productions
Distribution Company: Cinemation Industries

Flyboys (2006)
Director: Tony Bill

Producers: Dean Devlin, Marc Frydman
Screenplay: Phil Sears, Blake T. Evans, David S. Ward
Cast: James Franco, Martin Henderson, David Ellison
Production Company: Electric Entertainment
Distribution Company: MGM Distribution Company

War Horse (2011)
Director: Steven Spielberg
Producers: Steven Spielberg, Kathleen Kennedy
Screenplay: Lee Hall, Dick Curtis (based on the novel *War Horse* by Michael Morpurgo [New York, 1983] and the stage play of the same name by Nick Stafford [London, week of October 18, 2007])
Cast: Emily Watson, David Thewlis, Peter Mullan
Production Companies: DreamWorks Pictures, Reliance Entertainment, Amblin Entertainment, Kennedy/Marshall Company
Distribution Companies: Touchstone Pictures, DreamWorks SKG, Walt Disney Studios Motion Pictures

Wonder Woman (2017)
Director: Patty Jenkins
Producers: Charles Roven, Zack Snyder, Deborah Snyder, Richard Suckle
Screenplay: Allan Heinberg, Zack Snyder, Jason Fuchs (based on the comic book character Wonder Woman created by William Moulton Marston)
Cast: Gal Gadot, Chris Pine, Connie Nielsen
Production Companies: Warner Bros. Pictures, DC Comics, Atlas Entertainment, Cruel and Unusual Films
Distribution Companies: Warner Bros. Pictures

INDEX

100% American (1918), 5
1917 (2019), 10

Abie's Irish Rose (1928), 144
Adorée, Renée, 54, 105, 178, 190
Algonquin Round Table, 51, 54
Alice's Little Parade (1926), 89, 91
All Night Long (1924), 92–93
All Quiet on the Western Front (1930), 71, 79–80, 106, 173, 177–79, 193
American Cavalryman: A Liberian Romance, An (novel), 124, 132
Ames, Robert, 159
Anderson, Maxwell, 51, 57, 59, 61, 71
Apocalypse Now (1979), 207
Arbuckle, Roscoe "Fatty," 94
Archainbaud, George, 179, 182
Arlen, Richard, 42
Armstrong, Robert, 182
Army Nurse Corps, 136
Arthur, Jean, 77–78
Astor, Mary, 183
Aviator, The (2004), 67

Backwash of War, The (memoir), 136
Ball of Fire (1941), 170
Bancroft, George, 173–75
Band of Brothers (2001), 212
Barbed Wire (1927), 71
Barbusse, Henri, 51
Barrymore, Lionel, 187
Barthelmess, Richard, 41, 139, 162, 170, 181, 188

Bataan (1943), 124
Batman, 208
Batman Begins (2005), 208
Battle, The (1911), 20, 23, 26–29
Beaudine, William, 160
Behn, Harry, 53
Big Parade, The (1925), 9, 11, 35, 41, 48, 52–57, 59, 68, 89, 91, 93, 105, 141–44, 148, 154, 173, 178, 189–90
"Big Parade, The" (short story), 52–53, 64
Bill, Tony, 207
Biograph Company, 14–15, 18–20, 160
Birth of a Nation, The (1915), 18, 32, 110
Birthright (1924), 124, 131
Birthright (1939), 133–34
Block-Heads (1938), 93, 95
Blue Max, The (1966), 202–3
Boardman, Eleanor, 148, 155
Bobby Bumps, 82
Bond, The (1918), 5, 83
Bonus Army, 194
Borden, Mary, 136
Borzage, Frank, 86, 176–77
Bosko the Doughboy (1932), 96–101
Bottoms, Timothy, 205
Bow, Clara, 42, 145, 178, 190
Bowers, Charles, 82
Brady, Matthew, 5
Bray, J. R., 82
Brent, Evelyn, 161
Bridge on the River Kwai, The (1957), 104
Broken Lullaby (1932), 10, 71, 162, 179, 184–87, 191, 202

246

Broncho Production Company, 29
Brophy, Ed, 106
Brown, Johnny Mack, 181
Buckles, Frank, 3
Buñuel, Luis, 205
Butler, David, 141

Captain America, 208
Captain America: The First Avenger (2011), 209
Carroll, Nancy, 144–45, 162
Catholic Legion of Decency, 193
Ceiling Zero (1936), 170
Chandler, Helen, 162, 181
Chaplin, Charlie, 5, 82–83, 85–86, 108
Chaplin, Sydney, 82
Chase, Charley, 104, 108
Cher Ami, 123
Chestnutt, Charles, 130
City Lights (1931), 86
Civilization (1916), 32–33
Clive, Colin, 66
Clyde, June, 161
Cobb, Humphrey, 200
Cock of the Air (1932), 193
Coming Home (1979), 207
Committee on Public Information, 4, 113–16, 120
Cooper, Gary, 73, 75–76
Corporal Kate (1926), 142–45, 167
Cotter, Joseph Seamon, Jr., 124
Coward, The (1915), 32, 44
Cradle of Courage, The (1920), 35–38, 141, 173, 175, 191, 208, 212
Crane, Stephen, 11, 16–18, 20, 28
Creel, George, 114
Cromwell, John, 155, 173, 175
Cunard, Grace, 139

Daniels, Bebe, 83
Darby's Rangers (1958), 198
Darling Lili (1970), 202–3
Daughter of the Congo, A (1930), 130, 132–33
Dawn Patrol, The (1930), 64, 170–72, 195
Day, Marceline, 161

Deer Hunter, The (1978), 207
DeMille Pictures, 142
Dempster, Carol, 139
Dibb, Samuel, 10
Dickens, Charles, 15, 24
Dieterle, William, 71, 86, 179–80
Disney, Walt, 81, 89–91, 93, 96, 98–99, 108
Dix, Richard, 182
Dixon, Thomas, 110
Dos Passos, John, 6, 46, 51
Doughboys (1930), 93, 95, 100, 103–7
Doughboys: The Story of the AEF, 1917–1918, The (nonfiction), 79
Douglas, Kirk, 201
Downing, Henry Francis, 115, 124, 130
Downing Film Corporation, 115
Drummer of the 8th, The (1913), 23, 29
Du Bois, W. E. B., 121
Dumb Patrol, The (1931), 101, 104, 106
Dunbar-Nelson, Alice, 124
Duncan, Bud, 82–83

Ebony Film Corporation, 111–12, 116
Eddy, Helen Jerome, 158
Edeson, Arthur, 179
Edwards, Cliff "Ukelele" Ike, 103
Eilers, Sally, 95, 103
Eisenhower, Dwight, 194
Eisenstein, Sergei, 15
Enchanted Cottage, The (1924), 177
Evans, Maurice, 66

Fairbanks, Douglas, 85
Fairbanks, Douglas, Jr., 170
Farewell to Arms, A (1932), 193
Farewell to Arms, A (novel), 46
Farrell, Charles, 176
Faulkner, William, 24, 46, 48
Fazenda, Louise, 165
Felix the Cat, 86–89, 91, 98
Felix Turns the Tide (1922), 86–91, 97, 173
Finch, Flora, 82
First Blood (1982), 207
First World War: A Photographic History, The (nonfiction), 79

Fitzgerald, F. Scott, 6, 46
Fleischer Brothers, 89
Fleming, Victor, 144
Flyboys (2006), 207
Flying Ace, The (1926), 125–29
Forbidden Zone, The (memoir), 136
Ford, John, 71
Four Horsemen of the Apocalypse, The (1921), 35, 38–41
Four Horsemen of the Apocalypse, The (novel), 38
Four Sons (1928), 71
Fox, William, 57, 177
Fox Film Corporation, 59
Franco, James, 207
Frankenstein (1931), 79
Frantz (2016), 10
From Harlem to the Rhine (1920), 115–16
Fugitive, The (1910), 18, 23–26, 28

Gabriel Over the White House (1933), 193
Gance, Abel, 8
Gardner, Alexander, 5
Gaynor, Janet, 176
Gilbert, John, 53–54
Girl Who Stayed at Home, The (1919), 138–41
Gish, Lillian, 34, 122
Go Get 'Em! (memoir), 72, 74, 76
Gold Diggers of 1933 (1933), 194
Grand Army of the Republic, 15
Granddad (1913), 23, 30–31
Grande Illusion, La (1937), 8
Great Gatsby, The (novel), 46
Great Guns! (1927), 89–92, 96–97
Greatest Thing in Life, The (1918), 122, 124
Green-Eyed Monster, The (1920), 126
Griffith, D. W., 10–11, 14–29, 31, 34–35, 38, 45, 47, 81, 110, 122, 125, 138–40, 190, 211–12
Gumbin, Herman, 160

Half Shot at Sunrise (1930), 93–94, 102, 106
Hall, Beulah, 110
Hall, James, 67
Ham Agrees with Sherman (1916), 82
Hamilton, Lloyd, 82–83

Hamilton, Neil, 170
Hardy, Oliver, 93, 95, 101–2
Harlow, Jean, 67–68
Harman, Hugh, 96, 98–99, 108
Harron, Robert "Bobby," 34, 122, 139
Hart, Charles, 114
Hart, William S., 21–22, 35–38, 175
Hatari! (1962), 170
Hawks, Howard, 47, 170–71, 195
Hearst, William Randolph, 20
Hearts of the World (1918), 32, 34–35, 125, 141
Hell's Angels (1930), 48, 67–69, 177
Hell's Angels (play), 69–70
Hemingway, Ernest, 6, 46, 48
Heroes for Sale (1933), 79, 106, 179, 187–91, 193, 195
Heroic Negro Soldiers of the World War (1919), 115
High C's (1930), 104
Hillyer, Lambert, 35–36, 38, 175
His Master's Voice (1925), 35, 40–41, 141, 173
His Trust (1910), 18–19
His Trust Fulfilled (1910), 18–19
Holmes, Helen, 127, 138
Holmes, Phillips, 162, 184, 186, 202
Home of the Brave (2006), 213
Home to Harlem (novel), 124
Homesteader, The (1919), 130
Hoover, Herbert, 194
House with Closed Shutters, The (1910), 18, 23–24, 28, 44
Hughes, Howard, 67, 177
Hughes, Rupert, 146–48
Hunter, Tab, 199
Hurd, Earl, 82
Hurt Locker, The (2008), 214

Ibáñez, Vicente Blasco, 38
In Old Kentucky (1909), 19
In the Border States (1910), 18
In the Valley of Elah (2007), 213
Ince, Thomas, 10–11, 14–16, 20–24, 29–36, 45, 47, 81, 190
Independent Moving Pictures (IMP), 20
Informer, The (1912), 20

INDEX

Ingram, Rex, 38
Injustice (1919), 125–26, 129
Iron Man (2008), 208
Ising, Rudolf, 98–99

J'Accuse (1919), 8
Jackson, Peter, 10
Jenkins, Patty, 209–10
Johannah Enlists (1918), 141
Johnny Got His Gun (1971), 205–6, 212
Johnny Got His Gun (novel), 204–5
Johnson, George, 110–11, 113–16, 120–21, 130
Johnson, Noble, 110–11, 115, 120, 134
Jones, Bluebell, 161
Jones, Rosemary, 161
Journey's End (1930), 11, 48, 64, 67, 69–71, 195
Journey's End (2017), 10
Journey's End (play), 48, 65–68, 71
Jünger, Ernst, 51

Kay-Bee Production Company, 29
Keaton, Buster, 81–82, 93, 95, 100, 103–8
Keeler, Ruby, 194
Kicking the Germ Out of Germany (1918), 83–84
Kid, The (1921), 86
King, Burton, 122–24
King, Henry, 146, 148, 155
King Kong (1933), 120
Kubrick, Stanley, 198, 200–202, 204–6, 207, 209

Lafayette Escadrille, 207
Lafayette Escadrille (1958), 79, 198–200
Lafayette Flying Corps, 207
LaMotte, Ellen N., 136
Langdon, Harry, 92–95
Lasky, Jesse, 195
Last Flight, The (1931), 71, 86, 161–62, 179–82, 186, 190–91, 202
Laurel, Stan, 93, 95, 101–2
Lee, Dorothy, 102
Lee, Rowland, 71
Legion of the Condemned (1928), 48, 73–77

Legion of the Condemned (novelization), 73–76
Liberty Productions, 160
Lincoln Motion Picture Company, 110–14, 120–21, 134
Lindbergh, Charles, 42, 44
Little American, The (1917), 141
Little Caesar (1930), 193
Lloyd, Harold, 82–83
Lost Battalion, The (1919), 122–24, 139
Lost Squadron, The (1932), 179, 182–84, 186, 191, 202
Love Doctor, The (1929), 67
Lubin motion picture company, 110
Lubitsch, Ernst, 10, 71, 179, 184–87
Lucky Star (1929), 86, 176–77
Lukas, Paul, 77–78
Luke Joins the Navy (1916), 82–83
Luke's Preparedness Preparations (1916), 82–84
Lyon, Ben, 67

MacArthur, Douglas, 194
Macready, George, 201
Mad Parade, The (1931), 160–68, 213
Malloy, Dorothy, 160
Man I Killed, The (1932). See *Broken Lullaby*
Manners, David, 181
March, Joseph Moncure, 67
Marshall, Tully, 140
Mathis, June, 38
McCrea, Joel, 182
McKay, Claude, 124
Men with Wings (1938), 79
Mendes, Sam, 10
Menjou, Adolphe, 200–201
Messenger, The (2009), 214
Messmer, Otto, 81, 88–90, 92, 99, 108
Metro Goldwyn Mayer (MGM), 103, 107, 157
Micheaux, Oscar, 129–34
Mighty, The (1929), 155, 173–75, 179
Milestone, Lewis, 71, 177, 179
Mine Eyes Have Seen (play), 124

Mintz, Charles, 89
Mission in Action (1984), 207
Montgomery, Robert, 158
Mutt and Jeff, 82
Muybridge, Eadweard, 5
Mystery of the Leaping Fish, The (1916), 111

National Association for the Advancement of Colored People (NAACP), 110
National World War I Museum, 3
New York Motion Picture Company, 20
New York World, 51
Nissen, Greta, 67
Norman, Richard E., 126, 134
Norman Studios, 126–27
Nugent, Elliott, 181

Office of War Information, 4
Olivier, Laurence, 66
On the Fields of France (play), 124
Only Angels Have Wings (1939), 170
Orr, Gertrude, 160
Oswald the Lucky Rabbit, 89–92, 98
Our Colored Fighters (1919), 115
Our Hell Fighter's Return (1919), 115
Ozon, François, 10

Pack Up Your Troubles (1932), 101–2
Page, Anita, 158
Paramount Pictures, 42
Patent Leather Kid, The (1927), 35, 41–42
Paths of Glory (1957), 198, 200–202, 206
Paths of Glory (novel), 200
Patton, George, 194
Pickford, Mary, 5, 85
Plumes (novel), 48–53, 56–57, 59
Powell, Dick, 194
President Vanishes, The (1934), 193
Public Enemy, The (1931), 193

Ralston, Esther, 174
Ralston, Jobyna, 42
Realization of a Negro's Ambition, The (1916), 110

Red Badge of Courage, The (novel), 11, 16–18, 28, 45
Remarque, Erich Maria, 47, 79, 177
Renoir, Jean, 8
Return of the Soldier, The (novel), 51, 156
Rich, Irene, 161
Ridgeway, Fritzi, 161
Rio Bravo (1959), 170
Road Back, The (1937), 79
Rogers, Buddy, 42, 77–78, 144–45
Rostand, Maurice, 184
Rubens, Alma, 148

Sailor-Made Man, A (1921), 84
Sammy in Siberia, A (1918), 83–84
Sauerkraut Symphony (1916), 83
Saunders, John Monk, 47, 73, 170, 179
Saving Private Ryan (1998), 212
Scarface (1932), 193
Scorsese, Martin, 67
Scott, Emmett, 113
Selwyn, Edgar, 157
Sergeant York (1941), 195–97
Seymour, Clarine, 139
She Goes to War (1929), 146, 148–55, 157, 167
She Goes to War (novella), 146–49
Sherriff, R. C., 65, 70–71
Shop around the Corner (1940), 184
Shoulder Arms (1918), 83, 85–86
Single Lady (novel), 179
Smith, Albert, 13
Smith, Jimmy, 111
Soldier's Pay (novel), 46
South Pacific (1958), 104
Spielberg, Steven, 207
Spying the Spy (1918), 111–12
Stallings, Laurence, 11, 47–54, 57–61, 71, 75, 79–81, 144
Stone, Oliver, 213
Storm of Steel (memoir), 51
Stribling, T. S., 124, 130–32
Strictly Neutral (1915), 82
Stroheim, Erich von, 183
Submarine Pirate, A (1915), 82–83
Sullivan, Pat, 88–89

Summerville, Slim, 178
Superman, 208
Sutherland, Donald, 205
Swords and Hearts (1911), 18, 20

Tashman, Lilyan, 161
Temple, Shirley, 194
Terry, Alice, 39
Thalberg, Irving, 51–52
Thanhauser Company, 14
They Gave Him a Gun (1937), 107
They Shall Not Grow Old (2018), 10
This Day and Age (1933), 193
Three Soldiers (novel), 46, 51
Tolstoy, Leo, 24
Tone, Franchot, 107
Top Gun (1986), 172
Training of Colored Troops (1918), 116–21
Trooper of Troop K, The (1917), 110–11
Trouble in Paradise (1932), 184
Truffaut, François, 211
Trumbo, Dalton, 204–7

Uncommon Valor (1983), 207
Under Fire (novel), 51
United Confederate Veterans, 15

Valentino, Rudolph, 39–40
Vidor, King, 9, 41, 51–56, 59, 105, 144
Virgin of Seminole, The (1922), 131, 133
Vitagraph Company, 13–14
Von Richtofen and Brown (1971), 202–3

Walker, June, 158
Walsh, Raoul, 47, 57, 59, 63, 105
War Horse (2011), 207–8
War Nurse (1930), 157–61, 167
War Nurse: The Story of a Woman Who Lived, Loved and Suffered on the Western Front (novel), 156–59
Warner, Harry, 195
Warner, Jack, 194–95
Warner Bros., 194–95, 198
Washington, Booker T., 113

Wellman, William, 11, 42, 47–48, 64, 67, 71–81, 170, 179, 187–88, 198–200, 207
Wellman, William, Jr., 79
West, Rebecca, 51, 156
Westcott, Gordon, 188
Whale, James, 11, 47, 64–67, 69–71, 75, 77, 79–81, 177
What Price Glory? (1926), 48, 57, 59–64, 67, 71, 100, 105
What Price Glory? (play), 51, 53, 57–64
Wheeler, Bert, 93–94, 102, 106
When Washington Was in Vogue (novel), 124
White, Pearl, 127, 138
Whittlesey, Charles White, 123
"Wild Party, The" (narrative poem), 67
Williams, Edward Christopher, 124
Wilson, Woodrow, 32, 113
Wings (1927), 9, 35, 41–44, 48, 64, 67, 71–73, 75–77, 100, 145, 178, 189–90
Winkler, Margaret, 89
Within Our Gates (1920), 130
Wolheim, Louis, 178
Wonder Woman, 208–9
Wonder Woman (2017), 208
Woolsey, Robert, 93–94, 102, 106
World Trade Center (2006), 213
Wray, Fay, 73

York, Alvin C., 195–97
Young, Loretta, 190
Young Eagles (1930), 11, 48, 71, 73, 77–78

ABOUT THE AUTHOR

Jeffrey A. Hinkelman earned his PhD in literary and cultural studies from Carnegie Mellon University, where he has taught for many years. He is currently a senior lecturer in the Department of English and the director of the Film and Visual Media Program.

www.ingramcontent.com/pod-product-compliance
Lightning Source LLC
Chambersburg PA
CBHW030617230426
43661CB00053B/2027